WHEN THE COCK CROWS

WHEN THE COCK CROWS

A HISTORY OF THE PATHÉ EXCHANGE

RICHARD LEWIS WARD

Southern Illinois University Press
Carbondale

Southern Illinois University Press
www.siupress.com

Printed in the United States of America

19 18 17 16 4 3 2 1

Cover illustration: red rooster logo of the Pathé Exchange and five strips of Pathex 9.5-millimeter film

Cover design by Mary Rohrer

Library of Congress Cataloging-in-Publication Data
Names: Ward, Richard Lewis, 1953– author.
Title: When the cock crows : a history of the Pathé Exchange / Richard Lewis Ward.
Description: Carbondale : Southern Illinois University Press, 2016. | Includes bibliographical references and index.
Identifiers: LCCN 2015038657| ISBN 9780809334964 (paperback) | ISBN 9780809334971 (e-book)
Subjects: LCSH: Pathé Exchange—History.| BISAC: PERFORMING ARTS / Film & Video / History & Criticism. | PERFORMING ARTS / Film & Video / General.
Classification: LCC PN1999.P34 W37 2016 | DDC 384/.80979494—dc23
LC record available at http://lccn.loc.gov/2015038657

Printed on recycled paper. ♲

For Jane and my parents,
McInnis and Mary Catherine Ward

CONTENTS

PREFACE

I began work on this history of the Pathé Exchange in the spring of 2005, just after the publication of my *History of the Hal Roach Studios*. I had worked on the Roach book for so long that I experienced something of an "empty nest" syndrome once it was out in the world on its own. The Pathé Exchange seemed like a logical choice for my next work. It had been Hal Roach's theatrical distributor from 1915 to 1927, and in the course of my research on Roach, I had amassed a fair amount of material on Pathé. At the time it seemed that most of my research on Pathé had already been done. A full decade later I am finally wrapping things up.

During my journey through the history of the Pathé Exchange, my attitude toward the company shifted 180 degrees. Heavily influenced by the tone of the correspondence between the Hal Roach Studios and Pathé, I initially shared Roach's view that Pathé was inept, disorganized, and at times, in a word Roach used, "disgraceful." As my work went on, I came to the opinion that while some of Roach's criticism was merited, the missteps were just one facet of this endearingly eccentric and unique company. The Pathé rooster marched to the beat of its own drummer, for better or worse.

As I knew when I started my research for this book, there is no single repository for Pathé Exchange business records as there is for the Hal Roach Studios at the University of Southern California's Cinematic Arts Library. I did find business records for the Pathé Exchange's later years at the Margaret Herrick Library of the Academy of Motion Picture Arts and Sciences, in the United Artists Collection of the Wisconsin Center for Film and Theatre Research, and in the collection of Joseph P. Kennedy's personal papers at the John F. Kennedy Presidential Library. I cannot sufficiently express my gratitude to the staffs and management of those institutions for their helpfulness, professionalism, and hospitality.

In the absence of studio business records, the backbone of my research was countless hours of reading through microfilm copies of motion-picture-industry trade journals during the years the Pathé Exchange was in operation. Much of this work was accomplished, and the articles on Pathé copied and passed along to me, by a series of wonderful and tireless graduate assistants, including Rosalind Rountree, Marty Vignes, Evey Bell, Claire-Annick Melanson, Anna Smetanina, Gabby Rodriguez, John Kelsey, and Derrick Rodgers. I am indebted to Edwin J. Perkins, Patricia Mark, Sonja Sheffield, Rob Mobley, and David Pierce and the Media History Digital Library for their incredible generosity in sharing original research and resources, as well as for facilitating my research process. I am eternally grateful to my students and colleagues in the communication department at the University of South Alabama, who have given me a truly fulfilling professional home. Finally, cheers to Jane, Katie, Eddie, and Tiffany for always being there for me.

A subsection of the final chapter of this book is titled "Significant Passings." I have had several of these while working on this project. I began my research in earnest in July 2005 with my visit to the Margaret Herrick Library in Beverly Hills. Just one month later the town in which I live, Pass Christian, Mississippi, was virtually destroyed by Hurricane Katrina. I have watched with pride as the town has rebuilt itself from little more than a pile of rubble into a vibrant community.

The years following Katrina saw the births of my two grandchildren, Leighton and Edward, who have enriched my life beyond measure. Then, as the first draft of this project was entering its final stages in August 2013, my mother passed away. She and my late father were dedicated to giving my sister and me a thorough education, all the way through doctoral studies if we wanted to go that far. We did. Cathie became an MD, and I opted for the life of an academic. I offer this book as a memorial to McInnis and Mary Catherine Ward for making it possible for my sister and me to achieve our dreams.

WHEN THE COCK CROWS

INTRODUCTION

When someone is reciting the pantheon of studios that formed and dominated the American motion-picture industry for much of the twentieth century, the name of the Pathé Exchange will likely never be included in the list. The films that it released under its own name were almost exclusively made in the silent era, and those made by latter-day subsidiaries in the 1930s–60s were, by and large, not very memorable. Yet it was a film company like no other, and it really deserves a closer look.

While all of the other U.S. film studios were homegrown and those that survived for any period achieved a global reach that dominated much of the international cinema market, the Pathé Exchange was, in many ways, the exact opposite. It was established by a French parent firm, Pathé Frères, as just one more component in Charles Pathé's global media empire, his beachhead in America. Its very name suggests its intended function in the organization. The Pathé Exchange was planned only to be Pathé Frères' theatrical distributor in the United States, sending films to theaters across the country through a series of film exchanges, or distribution offices. Nothing more. As such, it really wasn't designed as a stand-alone entity. Initially, the brothers Pathé only produced enough films on U.S. soil to deflect or dilute the stigma connected with trying to sell a slate consisting entirely of European films to the largely isolationist American heartland. But then things changed.

At almost exactly the moment of the Pathé Exchange's inauguration at the end of 1914, Europe found itself embroiled in a continent-wide war that would last four brutal years. The prodigious flow of films from Pathé Frères' European filmmaking empire slowed to a trickle then reversed course. The once-unimportant American-based production units now became Pathé Frères' primary source of films to feed the rest of its worldwide distribution network.[1]

And during this period Pathé's U.S. producers, a mix of European émigrés and Americans, became extremely proficient at making one of the most popular film forms of the day, the movie serial. Although they didn't invent the form, the producers of the Pathé Exchange quickly made the serial their own and established with the moviegoing public an indelible link between the words *Pathé* and *serial*.[2]

Even at the peak of its importance to the rest of Pathé Frères, though, the U.S. operation was still run according to what Charles Pathé thought was best for the entire organization. Nearly a year *before* the beginning of the Pathé Exchange, Charles Pathé had announced that his American branch would shift its model of production to that which he was employing successfully elsewhere. Pathé was no longer interested in directly producing anything beyond his newsreel. Instead, he wished to adopt the paradigm of being a film publisher. Under this plan a trusted cadre of quasi-independent producers, many of them former employees of Pathé Frères, would handle the responsibilities (and the financial risks) of making films, which would then either be accepted or not by Pathé for theatrical distribution. This strategy made sense to Pathé, since it removed his own company from the uncertainties of film production and allowed his staff to pick only the best from finished product. The problem was, though, that the companies that were shortly to dominate the American film industry were taking the opposite, hands-on approach to film production.

Furthermore, Charles Pathé regarded big-budget filmmaking, anything epic or star-laden, to be a dangerous speculation.[3] He preferred to stick to lower-budgeted films like the serials and completely ignored the seismic shift going on in the American film industry, with Adolph Zukor and others increasing production costs and star power, and, most importantly, buying or building their own chains of theaters. For his part, Charles Pathé was not about to buy any theaters in the United States. In fact, after the First World War he was beginning to spin off parts of his global operation to concentrate on certain core aspects of his business in France.[4]

In 1921 the Pathé Exchange itself became the latest part of Pathé Freres to be spun off as an independent company, sold to the American investment firm of Merrill Lynch. Not particularly interested in the film company beyond its investment value, Merrill Lynch's conservative, "stay the course" approach ultimately proved ruinous for the Pathé Exchange. Even as late as 1921 Merrill Lynch may have been able to build the Pathé Exchange into a truly competitive film firm had it better appreciated and attempted to implement some of the business strategies of Pathé's competitors. But it did not, and, in effect, the

Pathé Exchange doomed itself to the margins of an industry in which it had been a pioneer. It may have taken pride in boasting that it was not a competitor but rather a protector of small, independent theater operators, staying out of the theater business and feeding its clients the types of short films and action features that played best in rural settings, but this strategy condemned it to be a minor player. By 1926 when Merrill Lynch awoke to the measures that needed to be taken to remain in business, the damage had largely been done. The Pathé's Exchange's subsequent owners made some efforts to correct the situation, constructing a somewhat flawed linkage to the Keith-Orpheum theater circuit and taking an active hand in film production, but even without the often self-serving machinations of latter-day management, it was probably too late to correct the course.

Despite the fact that the management of the Pathé Exchange had willingly embarked on a course that left it a greatly weakened organization, ripe for takeover by the coming of sound, the company was able to boast quite a number of accomplishments from 1910 to 1930. It occasionally flourished within the minor-league niche it had carved for itself. Among other things, it established the first and one of the most-trusted newsreels in the United States. It commissioned and distributed the early comedy films of Harold Lloyd, Harry Langdon, the team of Stan Laurel and Oliver Hardy, and the Our Gang series, and it distributed the groundbreaking documentary *Nanook of the North* (1922). And, as mentioned earlier, it and the earlier American production branch of Pathé Frères set the standard for movie serials beginning with the seminal *Perils of Pauline* (1914). An examination of this company, then, provides the reader with an alternate "what if" path for the development of the American film industry. It demonstrates what was and was not possible for a company that wanted to establish its own rules rather than imitate the competition and then finds itself outside of the vertically integrated oligopoly that controls its industry. Finally, the Pathé Exchange's continued existence after 1931 takes on the characteristics of a survival tale, in which an individual who has been left stranded manages to hike through a hostile landscape to an almost happy resolution.

CHAPTER ONE

CHARLES PATHÉ, FILM PUBLISHER

1908–14

Although the Pathé Exchange, Inc., didn't officially come into being until the end of 1914, its story actually begins a bit earlier. At the end of 1908, eight of the leading U.S. motion-picture production firms culminated a period of litigation and negotiation to form the Motion Picture Patents Company (MPPC). The purpose of the company was to guarantee its members a lock on the domestic film market to the exclusion of all new competitors through a pool of members' patents regarding the most fundamental technical processes of filmmaking. The reasoning went that unless a film studio had permission to use the processes, it would be unable to engage in filmmaking without being guilty of patent infringement, and the MPPC had no intention of granting such permission to anyone outside of its membership. While the idea seemed ironclad, it had a number of fatal flaws that would eventually doom it, along with most of its members.

In the first place, the process of investigating and litigating patent infringement was very time consuming and inefficient, and it proved to be a thoroughly ineffective way of controlling competition from "independent" producers outside of the MPPC. Secondly, the MPPC's policies to eliminate competition constituted a blatant restraint of trade in violation of the Sherman Antitrust Act. It was only a matter of time, in 1915 to be exact, before a federal court would order the MPPC's dissolution. Before that happened, though, the basic business plan of the MPPC locked its membership into a mode of production and distribution that was inflexible and unable to change with public tastes.

From the earliest days of the cinema, the industry had been built around the production and distribution of short films, initially running a matter of seconds and gradually increasing in length until, by 1910, the standard running time of a film was between ten and fifteen minutes, or a single thousand-foot reel of 35-millimeter film.[1] When the MPPC set up the General Film Company in 1910 to distribute its members' films to theaters, it established a formula that would accept from each member-producer roughly the same number of single-reel films per week. But then film lengths began to increase, first to two, then three, and then four or more reels, initially in the form of European imports and then, from 1911, as U.S. domestic productions. As a business based on the distribution of a certain number of single-reel films per week, General Film proved ill-suited to handle the longer films. It did eventually adapt to longer films to a rather limited degree, but by that time the "independent" producers outside of the MPPC, who had no such restrictions on film length and who ran more efficient and aggressive distribution organizations, were winning solidly both at the box office and in the courts. General Film and most of its MPPC producers would be out of business before 1920.

Pathé Frères, through its American successor the Pathé Exchange, Inc., was one of the few exceptions to the rule. Pathé Frères had been founded in France at the dawn of the cinema in 1895 by Charles, Émile, Jacques, and Théophile Pathé, each of whom reportedly invested the equivalent to $500 in U.S. dollars (in 1895 values). Initially the company ran a shop to sell phonographs and their accompanying records, but soon Charles became involved in the actual manufacture of records. Shortly thereafter he placed two flip-card motion-picture viewers at the shop. These were so successful that he soon purchased an additional twenty machines, placing them in stores in twenty different towns. To keep the film subjects fresh, and the income high, he developed a system of buying a set number of films at a time and rotating them to the different towns on his circuit. As Charles became more interested in film, leaving Émile to run the phonograph business,[2] he began producing his own short subjects, mostly "actuality" footage of trains passing by, chickens being fed, etc. As his filmmaking skills increased, the films became more elaborate. By 1905 Pathé Frères was at the top of the French filmmaking industry, a fact that its corporate logo of a proud, crowing red rooster seemed to confirm. It produced, among other things, some of the most elaborate trick films (surpassing the technical achievement of Georges Méliès in that genre) and inventive comedies, some of which starred Max Linder. Linder was arguably the first important cinema comedian and a strong influence on Charlie Chaplin and other architects of American film comedy. The studio's roster of directors included legendary pioneer Ferdinand Zecca, Albert Capellani, and Louis Gasnier, all of whom would later have some involvement with the

Pathé Exchange. At the same time, Pathé Frères began a program of expansion, setting up distribution channels throughout the world and establishing production studios in England, Italy, Russia, and, soon, the United States.[3]

Pathé Frères began distributing its films in the United States in 1904. The point man for this undertaking was Jacques A. Berst, an employee of Pathé Frères since 1896.[4] Thomas Edison, one of the primary film patent holders in the days before the MPPC, filed a patent-infringement suit against Pathé Frères to discourage the competition with his own film studio. The suit never came to trial, and in the interim Pathé Frères began selling its films in the United States at rates lower than Edison's. Between this product dumping (as it would be termed today) and the high quality of its productions, Pathé Frères' films constituted between one-third and one-half of the entire American market by October of 1906.[5] Pathé Frères had become such a major player in the U.S. film industry by 1908 that it was invited to become one of the founding members of the MPPC, one of only two non-U.S. firms included in the combine.

As Pathé Frères was poised to join the MPPC in 1908, the company made a substantial investment in its American operation when it purchased a building in East Bound Brook, New Jersey,[6] that had been built as a sanatorium and most recently had been home to the factory of the Ideal Cash Register Company. It converted the facility into a combination motion-picture studio, film processing and printing plant, film storage vault and editing rooms.[7] This plant would continue to be a key component of Pathé's American operations long after the company ceased active film production. The following year, Pathé Frères built a film production studio in Jersey City, some thirty-two miles from Bound Brook.[8] Perhaps more significantly, Jersey City was only six miles from the ready supply of acting, writing, and directing talent to be found in New York City and ten miles from the early film production center of Fort Lee, New Jersey. Cinematographer Arthur Miller remembered Pathé's Jersey City studio, with its arc lights and mercury-vapor tubes supplementing the natural sunlight coming in through the glass roof and sides, as "one of the most modern and well equipped of the time."[9] In addition, by 1910 the company was leasing an outdoor studio in the Los Angeles suburb of Edendale, largely used for the production of westerns.[10]

Pathé Frères' need for studio facilities to produce films on U.S. soil was not simply due to the French firm's ambition for a global media empire; it was a virtual necessity if the company were to remain competitive in the American market. As Richard Abel notes in *The Red Rooster Scare*, Pathé Frères' overwhelming success in the U.S. film market at the expense of its American competitors had made it a target for vilification in the press. Foreign films were increasingly portrayed as being dangerous to American values. While a European film of exceptional merit could still attract positive reviews and good box-office returns, the standard a European film had to meet for success was raised ever higher. This became even more problematic after 1910, as the quality of American films began to rise.

"WE DID IT"

Pathé Frères' U.S. productions were of variable quality, but some were quite interesting. The plot of *White Fawn's Devotion: A Play Acted by a Tribe of Red Indians in America* (1910), a film that still survives today, was pretty dated even in 1910, and the actors engage in the most extreme form of silent-film pantomime. Nevertheless, it survives as a fascinating document of the interaction between European American settlers and Native Americans as enacted by a mostly Native American cast. James Young Deer, *White Fawn*'s director, was of Native American heritage himself and was in charge of Pathé's Edendale-based productions. An unfortunate occurrence at the Edendale unit three years later would shine an unwanted spotlight on Pathé Frères. James Young Deer wanted a particularly thrilling stunt for the film *General Scott's Protégé* (1913) in which a horse and rider would fall off a precipice. The rider would save himself, but the horse would be "dashed to pieces." For the stunt, the crew used a horse that had been injured in one eye and had blood poisoning and, hence, was considered disposable. Although "half dead," the horse refused to make the jump off the cliff. The crew resorted to tying the horse's legs together so that it could be pushed off. The horse began to scream "like a human being" and to struggle. Some women who lived nearby rushed to investigate the commotion and saw the horse being pushed over the cliff. The horse rolled down the side of the hill and was injured (and presumably had to be put down, although the historical record on this is vague). Three members of the film unit, not including James Young Deer, were arrested and fined sixty dollars apiece for animal cruelty. "The incident has done immense undeserved harm to the motion picture industry in this city," wrote a *Moving Picture World* columnist, who went on to note that letters to local newspapers from readers "have been filled with general condemnation of the motion picture producers."[11] Further outrage occurred when the scene with the horse was actually included in the final picture, prompting *Moving Picture World* columnist George Blaisdell to write, "The fact that the objectionable scene is incorporated in the film as released makes the company responsible. It is incomprehensible that it should be released. It is regrettable that such cause should be given for public criticism."[12] Unbelievably, Pathé Frères made and released another film in early 1914 that contained an identical stunt, possibly reusing the scene from *General Scott's Protégé*. *Down Lone Gap Way*, the *Moving Picture World* noted, is "marred by the picture of a horse which is made to tumble head first down a steep incline. . . . This picture of a holdup and its consequences lacks convincing humanity in places where it isn't trite. It is one of the weakest Pathéplays by the Western company in some weeks."[13] Incidentally, the run-together trade name "Pathéplays" would be used with minor variations ("Pathépicture," "Pathécomedy," etc.) through the late 1920s.

The type of dramatic picture with which Pathé Frères would be most closely associated during much of the silent era was the serial (in Pathé Frères' case, the "Pathéserial"), thrill-oriented dramas whose story arc was spread over multiple episodes usually running between twenty and thirty minutes. The fact that serials had continuing story lines set them apart from other short-film series, which often had little more than a lead actor in common from one installment to the next. Serials could run from as few as eight episodes (with one 1960s homage to the form, *Captain Celluloid vs. the Film Pirates*, having only four) to Kalem's astonishing 119-episode *The Hazards of Helen* (1914–17), but in the second decade of the twentieth century most serials ran fourteen or fifteen episodes.

Although it didn't invent the form, Pathé Frères triumphed with its first effort in the field. *The Perils of Pauline* (1914), codirected by longtime Pathé Frères staffer Louis Gasnier, became the hallmark for the genre and earned its star, Pearl White, the title "Queen of the Serials." Initially planned for thirteen episodes but expanded to twenty by popular demand, the success of this series was so overwhelming that Pathé generated a then-record 147 film prints to serve theaters nationwide.[14] During the summer of 1914, while *Perils* was still in its original run, Pathé Frères was able to happily proclaim, "We Promised to Put Out the Greatest Serial Film Ever Produced—WE DID IT. The Perils of Pauline still continues its unprecedented success."[15] In a review of *Perils* in *Motion Picture News* the writer raves that episode 13 is the most thrilling yet and notes that "the title 'The Perils of Pauline' has become a household word. This speaks volumes for the popularity of the picture. Probably there is no surer test of the merits of anything."[16] Unlike later serials, individual entries in *Perils* did not conclude with cliff-hangers but, rather, ended with Pauline safe from whatever danger she had faced in that episode, only to have new perils arise in the next. The primary characters of Pauline, her fiancée, and her villainous guardian, who schemed to kill her so that he could claim her fortune, continued from one episode to the next.

Interestingly, the guardian, played by German-born Paul Panzer, was originally called Raymond Owen, but for a First World War–era reissue of *Perils* his name was changed to Kœrner to capitalize on anti-German sentiment. *The Perils of Pauline* was followed in rapid succession by *The Exploits of Elaine* (1914–15), *The New Exploits of Elaine* (1915), and *The Romance of Elaine* (1915), all starring Pearl White.[17]

Despite the popularity of the serials, it was another series in a different genre that would become Pathé Frères' standard-bearer, so much so that the name continued to have box-office value even after Pathé Frères and the Pathé Exchange had withdrawn from active film production. The *Pathé Weekly* newsreel started production in 1911,[18] the first such reel in the United States. It had been preceded in Charles Pathé's empire by the French *Pathé Journal* (beginning in 1907) and the British *Pathé Gazette* (beginning in 1908),[19] and it joined a family that included Pathé newsreels in Italy, Russia, Japan, and elsewhere.[20]

Getting the news to the public in a timely fashion was as important in the early twentieth century as it is today. As a Pathé Frères ad from 1914 stated, "nothing deteriorates in value with age more rapidly than news."[21] In the summer of 1913 the *Pathé Weekly* began to be issued twice weekly, on Mondays and Thursdays.[22] The following spring it became the *Pathé News* and was released as a short two-hundred to three-hundred-foot reel (roughly two and one-half to five minutes) five days a week.[23] At about the same time, the *Pathé News* began to be printed on Pathé-manufactured nonflammable safety film so that it could be shipped directly from Pathé Frères via U.S. mail to subscribing theaters. This bypassed the time-consuming routine of having to first ship the more commonly used, highly flammable nitrate film via courier to distribution exchanges and then on to individual theaters.[24]

No matter how frequently they came out, though, newsreels were inevitably bested by daily newspapers in the quest to disseminate the news rapidly. In an effort to have its newsreels project the credibility of newspapers, if not their speed, Pathé hired William P. Helm Jr., a former newspaper editor with Associated Press credentials as the *Pathé Weekly*'s editor at the beginning of 1914.[25] Helm contracted to get exclusive rights in the newsreel field to the United Press wire news service. In addition to receiving all of the United Press news stories, *Pathé Weekly*'s staff of thirty-seven cameramen would, under some circumstances, contribute still photos to United Press.[26]

Within two months of receiving the United Press service, the *Pathé Weekly* made further inroads into the world of print journalism, this time in the guise of cross promotion engineered by Edward A. McManus. While working for the McClure publishing company in 1912, it was McManus who had facilitated the weekly publication in *Ladies' World* of the story of the pioneering Edison serial *What Happened to Mary?*, resulting in added profits for both the serial and the magazine. Now in 1914 McManus was able to sell Pathé Frères and Hearst on the idea of the Hearst dailies in New York City, Boston, Chicago, Atlanta, Los Angeles, and San Francisco publishing stories in the morning paper that would be playing in the *Pathé Weekly* in theaters in those cities the same afternoon. Pathé predicted that this plan would bring a whole new group of people into movie theaters, creating such a huge demand for prints of the newsreels that it might have to set up "emergency" film exchanges outside of the General Film distribution system.[27]

Occasionally, when a major news story occurred in a big city that was home to one of Pathé Frères' offices, the news could be presented on local screens the same day it happened. The chronology of one of these events illustrates the process of getting the news onto the screen rapidly. One day in October 1915 a portion of a street in New York City caved in at 8 A.M. "burying a trolley car and killing and injuring a large number of persons." Within thirty minutes of the accident, three cameramen had arrived from the Pathé Frères studio in Jersey City. An hour later the film shot by the cameramen was in the lab being processed. By 11:30 A.M. the processed negative was on its way to be printed at Bound Brook, and two hours and fifteen minutes later, fifteen prints were being couriered to theaters in New York City. Seven additional prints followed within an hour, so that twenty-two theaters in New York City and Brooklyn were able to show it on their screens that afternoon and evening.[28]

"A DELIGHTFULLY VARIED ENTERTAINMENT"

In the motion-picture industry, the job of the distributor is roughly equivalent to that of the wholesaler in the retail business. The distributor runs the pipeline that takes the product from the producer to the marketplace: in the case of films, the theater. Pathé Frères had been one of the charter members of the MPPC's distribution arm, General Film, but there had been problems from the beginning. These problems had escalated by 1914 to a point that provides an interesting subtext to Pathé Frères' statements regarding "emergency" exchanges and a direct-mailing plan for its newsreel that bypassed General Film.

The first bump in the relationship between Pathé Frères and General Film was the inability of the latter to accept more than five short films from Pathé Frères per week, totaling between seven and nine films reels of a thousand feet.[29] This number was a bit lower than average for General Film's other producers, who supplied anywhere from four to seven short films totaling four to eleven reels per week.[30] But even if Pathé Frères' release schedule had been on the high end of General Film's scale, it still wouldn't have amounted to anything close to the one-third to one-half U.S. domestic market share Pathé Frères had enjoyed before it entered the MPPC. With Pathé's global studios cranking out films running the gamut from European-made features to American-made one- and two-reelers, Pathé Frères clearly had far more supply than General Film could handle. And then there was the problem of the "foreignness" of Pathé Frères' non-American product.

To address the latter issue Pathé Frères took out trade ads that cleverly promoted its European product released through General Film without reminding exhibitors (theater operators) that Pathé Frères itself was a French firm. It did this by identifying the foreign product not as Pathé Frères films but rather as CGPC films. CGPC, in fact, stood for Compagnie Genérale des Établissements Pathé Frères Phonographes & Cinématographes, the publicly traded parent company of Pathé Frères' film and phonograph interests. The CGPC ads used the films' foreignness as selling points, emphasizing their quality and the variety they would bring to a short film program. One example reads,

> MR. EXHIBITOR
> You need variety more than quantity in your
> shows to attract and hold your patronage.
> BOOK THE
> C. G. P. C. FILMS
> If you want the best the foreign market affords.
> C. G. P. C. SURPASSES ANYTHING AMERICA
> EVER PRODUCED! BOOK 'EM![31]

And another example reads,

> IN THE LICENSED FIELD THERE ARE THIRTY-
> SEVEN RELEASES WEEKLY. OF THESE
> Thirty-two are American.
> You Cannot Present a Variety to Your Patrons Unless You
> Have Something in Addition to American Films.
> C. G. P. C.
> FILLS THAT GAP AND WILL MAKE YOUR PROGRAM
> A DELIGHTFULLY VARIED ENTERTAINMENT.
> INSIST ON C. G. P. C. AT YOUR EXCHANGE.[32]

The solution to Pathé Frères' oversupply of films was met by seeking another distribution channel as an alternative to General Film. The new distributor was a company formed at the end of 1912 called Cosmopolitan Films. Before Cosmopolitan had released its first film, its management discovered that there had earlier been a film company with the same name. The company was promptly rechristened Eclectic Films.[33] Evidence indicates that Pathé Frères had a substantial ownership in Cosmopolitan/Eclectic from the start, although a later Pathé Frères' vice president would state in early 1915 that Pathé Frères didn't yet have a majority interest.[34] Still, while its early motto was "the cream of the European market selected for America," the company's trademark containing the words "Paris–New York" would seem to point toward Pathé Frères, as does the fact that the firm's first release, the Italian two-reeler *Lucretia Borgia*, was coproduced by Film d'Arte Italiana and SCAGL (Société Cinématographique des Auteurs et Gens de Lettres), a Pathé Frères affiliate.[35]

From the beginning of 1913 until early 1914, Pathé Frères continued to release its product through both General Film and Eclectic, with General Film handling the *Pathé Weekly*, most of the company's American-made dramas and comedies, and a few of its European productions, and Eclectic releasing the company's European product. Then, in the spring of 1914, Pathé Frères' relationship with General Film soured. Pathé Frères' management received reports from the field that films released through General Film were often unavailable at General's exchanges. Pathé Frères began to include an appeal in its print ads for exhibitors: "Insist upon this film at your exchange. If you cannot get it, write us."[36] The problem was particularly acute for the newly retitled *Pathé News*, where exhibitors reported that General Film was actively substituting a rival newsreel (*Hearst-Selig News*) and telling exhibitors that the *Pathé News* was not available. In an open letter to General Film published in the trade journals, Pathé Frères' lawyers asserted that General Film was engaged in "an organized effort . . . to suppress the use of [Pathé Frères'] films by exhibitors. This, in our opinion, constitutes a clear breach of your contract with Pathé."[37]

It was at this point that Pathé Frères' management decided to begin withdrawing from General Film. A week after the lawyers' letter was published, Pathé Frères' trade-journal ad announced that "[i]n order to prepare feature films for the future that are BIGGER AND BETTER in every way, beginning the week of May 25th the multiple [reel] release for Thursday will be discontinued. The Saturday multiple release will of course be retained."[38] However, less than a month later, the Saturday Pathé Frères release through General Film was dropped as well. At this point the remaining Monday–Wednesday single-reel releases through General Film consisted of the newsreel (which was also available for direct booking through Pathé Frères and Eclectic) and

European films, mostly travelogues (*Through the Bosporus, Historic St. Cloud*) and educational subjects (*Simple Experiments in Electricity, Venomous Serpents*). By mid-September and running through the end of 1914, the *Pathé News* was Pathé Frères' only General Film release.

Even before the open acrimony between Pathé Frères and General Film bubbled up in the trade journals, Pathé Frères had begun to shift the distribution of its more ambitious productions to Eclectic. *The Perils of Pauline*, which began its initial theatrical run at the end of March, was one of the first American Pathé Frères productions to go out through Eclectic. By August 8, 1914, the Pathé Frères–Eclectic release schedule looked like this:

> Every Wednesday and Friday "A Super-Excellent Multiple Reel Feature"
> Every Tuesday, "American made one or two reel comedy"
> Every Other Monday, "Perils of Pauline"
> "Mondays when Pauline is not released, Cartoon Comedy or Comedy and Short Scenic Educational subjects in Natural Colors."

The week this ad was published saw the release of an episode of *Perils*; an American Pathé Frères three-reeler titled *All Love Excelling* starring Crane Wilbur, who was also the romantic male lead in *Perils*; and *The Masked Motive*, a five-reel drama, presumably European.[39]

THE PATHÉ EXCHANGE, INC.

Despite the overwhelming success of its American production of *The Perils of Pauline*, Pathé Frères, in 1914, was on the verge of becoming a film distributor-packager only, withdrawing from active production of anything but its newsreel. This change was driven by Charles Pathé himself, and it began with his French operation in 1908. As Richard Abel has noted, Pathé, alarmed by a perceived oversupply of films in France, which drove down the prices that could be charged by producers and distributors, "began diverting the risks of production to the corporation's stable of smaller, quasi-independent affiliates . . . all of whose product . . . was then channeled through Pathé-Frères and its worldwide distribution agencies, eventually reaching up to 500 million people. The strategy secured a high, steady rate of dividends for Pathé stockholders, at least from 1908 to 1911, and helped to raise the corporation's capital stock to 15 million francs."[40]

Pathé first shared his thoughts on the matter of production versus distribution with the U.S. trade press during a visit to New York in January 1914:

> As far as I am concerned I have almost completely ceased producing on my own account. In my studios in France, Germany, Holland, Italy, Sweden, Russia, and elsewhere, I have selected those assistants and directors who have shown special talent and set them to producing on their own account. Under specified conditions I market their productions for them just as a publisher handles the books of his authors on a royalty basis. In the moving picture business this royalty is a percentage on each foot of positive film sold.
>
> Some of my directors have obtained extraordinary results. I will mention Max Linder, who is rather well known in America and very popular in Europe. This conscientious and hardworking artist, under the old system, earned some five to six thousand dollars a year. To-day working on his own account under the conditions which now prevail . . . he clears some forty to sixty thousand dollars a year, though he produces only one-third as much as he produced before. . . .[41]

Pathé concluded with the interesting observation that

> America is the best market in the world, but it has not been handled to the best advantage. . . . All our efforts hereafter will be directed toward the making of features. Time was when the multiple reel feature counted as the exception and the single reel constituted the rule—this order will now be reversed. . . .
>
> You have most excellent theaters here, but you change [film programs] almost everywhere every day, while in Europe the daily change is very rare indeed. That is the reason or one of the reasons why the average presentation is better in Europe. Yes, I mean projection and, of course, music [played live in the theater to accompany the film].[42]

While Pathé's new system might have the described benefits for top producers who consistently turned out quality work, the advantage was decidedly Pathé Frères'. As a producer-distributor, Pathé Frères was required to arrange production funding for every film and then would be faced with the task of marketing the finished product regardless of quality. As a distributor only, Pathé Frères could accept or reject any film for distribution with no obligation to market those it deemed substandard. Furthermore, it could advance production funding to its producers in any amount it desired or withhold funding completely. In short, this system permitted Pathé Frères to reap the benefits of its producers' best product while minimizing its risk in the event of a bad film.

The new system was phased in to Pathé's Frères' American operation around the middle of 1914. Thus, *The Perils of Pauline* was a Pathé Frères production, while its follow-up, *The Exploits of Elaine* and the two sequels in the *Elaine* franchise, were produced by Wharton, Inc.[43] In addition to changes in policy, this period saw considerable flux in Pathé Frères' previously stable American management. J. A. Berst, who had headed up the American branch from its inception in 1904, resigned in 1913 to become treasurer for General Film. Over the next few years he would become vice president and general manager of the Selig Polyscope production company, then president of General Film.[44] After more than a year under interim management that included L. P. Bonvillain,[45] Berst was officially replaced by Arthur Roussel, another émigré from Pathé Frères' Paris office, who was originally sent to the United States in 1910 to oversee Pathé Frères' Bound Brook processing facility. In 1913 he was installed by Charles Pathé as the head of Eclectic Films, and around the middle of 1914 he moved into the position of vice president and managing director at American Pathé Frères that had been vacated by Berst. During the fall of 1914, after only a few months on the job, Roussel became seriously ill and had to resign his position. He died around Christmas at the age of thirty-four.[46]

Roussel's successor was Felix Malitz, a native of Brandenburg, Germany, with an extensive business background, particularly in France. Malitz promised to put Pathé Frères' American branch "upon a scientific basis of commercial efficiency."[47] One of his first orders of business was the integration of the American branch with its new distribution arm. Charles Pathé had just purchased a controlling interest in Eclectic Films and renamed it the Pathé Exchange, Inc.[48]

CHAPTER TWO

"A PROGRAM WHICH WILL GO INTO EVERY PART OF THE WORLD" 1915–18

Charles Pathé spent two and a half months in the United States in late 1914. On the eve of his sailing back to France, now fully engaged in the First World War, Pathé addressed a dinner assembly of American Pathé's officers, directors, and department heads at the Hotel Brevoort in New York City on January 3, 1915. Speaking in French, Pathé opened with the announcement that

> the Eclectic concern is no longer and has been replaced by the Pathé Exchange, and . . . the Board of Directors of this new concern, as well as the one of the Pathé Frères, has appointed Mr. Malitz vice-president and assistant treasurer of both corporations, with Mr. [Charles] Dupuis as assistant director. They rely on you as I rely on them. . . . I can assure you that in following [Malitz's] instructions you will obtain very quickly the result we are all aiming at, namely, to obtain on the American Market what we have obtained on the world market.[1]

The formal acquisition of Eclectic by Pathé Frères had interesting side effects, some trivial and others with far-reaching consequences. While the Pathé Exchange shared a corporate office suite with the American branch of Pathé Frères, the two maintained a certain degree of separation. The former was incorporated under and subject to American law while the latter was a French concern. This led to such operational quirks as operating two separate cashier windows—one for each firm.

Of far greater impact to the future of the Pathé Exchange was the makeup of the board of directors of the new company. Pathé Frères' American attorney, Paul Fuller, approached a pair of young investors with whom he was acquainted named Charles Merrill and Edmund Lynch to take seats on the Pathé Exchange board for a salary of $50,000 per year. The reasons for the high salary are unclear, but it wasn't based on Merrill's and Lynch's reputations; they were both at the beginnings of their careers and had not yet established themselves. Merrill had only opened up his firm in 1914, with Lynch joining a few months later and the business being renamed Merrill, Lynch and Company in 1915. In *Wall Street to Main Street: Charles Merrill and Middle-Class Investors*, Edwin Perkins speculates that Charles Pathé may have believed that his firm might perform better if it had American businessmen looking after its fortunes and that Fuller suggested Merrill and Lynch.[2] Whatever the case, seating Merrill and Lynch on the board of directors of the Pathé Exchange would seal its destiny through the end of its existence as a film distributor.

THE GUIDING SPIRIT OF PATHÉ

The March 13, 1915, *Moving Picture World* article that served to introduce Felix Malitz to the theatrical end of the film industry runs a scant four paragraphs. After identifying Malitz as the vice president and managing director of Pathé Frères and the Pathé Exchange, Inc., it says that Malitz was asked for an autobiographical statement, but "Mr. Malitz was modestly disinclined to talk about himself."[3] What few biographical details that could be gleaned—that he attended the school where Bismarck had been a student and that he had spent years in "French business life"—were reported as coming from Malitz's coworkers. In all likelihood due to no action or suggestion on Malitz's part, the article was titled "Felix Malitz—Pathé Guiding Spirit."

Whether this title was Malitz's only "transgression" is unknown, but a mere two weeks after the article's publication came another in the *Moving Picture World* titled "Charles Pathé the Guiding Spirit." It consisted almost entirely of a prepared statement from Pathé:

> The guiding spirit of the House of Pathé always has been, at present is, and always will be Charles Pathé himself.
>
> The present directorate of the firm regrets being unable to give you a personal interview at the present time, but can only state that Felix Malitz no longer has any connection whatsoever with either Pathé Frères or Pathé Exchange, Inc. The offices formerly occupied by him are now held by Charles Dupuis and L. Gasnier. The latter, who has spent many years in the United States, occupying positions of trust with the house of Pathé, has just returned from Italy. He is thus recompensed for his long and faithful service, and his valuable experience in the film business recognized.

Paul Fuller, Jr., of the firm of Coudert Brothers, counsel for our firm, has been appointed a director.

Charles Pathé will continue to live in New York, and will devote his energies to the American branch of his great business.[4]

Under the new division of labor of the Pathé Exchange's top management, Louis Gasnier was named managing director and Charles Dupuis became vice president and technical director. Under this arrangement Gasnier's office was located in the Pathé Exchange headquarters at 25 West Forty-Fifth Street in New York City, while Dupuis spent most of his time at the Pathé Exchange's Jersey City studio.[5] The management staff was rounded out by Léon Madieu and, by the end of 1915, a person who would have a major impact on the Pathé Exchange's future, Paul Brunet.[6]

This new setup lasted less than a year. January of 1916 saw J. A. Berst resign the presidency of the faltering General Film distribution company and return to the Pathé Exchange as vice president and general manager, with Gasnier becoming "general director of productions."[7]

"THE CO-OPERATION OF THE BEST PRODUCERS"

At the beginning of 1915 Charles Pathé had restated yet again his vision of the future of his film "publication" business:

> The house of Pathé is unique in regard to its world-wide connections and a name for years universally synonymous with high class film productions. In the making up of this complete program I desire the co-operation of the best producers of both comedies and dramas. There is room for every really capable producer in the country to join with me in putting out the finest regular program ever seen, a program which will go into every part of the world and which will bring liberal profits and a world-wide fame to the men who make it possible.[8]

Under this policy, the American branch of Pathé Frères virtually exited the production business, and the Pathé Exchange, Inc., which for the sake of simplicity will be shortened to "Pathé" until Chapter 7, distributed films from a cadre of "affiliated" independent producers. Despite the populist overtones of Charles Pathé's statement, only occasionally during this period did Pathé distribute the films of producers outside of this circle, and, similarly, most of the affiliated producers distributed their entire output through Pathé. When a new producer did enter the fold, it was usually for a full schedule of films over the course of a year or more rather than an occasional single film from a truly independent producer.

The company with strongest ties to Pathé was the Astra Film Corporation, formed in the summer of 1916. Headed by Louis Gasnier, who left Pathé to start up the new company, Astra boasted the talents of former Pathé Frères scenarists George Fitzmaurice and George B. Seitz, former Pathé director Edward José, and *The Perils of Pauline* coproducer-director Donald MacKenzie.[9] An announcement in *Motion Picture News* in October 1916 stated that "[t]he Astra Film Corporation has at its disposal the financial resources of Pathé and the facilities of the Pathé Jersey City studios."[10] Astra's first production was *Via Wireless* (1916), a film version of a successful Broadway and touring-company thriller directed by Fitzmaurice.[11] Astra would produce over fifty feature films and serials for Pathé between 1916 and 1920. George B. Seitz left Astra in 1919 to set up his own company to produce Pathé serials. Coincidentally, the last serial to be produced by George B. Seitz Productions, *Plunder* (1923), was also the last serial for the "Queen of the Serials," Pearl White. Louis Gasnier moved to California in 1919, taking the Astra name with him and opening up a studio in Glendale.[12] He soon left Astra and directed for a variety of companies, including Robertson-Cole, for whom he made a highly successful version of *Kismet* (1920) with Otis Skinner.[13] Gasnier landed at Paramount in 1929, first working as a staff director in Hollywood and then, because of his origins, at Paramount's French subsidiary. When Paramount closed its French studio in 1934, Gasnier continued to work in various European studios for a time, then returned to Hollywood. After a period of unemployment following one final film for Paramount, Gasnier was forced to accept a job directing ultra-low-budget pictures for independent producer George A. Hirliman. With only a few equally micro-budgeted exceptions, he would spend the remainder of his career working for Hirliman. Ironically, this descent into low-budget pictures led to the production of Gasnier's best-remembered film. His first film for Hirliman in 1936 was *Tell Your Children*, better known today by its reissue title, *Reefer Madness*.[14]

Wharton, Inc., founded in 1914 by brothers Theodore and Leopold Wharton, distributed its productions first through Eclectic and then through Pathé. However, the brothers were among the first Pathé producers to complain about Pathé's policy, to be discussed later, of wanting all of its features to run a standardized five reels. The Whartons began shopping their productions to other distributors in 1916 in the hopes of being able to do longer and more elaborate features in their amusement-park-cum-film-studio in Ithaca, New York.[15] Although they remained in business until 1919, they were never able to attract the quality of distribution they desired for their films after leaving Pathé, and they actually wound up often having to act as their own distributors.

A final twist in their relationship with Pathé came in 1917, when they were producing their third serial for release through William Randolph Hearst's International Film Service. As the first episode of *Patria*, starring Irene Castle, was beginning its theatrical run, International announced that it was closing its distribution offices and shifting its distribution to Pathé.[16] *Patria* opened to rave reviews,[17] and Irene Castle signed a long-term contract with Pathé, who put the production of her future features in the hands of Astra, not Wharton.[18]

The Arrow Film Corporation was another Pathé producer that chafed at Pathé's length restrictions, but it was one that had a reasonably successful life after it and Pathé had parted company. Its relationship with Pathé got off to a very rocky start. In 1915 Arrow's president, W. E. Shallenberger, leased space in the Yonkers, New York, studio of the Standard Film Print Corporation for the production of short films and four-to-five-reel features for Pathé.[19]

The first production was to be a serial titled *Who Is Guilty?* Members of the trade press were given a tour of the studio early in the production, and one reporter described it as being "criss-crossed by the serpentine electric cables and partly choked with the lumber of pictures passed and yet to be."[20] While the reporter seemed thoroughly charmed by the cast, headed by Emmy Wehlen and Howard Estabrook, the production was a troubled one. In late November Pathé announced that a serial titled *The Red Circle* would take the place of *Who Is Guilty?* in its December release schedule. *The Red Circle* was produced by Balboa, Pathé's primary West Coast production affiliate. Ironically, Balboa had originally been announced as the producer of *Who Is Guilty?*, only to have the serial reassigned to Arrow. The reason given for the substitution was frank, if just a bit cryptic. Pathé and Arrow, the announcement said, were committed to pictures of the highest quality: "The first episode, when screened, proved to be disappointing for causes which have now been removed. At great financial loss the episode was scrapped and will be entirely made over."[21] The "causes which have now been removed" evidently were the actors who had so charmed the trade press, because when the serial finally surfaced in May 1916, it did so with a new cast headed by Anna Q. Nilsson and Tom Moore.[22] It also had the slightly shorter title of *Who's Guilty?* The changes apparently paid off, because Pathé happily reported in early June that it had to increase its order of film prints for theatrical showing from 100 to 117 and that prints originally intended for Canada had to be redirected to the U.S. West Coast to satisfy the demand.[23]

Despite this success Arrow's president was almost immediately dissatisfied by the reel limits on Pathé features. In September 1916 he announced that while Arrow wouldn't abandon "program features," he felt that the company's future lay in the longer special pictures: "Mr. Shallenberger feels that it is best not to agree to make nothing but five-reel productions, turning every available plot into 5,000 feet of film regardless of whether it should be told in 3,000 or 7,000 feet." Similarly, the number of episodes of Arrow's future serials would be determined by the plot.[24] While Arrow, like Wharton, would eventually resort to distributing much of its own product, it managed to survive into the mid-1920s.[25]

Perhaps the affiliated producer with the longest history prior to releasing through Pathé was the Thanhouser Film Corporation, which had been established in 1910 in the New York City suburb of New Rochelle by theatrical manager Edwin Thanhouser. After two very successful years, Thanhouser sold the company to a group of investors, including Charles J. Hite and future Arrow president W. E. Shallenberger,[26] and took his family on a two-year visit to Europe with the proceeds. Hite was named president of Thanhouser, but when he died after a 1914 automobile accident, the studio was left without an obvious successor, and it drifted into disarray. By coincidence it was not long afterward that Edwin Thanhouser and his family returned to the United States, having left Europe with the outbreak of the First World War. The Thanhouser Film Corporation's board of directors asked Thanhouser to return to the presidency of his namesake studio.[27]

From its inception Thanhouser had been an independent producer, operating outside of the Motion Picture Patents Company. As such, it was unable to distribute its productions through General Film. Initially the company distributed its own product, then it turned to a pair of established independent distributors: first the Motion Picture Distributing and Sales Company and then the Film Supply Company. After the 1912 sale to Hite et al., Thanhouser switched its distribution to the more powerful Mutual Film Corporation, a company cofounded by Hite and one in which he was vice president, treasurer, and board member.[28] Even after Hite's death Thanhouser continued releasing through Mutual until mid-1916, when it signed on with Pathé.

Under the contract with Pathé, Thanhouser would produce two five-reel features per month at its New Rochelle and Jacksonville, Florida, studios. While Edwin Thanhouser noted that this would constitute only one-fourth of the monthly output of shorts and features Thanhouser had made for Mutual, it would actually make Thanhouser Pathé's largest supplier of the period.[29] Pathé would distribute twenty-eight Thanhouser features between August 14, 1916, and October 7, 1917.

Thanhouser's decision to cease production in 1917 apparently was a sudden one. In July Edwin Thanhouser announced that he would not join five producers who had recently stopped giving advance screenings of their films for critics, asserting that he was "a firm believer in giving the exhibitor [the] earliest information possible."[30] His belief in the continuing quality of his productions was solid: "I think the [Pathé] Gold Rooster Plays we have produced since last August . . . have demonstrated the meaning of Thanhouser methods when applied to features." He went on to say that the films had been so successful that it was hard to single out the best, although *The Vicar of Wakefield* "has made a particular impression."[31] Yet less than two weeks after these proclamations came the news that Clara Kimball Young had leased Thanhouser's New Rochelle studio for the production of her next film.[32] October brought the release of what would be Thanhouser's final film, *The Heart of Ezra Greer*, along with word of another lease tenant moving into the studio.[33] By 1920 when Edward José directed *The Riddle: Woman* in the facility, the trade papers were referring to it as "the old Thanhouser studio."

As for Edwin Thanhouser, he announced his retirement in March 1918, saying that his 1915 return to the studio's helm had been done with the understanding that he would stay for only three years. He put the finishing touches on his estate on Long Island Sound[34] and settled into a long and prosperous retirement, dying at the age of ninety in 1956.[35]

Pathé's principal West Coast production affiliate was the Balboa Amusement Producing Company located in Long Beach, California. Balboa was established in 1913 and released its mostly short-film product through several distributors before signing with Eclectic at the end of 1914. At that time Charles Pathé declared Balboa's two-, three-, and four-reel dramas and one-reel comedies "to be the finest American made pictures he had ever seen upon the screen."[36] Also in December 1914 Ruth Roland signed a three-year contract with Balboa for a reported $1,000 per week. From the onset of her film career, beginning in 1908, Roland had acted for the Kalem Company. Like many early film companies Kalem resisted giving its stars on-screen billing, fearing that if the stars became known by name to the moviegoing public, they would be in a position to insist upon higher pay when their contracts came up for renewal. These studios chose instead to identify actors by generic screen names so that they could substitute another actor if the original's salary demands became too high. Hence, prior to signing with Balboa, Ruth Roland had been known to theater audiences as "The Kalem Girl."[37] She would soon become the new "Queen of the Serials" as Pearl White attempted to shift away from serials toward feature dramas.

Also joining Balboa at the end of 1914 was Henry B. Walthall, a former D. W. Griffith star whose most memorable role was the male lead in Griffith's

Birth of a Nation. Walthall would become famous when the movie was released within a few months. Walthall only made two features for Balboa, neither of which was released through Pathé. Of far more significance to Balboa (and film history) was the presence on the payroll of an actor named Henry King. King had joined Balboa in early 1914, and while he was still primarily an actor at the time Balboa began releasing through Pathé, he would soon turn to directing and would go on to pilot over a hundred features through the early 1960s, including *Twelve O'Clock High* (1949), *The Gunfighter* (1950), and *The Sun Also Rises* (1957).

One of Balboa's first productions for Pathé was an unusual series of shorts starring Roland and King titled *Who Pays?* Presented (and referred to in the trade press) as a serial with each entry given a chapter number in typical serial fashion, *Who Pays?* eschewed a continuing story line and characters from one episode to the next; the common thread here was a central theme shared by all of the installments. Each chapter presents a self-contained story in which some miscarriage of justice or societal inequality brings ruin to its characters in an unhappy ending. The success of *Who Pays?* would lead to a similar series from Balboa, also starring Ruth Roland, titled *The Price of Folly.* However, by the time *The Price of Folly* hit theater screens in 1918, Balboa was reaching the end of its road.

Balboa's demise was most likely the result of overexpansion. Balboa had begun a program of new construction on its lot in mid-1915; within a year it proclaimed itself to be "the fastest growing and the largest actually independent moving picture producing studio in the world." This was a golden period for the company, with its serials *Neal of the Navy* and *The Red Circle* (both in 1915, the latter starring Ruth Roland) being popular successes,[38] and with its features *The Shrine of Happiness* and *Adventures of a Madcap* (both in 1915) being selected as two of the first "Gold Rooster" productions to be sent to France to be colored with the Pathécolor process (which will be discussed later).[39]

During this heyday for his company, studio president H. M. Horkheimer opined that "[a] studio is not a factory." He went on to explain that the waste that others, including some producers, saw in the filmmaking process was "time given to turning out of careful and artistic work. If your purpose is primarily to 'manufacture film,' then of course you can rush your output. But the result will tell on the screen. Each silent drama put on is a separate problem. The studio's business is not like that of a shoe factory, which makes thousands of duplicates of a given pattern."[40] In a bit of self-contradiction Horkheimer proudly noted that his company had a weekly production capacity of twenty thousand feet of film.[41]

By late 1916 Balboa boasted eighteen buildings, including a papier-mâché department to turn out "sculptural props," a blacksmith shop, two warehouses of props, and a concrete vault to protect the cameras and other equipment.[42] By the beginning of 1917 Balboa's output of films was greater than Pathé was willing to take; the excess product was distributed by General Film. The strain was beginning to show in the quality of the work. Of the early 1917 release *Sold at Auction*, the *Motion Picture News* commented that Balboa produced "typical pictures. For form's sake and as a matter of course they deal in pictures molded along popular lines. If they have a point to make . . . it must be obvious, not subtle. . . . 'Sold at Auction' is ripe melodrama at its ripest."[43]

The second half of 1917 saw a dramatic curtailment of production at Balboa. The first public hint of impending disaster came at the beginning of 1918, when J. A. Berst announced that the studios of Paralta Plays would be Pathé's future West Coast production center.[44] By spring 1918 production at Balboa had ceased completely, and in October Balboa's creditors met to discuss liquidation of Balboa's $60,000 outstanding debt. An inventory of the facility revealed that "in the property rooms is a collection of material from practically all over the world. Included in the equipment are several automobiles and a number of valuable cameras."[45] The studio changed ownership and soldiered on for a few more years as a rental facility for independent producers before finally being demolished in the mid-1920s.

A final legacy of Balboa was a pair of spin-off production companies. The first was the Diando, established by W. A. S. Douglas and L. T. Osborne (D and O, or Diando), formed in Glendale, California, in 1917 exclusively to produce the films of former Balboa star "Baby" Marie Osborne.[46] The studio made a few films featuring other stars as well before it expired, with its maturing star's career, in 1919.[47] Pathé was its only distributor. The other company to rise from Balboa's ashes was Ruth Roland Serials, Inc. When Balboa ceased operations shortly after the production of *The Price of Folly*, Roland's association with Pathé continued, first through a pair of serials produced by Astra, then with seven serials produced between 1919 and 1923 for her own firm. As with Diando, Ruth Roland Serials released all of its product through Pathé.

While the studios discussed above were capable of handling dramatic features and serials, along with the occasional romantic or situational feature comedy, Pathé also needed a reliable supply of slapstick short comedies to provide balance to its release schedule. This type of film had first been popularized in the United States by French imports, mostly from Pathé Frères, in the years before 1912. Beginning in 1912 this style of visual comedy, emphasizing fast action and physical stunts, was appropriated and Americanized by Mack Sennett's Keystone studio and a host of subsequent imitators. The belief at the time, that slapstick comedy could only be produced by a company that specialized in the form, would seem to be borne out by Balboa's efforts in the field. Its short-comedy series featuring a character called Ima Simp merited only three episodes, produced during the first half of 1915.

One studio that specialized in comedy was founded by four theatrical-producer brothers from Kalamazoo, Michigan. In late 1913 Aubrey, Harry, Isaac, and Sam Mittenthal established the Mittenthal Film Company in a small studio in Yonkers, New York. They initially produced short dramas, but late in 1914 switched to single-reel comedies. Starting in early 1915 most of their comedies centered on a pair of burlesque characters billed as Heinie and Louie, played by Jimmy Aubrey and Walter Kendig.[48] Pathé began distribution of these films in mid-1915, and the series continued, often to very good reviews, until the Mittenthal brothers withdrew from film production in 1917.[49]

By far and away, Pathé's most successful comedy specialist, in fact the most successful of its production affiliates in any genre, was the studio headed by Hal Roach. Established as the Rolin Film Company in the summer of 1914, the firm operated in a series of rented studio facilities in the Los Angeles area until it built a permanent home in Culver City, California, in 1920 and changed its corporate name to the Hal Roach Studios.

Like Mittenthal, Rolin didn't start out to be a comedy specialist. Its early productions included both short dramas and comedies. Unlike Mittenthal, though, Rolin experienced great difficulty getting its early productions distributed theatrically. During the first nine months of its existence, Rolin teetered on the edge of bankruptcy as it produced films for which it could find no market. Finally, in the spring of 1915, it sold a single comedy starring future comedy titan Harold Lloyd to Pathé. For the next six months Rolin continued to produce comedies featuring Lloyd on speculation, to be accepted or rejected by Pathé on a case-by-case basis. In October 1915 Pathé was sufficiently satisfied with the quality and reliability of Rolin's output to offer the studio a long-term contract for a series of one-reel comedies featuring Harold Lloyd as a character named Lonesome Luke.[50]

Many of the business records for Rolin and the Hal Roach Studios still exist, housed at the University of Southern California. These records permit detailed study of the relationship between Pathé and an affiliated producer who began in a position of real weakness, impoverished and begging for distribution of its accumulated productions, but whose bargaining power rose steadily as Harold Lloyd's popularity skyrocketed. An examination of the

Pathé-Rolin relationship has already been undertaken in *A History of the Hal Roach Studios*, but a brief review might be helpful now since, presumably, the system of quality control Pathé exercised on Rolin's films was similar to its dealings with its other production partners.

All material submitted by Rolin to Pathé had to pass muster with a screening committee of six judges, made up of staff members of Pathé's New York City headquarters. Of Rolin's initial submission of nine one-reel comedies and three two-reel dramas in March 1915, the committee rejected the dramas outright and complained that the comedies were crude, vulgar, and full of censorable material. The committee also noted the inferior technical qualities of the films, with mediocre photography and onlookers photographed in the background.[51] Despite this, Pathé did accept a comedy in which Harold Lloyd played a character named Willie Work for distribution and asked Rolin to produce more like it, correcting the defects that the screening committee had pointed out. The Willie Work character was modified, and Lonesome Luke was born.

Even after Rolin entered into the long-term contract with Pathé in October 1915, its films were still reviewed by the screening committee, which had the power to demand changes and to reject films outright. Rejected films became the producer's loss, with Pathé under no obligation to pay for them. The power wielded by this committee was all too apparent when Rolin attempted to start up a second comedy series in addition to the Lonesome Luke films. This series featured an Italian circus clown named Armando Novello who billed himself as Toto. When Hal Roach's associate Dwight Whiting, in New York on a business trip, sent Roach a telegram saying that the screening committee wanted a 1918 Toto film reedited, Roach angrily wired back observing that Pathé's executives knew nothing about comedy and that he would not make any changes. Pathé could take the film as it was or not at all.[52] The following day Whiting relayed the news that Pathé had called Roach's bluff and rejected the Toto film entirely. The committee believed that the only good material in the film was that set on a streetcar, and they suggested that the streetcar material should be expanded to consume the bulk of the film's running time. Whiting concluded with his own belief that the Toto series was a doomed enterprise and that after production wrapped on "Toto Three," Roach should fire the Toto company.[53]

The day he received the first telegram from Whiting, Roach had desperately tried to find a new distributor for the Toto films. He met with rejection at every turn. He then asked Whiting to speak again to the committee, asserting that as funny as the streetcar material was, it would not carry the whole film.[54] While no copy of the Toto film in question is known to exist, the fact that it was ultimately released as *Fare, Please*, a title that emphasizes the streetcar material, suggests that Roach, faced with the hard reality of remaking the film Pathé's way or taking a loss, chose the former path.

One final note that speaks to the committee's authority in style as well as substance, Whiting told Roach to inform Toto's cinematographer to stop panning the camera so much. No less than J. A. Berst himself advised Whiting that Pathé discouraged the use of pans and that "nearly every scene in Toto Three had panning needlessly up and down or sideways. . . ."[55]

GOLD ROOSTER PLAYS

Around 1915 U.S. film lengths underwent a significant change. Before then practically all films ran thirty minutes or less. By late 1914 a survey of theaters in twenty-seven cities of varying sizes revealed a growing preference for feature-length pictures over all-shorts programs. Whether short films, features, or a combination of both, program length varied widely from three or four reels (forty-five minutes to an hour) in Birmingham, Alabama, to a maximum of eight reels (two hours) in five of the cities.[56]

Then as now, films based on a known literary work had the advantage of a ready-made audience. Members of the public familiar with a published work, or those who had at least heard good things in connection with its title, were more likely to see a film version. The shift from short films to features meant a shift from short stories to novels and plays for those films with a literary precedent.

Perhaps because of its connections to Europe, where the practice of making longer films based on known works predated that in the United States, Pathé seized upon this idea for its American productions. As early as 1913 Pathé announced that it had secured the film rights to stage successes recently produced by Henry W. Savage, including what would be the first screen version of the oft-remade *Madame X*. The *Moving Picture World* remarked that "[a]s a result of this deal, Pathé, before so strongly fortified with photoplay material, becomes almost a monopolist in the possession of stage successes."[57] In 1915 Pathé made a similar deal with stage producer A. H. Woods.[58] The same year, Pathé secured the screen rights to *The Light That Failed*, the first work by Rudyard Kipling "to be put into pictures."[59]

Pathé had sought a link to the stage and "legitimate" drama early on by releasing many of its short films under the trade name "Pathéplays." Beginning in September 1915 the company launched a new series of feature-length films under the banner "Pathé Gold Rooster Plays." Announcing the series, Pathé boasted that it "has arranged a feature campaign . . . that will be without parallel."[60]

The groundwork, it said, had been laid months earlier with the acquisition of film rights to famous books and plays. The films would be strictly American productions, with the rare exception of a top European film like the Paris-produced *Les Misérables* (1912). "Pathé Frères," the article continued, "is thought to be the biggest and most important motion picture company in the world. The American branch is now receiving the most attention of any of its subsidiary concerns, Charles G. Pathé himself having spent much of his time recently in this country."[61] As an added incentive, theaters booking Gold Rooster Plays would receive a free musical cue sheet with each film. The cue sheet would assist the theater's musicians by suggesting certain stock songs to be played with each scene in the film.[62] Curiously, although the Gold Rooster Plays were intended as the top of Pathé's production line, the company rigidly held its producers to film lengths of five reels, running between sixty and seventy-five minutes. This put the features in the category of "program pictures": films considered standard and unexceptional, designed to provide fairly routine entertainment. By their very nature, program pictures could not rise to the level of ambition and renown of longer "special features" made by the top stars and directors.

One final item in the article announcing the Gold Rooster Plays was that some of them would be presented in Pathécolor. From the earliest days of the motion picture, filmmakers had sought various ways of artificially introducing color into black and white films until a "natural color" process capable of photographing all the hues of nature could be developed. The first "color" films were hand colored. Rooms full of employees, usually women, painstakingly colored the images on a film print one frame at a time.[63] Considering the facts that a frame of 35-millimeter film is roughly the size of a postage stamp containing images so tiny that the colorists often had to use paintbrushes with a single horse hair; that one had to paint sixteen or more frames to get one second's worth of film; and that there was no way to duplicate the color from one print to another, meaning that every copy of the film had to be colored individually, this was a very inefficient and unsatisfactory color system. The small size of the frame and the heavy labor demands meant that only certain objects were colored, leaving the rest of the image in black and white, and the colors often wobbled beyond the boundaries of the object being painted.[64]

Pathécolor represented a vast improvement over hand coloring. The intricate process is described by Brian Coe in *The History of Movie Photography*:

> A print of the film to be coloured was projected one frame at a time onto a small screen. The operator moved a pointer over the enlarged picture, outlining all the areas to be tinted in a particular colour. A pantographic

> mechanical linkage connected to the pointer moved a cutter over another film strip, cutting out all these areas. As many as six stencil films might be prepared for as many different colours.[65] The stencil films were run in contact with a new print through staining machines which applied dyes of suitable colours through the holes.[66]

Although the process of cutting the stencil films was still labor intensive, taking "a good worker an hour to cut only three feet of stencil strip for a single tinting,"[67] the advantages of Pathécolor were that the colors could be applied to the smallest item in the frame with a precision that kept the dye within the boundaries of the object being colored, and, unlike hand coloring, once the stencils were cut the results could be machine-duplicated on as many prints as desired. Pathé's "colorists" had a palate of nine different dyes from which to work, and surviving Pathécolor prints possess a charm and beauty that is unique.[68] As Joshua Yumibe notes, the success of Pathécolor established the company as "the leading producer of colored films around the world. The popularity of these films in part fueled Pathé's global success during the early years of the 1900s."[69] In the case of the Pathé Exchange, use of Pathécolor segments extended all the way into the early talking-picture era.

Commenting on the use of Pathécolor one year into the Gold Rooster program, J. A. Berst expressed his belief that color both enhanced dramatic realism and fattened the box-office take, justifying the extra time and money spent to color a film. He observed that "blackberry patches, outdoor swimming pools washing up on the lips of mossy banks, fruit orchards, country estates, flower-fringed roads and lastly, the [*sic*] not leastly, the charming summer dresses worn by Miss Roland insisted on COLOR. So we sent 'A Matrimonial Martyr' abroad to our Paris laboratories, there to be treated to the tedious and expensive process of Pathécolor. And the feature, returned, endorses our efforts on it."[70]

The Gold Rooster Plays started off strong and were initially released at the rate of one per week. The *Moving Picture World* commented that *The Galloper* (1915) was the first of the Gold Rooster Plays and "is worthy of the honor thus given to it."[71] Of *Comrade John* (1915) the *Motion Picture News* said, "It is seldom we see as good a picture as this new member of the Gold Rooster Family."[72] Pathécolor came in for its share of praise. The *Moving Picture World* said that *The Shrine of Happiness* (1916) should "attract widespread attention. The play was produced in Southern California by Balboa, and the locations chosen were so beautiful as to lend themselves particularly well to Pathécolor."[73] Reviews of Pathécolor were overwhelmingly, but not universally, positive. The *Moving*

Picture World grumbled that the travelogue *Here and There in Spain* (1916) "is colored, but not always artistically."[74] Despite the references to colorists and commendations to producers for choosing photogenic locations, the theme running through practically all of the period reviews of Pathécolor emphasizes its almost photographic verisimilitude. *Motion Picture News* raved that after Pathé sent Gold Rooster *Sultana* (1916) to France to be colored, it came back as "a splendid example of color photography."[75] The following month *Motion Picture News* actually found Pathécolor practically the only reason to see *Adventures of a Madcap*, saying that "artistically colored prints add to the attractiveness of this story of rural, city and gypsy life. The story apparently was created to give Jackie Saunders one of the hoyden parts in which she delights, and has little strength or originality to carry it. The settings, however, are amid woodland glades, flower gardens and ivy clad mansions, and these lend themselves excellently to the pencil of the colorist."[76]

It was evident by the spring of 1916 that the weekly Gold Rooster releases weren't paying off as anticipated. J. A. Berst had just returned to the company, replacing the team of Gasnier and Dupuis. He immediately shifted more of Pathé's resources into its highly popular and successful serial production, likely at the insistence of Charles Pathé, and the output of Gold Rooster Plays dropped from one per week to one per month. This seemingly regressive move can best be seen in the career track of Edward José. José perhaps left his most lasting mark on film history playing the family man lured to his doom by Theda Bara in *A Fool There Was* (1915), but in 1915 he was turning his sights from acting to directing. During the latter part of 1915 José directed no fewer than four Gold Rooster Plays at Astra. The last of the four, *The Beloved Vagabond*, drew interestingly mixed reviews. The generally affable *Moving Picture World* gushed that "[t]he film, made here in America, was sent to Paris to be hand colored, the result being a delightful enhancement of an already beautiful production."[77] The somewhat more acerbic *Motion Picture News* sarcastically sneered, "It is a high class picture, strictly so. It is fit for the patrons of two-dollar psychological plays. It is quaint, subtle and artistic. In fact, it is so exceedingly high class that it may sail serenely over the heads of the patrons who want the 'movie' type of entertainment."[78]

By early 1916 Pathé had José, who had just incorporated himself as Edward José Productions, directing their latest Pearl White serial *The Iron Claw*. Trying to put the best face on the situation, an advertisement in the *Moving Picture World* said that "Pathé, after seeing 'The Beloved Vagabond,' 'Simon the Jester,' 'The Closing Net' and 'Nedra,' entrusted to Edward José the direction of its greatest serial."[79] As had been the case with *The Perils of Pauline*, *The*

Iron Claw was popular enough that its run was extended from the originally planned fourteen or fifteen episodes to twenty.[80]

As they formulated their production plans for the movie season beginning in the fall of 1916 and running through the summer of 1917, Berst and his staff continued their focus on serials, announcing that the company's affiliates would produce seven during the year.[81] The serials were generally released in a pattern that saw two different series in the theaters at any given time. The releases were staggered, so that as one serial ended (to be replaced by a new one the next week), the other was in "midlife," approximately halfway through its run.

Two of Pathé's serials for the upcoming season would be based on published works. The Balboa-produced Ruth Roland serial *The Neglected Wife* (1917) was based on the novel *The Journal of a Neglected Wife* and its sequel *The Woman Alone*. Astra's *The Mystery of the Double Cross* (1917), in which Mollie King substituted for intended star Pearl White, was based on the novel *The Double Cross*.[82] At the same time, the serials would adhere to the core values that had made them so popular. In an article titled "What the Public Wants in 'Shielding Shadow,'" Louis Gasnier said, "In 'The Shielding Shadow' we have combined everything which experience has shown that the motion picture wants. . . . We have adventure, love, mystery, and a strong element of suspense throughout. . . . There are more thrills, greater thrills, than there ever have been in any other serials."[83]

Despite the new emphasis on serials, Berst decided to make another run at the feature market for the new movie season. In July he announced that Pathé would release two Gold Rooster plays per month.[84] By October the number was back up to one Gold Rooster per week.[85] Berst expressed his hope that the five-reeler would equal the serial as a box-office attraction and "that in the future the five-reeler will be emphasized in the Pathé program."[86] Again, as to the career of Edward José, the 1916–17 movie season saw him alternating feature and serial work. His initial offering was the feature version of *The Light That Failed* (1916), followed by the serial *Pearl of the Army* (1916–17) and the feature *Mayblossom* (1917), both starring Pearl White. After that, he left Pathé for a career directing features for a variety of companies, including future Pathé affiliate Associated Exhibitors. In the early 1920s he moved to France, where he ended his directing career with a feature that was also Pearl White's last, *Terror* (1924).

In addition to features from Astra, Arrow, Thanhouser, and Balboa, the expanded feature output for 1916–17 included one feature each from the pioneering female filmmaker Alice Guy and her husband Herbert Blaché. Guy had been one of French filmmaker Leon Gaumont's first directors in the late

1890s and had established her own production company, Solax, in the United States in 1910. But her studio had closed at mid-decade, and by 1917 when her first Pathé-released film, *The Empress*, appeared, it drew a resounding raspberry from *Motion Picture News* critic Peter Milne, who noted that "not only is the production conventional in plot, but its treatment is hackneyed and its settings are undeniably cheap."[87] Of her remaining seven directorial efforts, Guy would direct two more films for Pathé release: *The Great Adventure* with Bessie Love appeared in 1918,[88] and her final film, *Tarnished Reputations*, codirected by Herbert Blaché and produced by fellow Gaumont alumnus Léonce Perret, was released in 1920.

"HIS WORK UPON THE SCREEN WILL LIVE WHEN HE IS DEAD"

Today the vast majority of films produced during the silent era are gone, victims of decay and neglect. Of those films that do survive, most are locked away in film archives and may only be viewed, if at all, by making a trip to the archive. Only a small subset of surviving silent films is available on video disc, via streaming video, or online, for the same reason that so many were allowed to disintegrate in the first place: there is little commercial value in present-day reissues of silent films. Compared to the number of people who will buy or rent the latest big-budget Hollywood production, the number of those who seek out silent-film releases is too small to make the effort worthwhile to any but a handful of dedicated firms.

Five of Thanhouser's twenty-eight Gold Rooster Plays are known to have survived and are available at the time of this writing due to the efforts of Edwin Thanhouser's grandson, Ned Thanhouser, and his Thanhouser Company Film Preservation, Inc. Of the five, *King Lear* (1916) and *The Fires of Youth* (1917) exist only as half-hour abridgements. *The World and the Woman* (1916) and *The Woman in White* (1917) survive mostly intact as reissue versions in which the original subtitles have been replaced. With the exception of a replaced main title card, *The Vicar of Wakefield* (1917) alone exists in its original form, complete with the words "Pathé Gold Rooster Play" emblazoned across the top of many of its subtitles.

If only one of Thanhouser's Gold Rooster Plays could survive completely intact, *The Vicar of Wakefield* is a fortunate choice. It was Edwin Thanhouser's favorite of the group and also was the most successful. A year after its original release Pathé reclassified it from Gold Rooster to "Super-Feature" for reissue.[89] Viewing the film today, one is impressed by the good costumes and the substantial sets and locations, which give an authentic mid-eighteenth-century atmosphere to the proceedings. This stands in sharp contrast to an Arrow Gold Rooster Play, *Crime and Punishment*, released the same day as *Vicar*. About *Crime and Punishment*, Peter Milne of the *Motion Picture News* complained that "in the matter of production, 'Crime and Punishment' is hardly consistent with the Pathé Standard. The scenes of poverty and squalor . . . are realistic to a degree, but in some of the scenes, mainly in the office where a backdrop that is undeniably a backdrop is hung, the mechanics of the studio are quite obviously revealed."[90] The same reviewer admired the authentic period atmosphere and "charming pictures of rural life" contained in *Vicar*, although he found Frederick Warde's performance to be "full of ultra-Shakespearian gesticulations" and said that Warde "forgets he is acting for the camera and not on the stage."[91] This description conjures up images of a stilted and over-exaggerated performance, which would have to be accepted at face value had the film not survived. It does exist, though, and while the acting style of the classically stage-trained Warde does seem a bit mannered at times, it is more often rather subdued and charming.

Not long after *The Vicar of Wakefield* was released, Frederick Warde wrote a story for the *Moving Picture World* in which he detailed his transition from stage to film acting: "My experience in moving pictures has been limited; my knowledge of the stage is of nearly half a century. . . . When I entered the moving picture business I found I had much of this to unlearn. Not that it was necessary to be unnatural before the camera, but to curb the natural tendency to spontaneity, and to synchronize one's emotions and movements to the action of the machine."[92] Warde noted that his Thanhouser films to date had all been

> pronounced successes. They all demanded acting as well as appearance, and without the experienced legitimate actor, would not have created the impression they did. . . . Physical beauty is a powerful asset for a picture, and for a time was practically the only one, but the development of its dramatic possibilities has created a demand for something more than attractive personality in the illustration of a story. The expression of the face must carry with it the conviction of sincere emotion. The walk, the carriage of the limbs, every action must be in harmony with the feeling of the moment or the effect is only artificial and worthless. . . . The actor's work upon the stage leaves but a memory, sweet and often tender, as it is, but his work upon the screen will live when he is dead, and many friends and admirers will look upon his features as in life, and recall those memories; while new generations will admire and praise his art and skill long after he is dead.[93]

With this last thought in mind, it is a happy coincidence that in addition to *The Vicar of Wakefield*, at least four other films starring Warde still exist: *The Life and Death of King Richard III* (1912) and abridgements of the Thanhouser-produced *Silas Marner* (released by Mutual in 1916), *King Lear*, and *The Fires of Youth*.

Another of Thanhouser's surviving films is noteworthy for its intricate plot structure, effective use of parallel action and crosscutting, and, again, its use of authentic settings. Set largely in the Adirondack Mountains, *The World and the Woman* is the second film appearance of tragic silent-screen legend Jeanne Eagels. At first glance it seems a straightforward, at times preposterous, story of redemption, but upon reflection it becomes apparent that the redemption actually involves an intricate dance of multiple characters whose interaction enables each to shed his or her personal baggage.

PATHÉ PLAYS

As Berst and his team were planning their strategy for the 1917–18 movie season, Pathé sat somewhere in the middle of the movie-studio hierarchy and seemed poised to move higher. With one five-reel feature and nine reels of short subjects per week, its output was less than that of Paramount, Universal, Triangle, Mutual, and K-E-S-E (Kleine, Edison, Selig, and Essanay), but the last three of these companies would soon be out of business. Pathé's output was greater than that of Fox, Metro, Vitagraph (which would be folded into Warner Brothers in the mid-1920s), World, and a host of ephemeral studios.[94] The main difference between Pathé and its competitors, though, was Charles Pathé's book-publishing model, his belief in a decentralized system of production. As will be demonstrated shortly, Pathé's ideas ran contrary to the business plans of those running the production companies that would become the major studios, for whom consolidation was the order of the day.

In addition to consolidation, problems with an overproduction of features, leading to a glut of films on the market; a devastating influenza epidemic that would compel health authorities in many cities to order theaters to close for weeks, in some cases months; and challenges from forces in the United States who wanted to see films censored and movie theaters closed nationwide on Sunday lay just over the horizon in the summer of 1917. But a problem very much on the minds of producers, as Berst and his associates set their eyes on the future, was a dramatic increase in the salary expectation of the industry's top stars. Just as the members of the Motion Picture Patents Company had feared, allowing stars to be billed by name made them bankable commodities, and the stars were eager to exploit that fact. The point was driven home in an editorial cartoon in the *Motion Picture News* from March 1917, in which a female star wearing furs, carrying a bag of money, and preparing to get into a diamond-encrusted limousine throws a handful of pocket change to a couple of beggars who are in the gutter fighting over it. One of the beggars is identified as "Producers," and the other is "Exhibitors."[95]

So it was that for the 1917–18 film season Berst announced a new feature policy that "will embrace the following box office stars: Fannie Ward, Frank Keenan, Bessie Love, Bryant Washburn, Pearl White and Mrs. Vernon Castle." The new series of star features would be known as Pathé Plays. The two-year-old Gold Rooster brand was downgraded to secondary status, featuring Antonio Moreno, Gladys Hulette, and Baby Marie Osborne. The final Gold Rooster Play would be released in March 1918. In a departure from its past practices, but in keeping with industry trends, Pathé abandoned its "open booking" policy in which exhibitors could book films individually. Exhibitors would now be forced to take either the entire output of one or more of the identified star players or, if they wished, could book the entire Pathé Plays series. *The Vicar of Wakefield* and a 1912 French version of *Les Misérables* would go into reissue as "Super-Features," as would a pair of Harry Rapf–produced features: *To-Day* and *The Mad Lover*.[96]

One independent production not released as a Super-Feature was Marion Davies' film debut. *Runaway Romany* (1917) was written by Davies herself, and prior to its release it had been the subject of a three-month publicity barrage in the form of large advertisements in newspaper Sunday supplements and a serialization of the film's story published in forty newspapers.[97] Despite this, the film quietly slipped in and out of theaters as a Gold Rooster Play beginning Christmas week 1917. *Motion Picture News* critic Peter Milne noted that the film had been "long-heralded and widely advertised" but observed that Davies' "abilities in the dramatic line are not to be compared with those which have gained her popularity on New York's Broadway." Milne found the film's climax to lack "the punch usually associated with such momentous points. Probably this latter lacking is partially due to the fact that the essentials of 'Runaway Romany' are more or less familiar, but skillful treatment has oftentimes made much of mere conventionality."[98]

Reviewing his company's business plan in October 1917, J. A. Berst sought to reassure theater owners that Pathé had no desire to buy any theaters, unlike the growing Paramount conglomerate. "The best for the least" would be the motto, said Berst. Offering a quality product at low prices, Pathé would concentrate on distribution:

> We cannot accomplish this if we are occupying ourselves with the exhibiting end of the business. No one man can conquer the entire world. . . . We are working to build up the producing and manufacturing end of our business. . . . We will leave it to some one else to handle the exhibiting end. . . . We want the name "Pathé" to mean the best and most in the motion picture, so that when a person mentions "motion pictures" he will think of "Pathé" just as today every one thinks of Pathé when they mention "News Film" or "Serials."[99]

The expanded feature output meant a need for greater studio capacity. In October 1917 Astra was occupying four studios in Jérsey City and Fort Lee, New Jersey, and Pathé leased space in three additional studios: the Sanger Studio at 134th Street and Park Avenue and the Norma Talmadge Studio on Forty-Eighth Street, both in New York City, and the Kalem Studio in Los Angeles.[100]

RUSSIAN ART FILMS

As noted earlier, U.S. distribution of the films produced by Pathé's worldwide network of affiliated producers was a bit problematic. Almost from cinema's outset, American producers had resented the competition presented by European films, especially when the films were sold on the U.S. market at prices below those at which American producers could profitably operate.[101] Exacerbating the problem was the fact that most American films before 1915 were technically and artistically inferior to the best European product. Acting in what they perceived as the American industry's best interests, the popular press and trade publications sought to vilify European productions as depicting morals and lifestyles that were damaging to American values, particularly when it came to young people. The trade press often disdainfully commented upon a film's obvious Europeanness. As an example, consider the *Motion Picture News* review of Italian import *The Shadow of Her Past*:

> The emotionalism of the continental players has never been so clearly evinced as in this Gold Rooster play. . . . Lucien Muratore . . . is violently profuse in gesture and expression. The story . . . is mediocre as compared with the average Pathé project. The box office value of "The Shadow of Her Past" will depend more on the sensations conveyed by the title than in its net contents. . . . It moves slower than the average five reeler. . . . The production is good in the matter of settings and photography.[102]

Still, there were exceptions. At the beginning of 1914 Pathé released in the United States, with heavy publicity, *Germinal*, a five-reel adaptation of an Émile Zola novel produced in 1913 by Pathé's French affiliate SCAGL (Société

Cinématographique des Auteurs et Gens de Lettres). In his review of the film for the *Moving Picture World*, W. Stephen Bush wrote that "at their best the Pathé productions are unbeatable. . . . It is at its best in 'Germinal.'"[103] He went on to proclaim the film a true masterpiece. Similarly, French comedies, particularly those starring Max Linder, remained popular when other foreign imports were being condemned, and *The Life of Our Savior*, a Pathécolor French biography of Jesus Christ shot on locations in Palestine and Egypt, became a perennial Christmas favorite for several years, beginning in 1915.

Attitudes toward foreign films began to change a bit around mid-decade, in the trade press anyway. Late in 1916, W. Stephen Bush wrote,

> We have in the past hesitated to concur in the prevailing opinion that the foreign-made film of just ordinary quality has no more chance in the American market. Today we feel convinced that the prevailing opinion is right.
>
> We believe that two simple causes have been operating to bring about this result. The first cause we think is the steady improvement of American made film; the second is the deterioration of the European film.[104]

To prove his point Bush goes on to quote Umberto Paradisi, critic for the Italian film trade journal *La Vita Cinematografica*, as saying, "The Americans have beaten us."

This perceived decline in the quality of European films may have made them seem to be less of a competitive threat to American productions, creating an environment in which a "good," as opposed to "ordinary," European film could be openly admired for its artistry and could be a popular success. While the word *foreign* retained some of its pejorative bite, *Motion Picture News* denounced the 1917 Pathé Gold Rooster release of Abel Gance's *The Torture of Silence* as "typically foreign," a European film could, under the right circumstances, do remarkably well. One case in point was Pathé's rerelease *Les Misérables*. A big success in the United States in 1913–14, the 1917 reissue opened to capacity crowds in Chicago.[105] It continued to draw well throughout the United States, with one exhibitor calling it "old but appreciated."[106]

This evolving attitude toward foreign films of "artistic merit" may have been a factor in J. A. Berst's decision to take a gamble and release an entire series of foreign films in the 1917–18 season. To the likely consternation of Charles Pathé, the films would not be drawn from Pathé Frères' large catalog of current and past releases, but instead would be "a series of special Russian Art Films, which are so beautiful in production, so powerful in story, and so remarkable in acting that they are confidently expected to create a sensation."[107] The Russian films, which would run five or six reels each, could be booked in series or individually and would be released at the rate of one every four weeks.

In an early trade-press story on the series, N. S. Kaplan, president of the Russian Art Film Corporation, tackled the "foreignness" issue head on.

> Promise is made by the Russian Art Films that exhibitors who have in the past complained that they found foreign films unprofitable because of the character of the productions, exaggerated gestures of the actor and general lack of efficient and intelligent direction, will have cause to revise their opinion when the first productions of this company are presented to the trade within a few weeks. . . . They are said to be consistently artistic, revealing the highest and best taste in studio preparation, keen discernment in the casting of the various roles and a high level of direction.[108]

Although the films presented to the film trade in September 1917 had, obviously, already been completed, Berst contracted with Kaplan to produce an additional twenty-six features. Kaplan set sail for home in October 1917 with an American cameraman and lab manager in tow, to guarantee that the photographic elements of the films were "up to U.S. standards." Upon leaving, Kaplan predicted that "[t]he time is not far distant when America and Russia will be working side by side for the achievement and advancement of the most popular expression of art—the motion picture."[109]

As history would record, October 1917 was not a good time for a Russian business to make plans to export its product. That month the Bolsheviks succeeded in overthrowing the government of Alexander Kerensky, which had itself only been in power since the overthrow of the czar the previous February. The Russian film industry was nationalized soon thereafter. No new Russian Art Films would ever reach Pathé, leaving the company with only the eight completed films that had been deposited by Kaplan during his visit and that had served as the basis for Pathé's contract. The films were released at the rate of one per month from October 1917 through May 1918. They were mostly 1916 productions of the Joseph Yermoliev studio, although there was at least one film, released in the United States as *Her Sister's Rival*, produced by Yermoliev's competitor Aleksandr Khanzhonkov. Five of the films featured czarist Russia's premier film actor Ivan Mozzhukhin, who received a permanent place in film-history texts because of his "starring role" in Lev Kuleshov's famous editing experiment.

At least two of the Russian Art Films, *Her Sister's Rival* and *The Queen of Spades*, have survived and are widely available for review. *The Queen of Spades* may be the slightly more interesting of the two, if for no other reason than the fact that it has the legendary Mozzhukhin in the leading role. Just one month after complaining about the "typically foreign" nature of Gance's *The Torture of Silence* (also still available for review), *Motion Picture News* critic Peter Milne raved that *The Queen of Spades*

> is a striking example of the manner in which skilled acting and the playing upon a single situation, a man's overwhelming passion for money, can carry the interest through from start to finish without once faltering. Much has been said regarding the ability of the players appearing in these pictures and here, in this drama, they prove that the praise heaped upon them by the press agent is far from undeserved. Notably does I. Mosukin [*sic*], as the man, give a performance of utmost skill. . . .
>
> The manner in which the director . . . has built up the suspense from the time that Herman hears of the story of the secret cards until the finale is little short of marvelous. The tension is high from this minute on and never once is there the slightest suggestion of a letdown.[110]

Milne's review of the next Russian Art Film to be released, the third in the series following *The Painted Doll* and *The Queen of Spades*, opened similarly with praise: "'Her Sister's Rival' is the best of the Russian Art subjects yet shown. A faint recollection calls to mind the fact that the same statement was made regarding the last one. But such is the case."[111]

THE *HEARST-PATHÉ NEWS*

Even as Pathé farmed the production of its films out to affiliated producers, it maintained in-house control of one of its flagship series, the *Pathé News*. This changed somewhat in January 1917, although the extent of the change was later the subject of some controversy. Pathé entered into a contract to distribute the output of William Randolph Hearst's International Film Service. This meant the distribution of cartoon series featuring characters appearing in Hearst newspapers, including the Katzenjammer Kids, Krazy Kat, Happy Hooligan, and Abe Kabibble.[112] These cartoons were quite short, and to fill out a thousand-foot reel they were combined with informational subjects with titles like *New York's Giant Barge Canal* and *Lace Making*, which were also produced by International. As noted earlier, Pathé also picked up distribution of the Wharton-produced Irene Castle serial *Patria*.[113]

Most significant in the arrangement with International, however, was the combination of the *Pathé News* with the *Hearst International News Pictorial* to form the *Hearst-Pathé News*. Hearst had entered the newsreel business in

1913, when he allied himself with Selig Polyscope to form the *Hearst-Selig Weekly*. In 1914 he left that arrangement to start the *Hearst-Vitagraph Weekly*. At some point thereafter he established International to produce and distribute the newsreel and cartoons.[114]

Under the announced terms of the newsreel merger, the editing, processing, and printing would be handled by Pathé, which would also contribute much of the European coverage. Hearst would handle much of the domestic news gathering and photography. The *Hearst-Pathé News* would be issued twice a week.[115]

The real reason Pathé was willing to combine its highly successful newsreel with Hearst's probably had less to do with the newsreel than it did with the free publicity the rest of its product line would receive through Hearst newspapers, including the popular promotional tactic of printing the stories of serials in the press.[116] Pathé had actually enjoyed this type of publicity tie-in with Hearst going back to *The Perils of Pauline*.[117] The new alignment with Hearst promised to be just as beneficial for the newsreel. Just a few months into the distribution arrangement with International, Pathé would happily report a 26 percent increase in its newsreel business, really no surprise since the combined reel went out to the theaters that had previously played the Hearst reel in addition to Pathé's existing customers. Pathé also claimed at that time that it was already seeing increased business for its other product due to the backing and publicity it was receiving in Hearst's newspapers.[118]

Within a short time, though, the honeymoon soured as Pathé learned how much baggage was associated with the Hearst name. As Ed Hulse has described in *Distressed Damsels and Masked Marauders*, the troubles started with the serial *Patria*, which had as a major plot component Japanese emissaries attempting to persuade Mexico to invade the United States. The British had just made public the information that Germany, not Japan, had attempted to engineer an invasion of the still-neutral United States through Mexico, and, to make matters worse, the United States had just signed an alliance with Japan in the event of war. The Japanese lodged a formal protest with the U.S. government at being portrayed as the villains in *Patria*. Their case was taken up by no less than the president of the United States, who wrote to Berst that he had seen part of the film "and was disturbed by the character of the story. It is extremely unfair to the Japanese and I fear that it is calculated to stir up a great deal of hostility which will be far from beneficial to the country, indeed will, particularly in the present circumstances, be extremely hurtful. I take the liberty, therefore, of asking whether the Pathé Company would not be willing to withdraw it if it is still being exhibited."[119] After extended negotiations among the government, Pathé, and Hearst, the film remained in release with only the most minor of cosmetic edits. The most significant of these was to remake the title cards to give the obviously Japanese characters Hispanic names in a pale attempt to make it appear that the Mexican plot was homegrown.[120]

The *Patria* affair was but a harbinger of what was to come. Hearst's reputation for journalistic bias in his news operation and his blatantly pro-German stance in the run up to the United States' entry into the First World War began to taint the Pathé newsreel's good reputation. As Pathé vice president Paul Brunet explained in October 1918, "Ever since the American public became incensed over the lack of patriotism exhibited by Hearst and his newspapers, we have spent a good share of our time apologizing and explaining Hearst's connection with the pictures."[121] That connection, Brunet asserted, went no further than International cameramen providing Pathé with raw footage and that complete editorial control had always been Pathé's. Although the contract with Hearst ran until the end of 1918, and the Hearst name remained on the reel until that time, Pathé refused to take any more footage from International cameramen after early October, despite the fact that it still had to pay Hearst $25,000 for his cameramen's services for the remainder of the contract.[122] As the United States became embroiled in the First World War, Pathé distributed documentary shorts and features about the war prepared by the governmental Committee on Public Information, perhaps in an effort to put more distance between itself and Hearst.[123]

"GOOD PICTURE, EXCELLENTLY PHOTOGRAPHED"

In February 1918 Pathé released a film based on another Rudyard Kipling work that it asserted was the most expensive ever produced by any firm up to that time. Even with a reported cost of over $100,000, *The Naulahka*'s claim to the title of most expensive is blatantly false. There had certainly been costlier productions prior to 1918, but it was nevertheless a very expensive film by Pathé's standards.[124] As edited at Astra, the film ran eight reels, but it was shortened to six to make it more exhibitor friendly.[125] Even in its truncated form, *Motion Picture News* observed that it was a reel longer than normal pictures and was "proportionately greater." However, in the film-industry climate of late 1917 and early 1918, making an expensive film was hardly a badge of honor. The widespread belief that costs had spiraled out of control was summed up by Samuel Goldfish,[126] president of Goldwyn Pictures Corporation, who declared that the industry was close to disaster: "Obviously, the producer is paying too much, the exhibitor is paying too much, and the public—through all this extravagance—is paying too much. It is a vicious circle that only the producer can break."[127] To make matters worse, the U.S. federal government had just instituted a war excise tax on exhibitors of fifteen cents per reel per day, further diminishing theatrical profits.[128]

Addressing the complaint of many exhibitors that they were paying too much for films to be able to turn a profit, Stanley Mastbaum, a Philadelphia-based exhibitor, suggested that the industry consolidate, with fewer distributors and exchanges and less production and advertising.[129] To this, J. A. Berst responded, "The so-called waste and overproduction about which you complain in your 833-word telegram of November 26 mean the salvation of the exhibitors of the United States and not their destruction as you seem to believe." He said that while it was true that there were some bad companies with bad product, Pathé and the other reputable companies were prospering, and the current climate of competition was healthy and kept the costs to the exhibitor down and the quality up.[130]

This assertion, and the notion that Pathé was the friend of the cost-conscious exhibitor, would become central to Pathé's advertising at the end of 1917. A two-page Pathé ad in the *Moving Picture World* offered a testimonial from C. L. Dooley, manager of two theaters in Patterson, New Jersey. Dooley stated that his theaters had recently discontinued booking expensive pictures to be able to stay in business: "No star is big enough to earn a profit for the exhibitor if the picture is too costly. My opinion is that entirely too much attention is being paid to the star, and entirely too little attention to the story. Audiences demand good stories. We exhibitors cannot support fabulous priced stars by paying for these pictures more than is justified by our box office returns." In another part of the ad, Berst noted that Dooley had canceled thirteen star series to stay in business. Pathé's policy of quality films at affordable prices, Berst continued, offered salvation to the exhibitor.[131] In a later ad Berst asked exhibitors if they were tired of paying $100 a day for a film worth $25 a day and asked producers if they were tired of paying a star worth $200 a week a weekly salary of $2,000. The answer, he said, was Pathé. He cited a recent deal in which the manager of eighteen theaters in the Washington, D.C., area canceled ninety contracts with "a certain company" and picked up Pathé.[132]

The fact, though, was that the vast majority of Pathé's films of the period were only doing average business at the box office.[133] What had to be maddening to Berst and his associates was the fact that many of the films got excellent reviews from critics and exhibitors alike. All too typical was a western U.S. exhibitor's assessment of the Astra-produced Irene Castle Pathé Play titled *The Mark of Cain*: "Good picture, excellently photographed, beautiful settings, no pulling power."[134] Only the reissues of *Les Misérables* and *The Vicar of Wakefield* were reported as good audience draws.

Given the situation, Pathé had little choice but to cut back on feature production, from one per week to one every two weeks. Overproduction in the industry leading to a glut of features on the market was given as the cause for decreasing the output, but exhibitors were assured that this would be accompanied by an increase in the quality of the features that Pathé did release. This, the press release continued, would allow Pathé to have "the advantages of the star system without its evils."[135] Saying that "[t]he most serious situation that the industry confronts today is the inclination toward hysteria that is apparent in some quarters," Berst insisted that he was still an optimist. While he admitted that theater attendance was down, he blamed the hysteria on "calamity howlers [who] begin to yelp and whine. Unfortunately they seldom, if ever, represent the true spirit of the industry, but their cries nevertheless are bound to have their evil results."[136]

Following a trip to California, Berst, as noted earlier, named the studios of Paralta Plays as Pathé's future West Coast center of production. As he did so, he added, "For some time past there has been a growing belief that a great deal of the present waste in production could be eliminated by centralizing production activities in two or three studios."[137] With the promise of new production, the owners of Paralta began plans to expand their studio.[138] Then, in a March 7, 1918, meeting of the board of directors of Pathé, J. A. Berst was dismissed as vice president and general manager.[139]

CHAPTER THREE

"IN CLOSER TOUCH WITH THE WORLD ORGANIZATION OF PATHÉ" 1918–21

That "certain company" to which J. A. Berst had referred in the January 1918 ad was on the mind of practically every actor, producer, and exhibitor in the years leading up to 1920. The company seemingly had a corner on the most valuable actors and directors in the business, meaning it could force exhibitors to pay top dollar for its productions and to take the productions in groups, rather than individually. This way it could package its good films with its bad ones and make a profit on all without any concern for whether the exhibitor played the bad films to empty theaters. As if all of that were not bad enough for the exhibitor, the company was beginning to purchase its own theaters that operated in direct competition with the established houses. Producers as well as exhibitors based many of their business strategies after 1915 on how best to protect their own interests and keep the company from further dominating the industry. The company was Paramount Pictures.

Paramount was established by W. W. Hodkinson in 1914 as a national distributor set up to handle the films of producers not belonging to the Motion Picture Patents Company. According to legend, Hodkinson was responsible for the company's famous mountain and stars logo, basing it on a mountain in the American West he remembered seeing as a child. Among the earliest producers to use Paramount's distribution services were Adolph Zukor's Famous Players Film Company, the Jesse L. Lasky Feature Play Company, and Bosworth, Inc.[1]

Paramount's drive of consolidation and conquest began in July 1916, when Famous Players and Lasky merged to form what the *Motion Picture News* called "[t]he greatest merger of producing interests in the history of the motion picture industry."[2] Adolph Zukor, who charted the course of this and many other mergers and acquisitions to come, was president of the new Famous Players–Lasky Company, with Lasky as vice president and Samuel Goldfish as chairman of the board. Within two months Goldfish would leave the company.[3]

October 1916 brought news of another merger. The Oliver Morosco Photoplay Company and Pallas Pictures, two of Paramount's other producers, were folded into Famous Players–Lasky.[4] In December Zukor achieved the next logical step in his program of consolidation. Famous Players–Lasky arranged a takeover of Paramount.[5] Although the production end of the business would officially operate under variations of the Famous Players–Lasky name through the 1920s, the brand name by which the public knew the company was Paramount Pictures.[6] In the years leading up to 1920 Zukor was starting to acquire theaters. One of Zukor's first acts after gaining control of Paramount was to oust the man who had founded it, W. W. Hodkinson.

"EXTRA-SELECTED STAR PHOTOPLAYS"

As is usually the case in such circumstances, neither J. A. Berst nor Pathé released a statement explaining his March 1918 departure from the company. Instead, press releases extolled the management skills of Pathé's new vice president and general manager, Paul Brunet. Unlike Berst, Roussel, and Gasnier before him, Brunet did not have a long history with Pathé Frères. Nevertheless, Brunet had quickly worked his way into Charles Pathé's confidence and would enjoy a high place in the firm for a number of years, including a seat on the board of directors of Pathé-Cinema, the motion-picture successor of Pathé Frères. With a background in French business (much like Felix Malitz), Brunet had joined Pathé in 1914, and since 1916 he had been the Pathé Exchange's comptroller, assistant treasurer, and a member of the board of directors. In anointing his new emissary in America, Charles Pathé declared that Brunet had run the best organized and directed of all of Pathé's departments, adding that Brunet "has been in close touch with the financial and exchange ends of the business, and his system of exchange control has been responsible for a marked increase in efficiency."[7] For his part, Brunet promised that the Pathé Exchange "will be in closer touch with the world organization of Pathé,"[8] a statement that spoke volumes about the likely reason for Berst's departure. Indeed, one of the chief reasons Berst was replaced, according to Stephanie Salmon, was his inability to control costs, particularly on Pathé's high-end Gold Rooster pictures. Charles Pathé considered this wasteful and preferred to see production money plowed into the much cheaper and more financially successful serials.[9]

Charles Pathé's concern about Berst's extravagance went beyond an apparent case of micromanagement. The First World War had severely curtailed the film production activities at most European studios. During the war, and even after, the Pathé Exchange was Charles Pathé's only reliable source of films to feed to European theaters, becoming, in a word that means the same in French as in English, *indispensable* to his global organization.[10] However, time would prove that following a course of action that was best for Pathé's international operations was not necessarily beneficial for the Pathé Exchange's long-term prospects as a competitive American film producer.

As part of the management change, Ferdinand Zecca was named the new director general of productions.[11] Zecca was a French film pioneer who had been with Charles Pathé since 1901. His appointment as Pathé's production manager was perhaps intended to compensate for Brunet's lack of production experience. In any case, Zecca would be back in France by 1919.

Brunet's first order of business was to cancel the contract with Paralta Plays.[12] Pathé's West Coast production was moved temporarily to Universal City, where Pathé was already leasing space for the Fannie Ward–starring vehicle *A Japanese Nightingale*.[13] In short order a new contract was negotiated with Anderson-Brunton Productions, a reorganized version of Paralta.[14] Beyond that, Brunet announced that on Charles Pathé's orders, the company would emphasize production of serials to "a new standard of quality."[15] Many in the industry interpreted this as meaning that Pathé would abandon features to concentrate on short-film production, prompting a rebuttal from Pathé: "All reports to the contrary, Pathé will continue to release feature pictures of the highest quality. The rumor has been spread, and presumably by persons who are not disinterested, that Pathé would discontinue the release of feature pictures. The rumor has no basis of truth."[16]

Brunet also reversed Berst's recent policy, which had followed the industry trend of requiring exhibitors to book some films only in groups. The Pathé Selective Feature Program would allow theater operators the option of booking films individually, if they wished, although the films could still be booked in series for a lower rate per film.[17]

By August 1918 when he announced Pathé's policy for the 1918–19 movie season, Brunet had gained a good grasp of the problems created by the overproduction of feature-length films. By his estimate, the current output of five-to-six-reel features exceeded demand by four to one, and the market for features would be "super-saturated" during the upcoming year.[18] Brunet's assessment of the situation, which would only get worse over the next few seasons, was echoed by a *Moving Picture World* editorial in December 1920, which observed that the "flooded feature market . . . will receive eight hundred big productions this year when the first run market can only absorb two hundred of them under the most favorable conditions. . . ."[19]

To counter this, Brunet claimed that Pathé had been putting aside its best feature product for "the proper time. Now we are fully prepared to enter the field of specialized features with a year's supply of Extra-Selected Star Photoplays. We will release them one every four weeks."[20] In addition to its top-of-the-line series of features, "From time to time we intend to release others, the product of our present contributing studios and outside producers. We will release no features under the Pathé name, however, that do not thoroughly satisfy us as to quality, and our plans do not contemplate a greater quantity than one Pathé feature every other week."[21] The designation for Pathé's new top line of films created a rather awkward mouthful, as the name of the star was actually inserted. A film starring Fannie Ward became an "Extra-Selected Fannie Ward Photoplay." After the 1918–19 season, the series name was retired, and a top feature was promoted simply as a "Special Feature."

ON BROADWAY

An important publicity tactic during the early years of Paul Brunet's administration, and one that was not unique to Pathé, was getting films booked into large New York City theaters, then using the fact that they had played in these prestigious venues to promote them nationwide. The sales job was made even easier if the theaters' managers could be induced to give the films an endorsement. In June 1918 Pathé was able to boast that the Astra-produced Fannie Ward vehicle *The Yellow Ticket* was playing at the Rialto, while the Anderson-Brunton Company's *More Trouble* was in the Rivoli.[22]

From 1910 until the early 1920s, movie-theater attendance dropped notably during the summer due to the lack of any type of air-cooling system in most theaters[23] and the fact that the longer daylight hours in summer saw people more engaged in outdoor activities and less prone to go to the movies. Some small theaters closed completely during the summer. Because of this, most film companies released their least attractive films during the summer season, assuming that they would do poor business anyway. In an attempt to counter this trend (and to seize what business there was to be had while competition was low), Pathé announced a "big feature push" in the summer of 1920 to "give exhibitors the highest class type of features for summer consumption."[24] In the vanguard was distinguished actor H. B. Warner in his Pathé debut, *One Hour before Dawn*. Pathé was able to get the film booked into Broadway's Capitol Theater, together with the Harold Lloyd short film *High and Dizzy*. At the same time, Pathé's *Man and His Woman* played at the Broadway Theater.[25] Broadway's manager, B. S. Moss, became a real friend to Pathé during this period, booking the first "comeback" film featuring Blanche Sweet, a former D. W. Griffith star. Moss was happy enough with the results to book Sweet's next three Pathé films in the Broadway as well.[26] At the same time, the Capitol Theater booked all four of Pathé's *After Thirty* short films.[27] Assessing the trend of booking films on Broadway, Paramount's Adolph Zukor predicted at the end of 1920 that individual films would eventually play for an entire year on the Great White Way, imitating the runs of theatrical performances.[28]

Charles Pathé returned to the United States for a two-month visit in April 1919, his first in two years.[29] Before he left, he gave Brunet a ringing endorsement, saying that he was largely responsible for the company's current success.[30] Perhaps emboldened by his boss's praise, Brunet embarked on a program of expansion to include a greater array of producers than ever before. They included Pathé stalwarts like George B. Seitz, Hal Roach, Louis Gasnier, and new producers including Albert Cappellani (like Gasnier, an alumnus of Pathé Frères in France); Leonce Perret (who had worked for Pathé Frères' rival Leon Gaumont); Mrs. Sidney (Lucille) Drew, whose work will be discussed shortly; and J. Stuart Blackton.[31]

British-born, American-raised J. Stuart Blackton was employed as a cartoonist for the *New York Evening World* newspaper in 1896 when he was invited to demonstrate his abilities as a rapid sketch artist in three films made by Thomas Edison's studio. Blackton was so taken with the potential of film that he and fellow Englishman Albert E. Smith formed the Vitagraph Studios in 1897, becoming some of Edison's earliest competition. Blackton left Vitagraph in 1917 to begin independent production. His films from this period were distributed by several companies, of which Pathé was the most recent. Pathé's arrangement with "Commodore" Blackton called for him to produce and direct between six and ten features per year, each of which would be released as "specials."[32] To accomplish this, Blackton overhauled his Brooklyn studio, adding improvements and doubling its size.[33]

While some of the nine films he would distribute through Pathé in 1919 and 1920 received good reviews, more typical was the *Motion Picture News*' description of Blackton's inaugural effort, *The Moonshine Trail*: "The film as a whole seems to have been produced in a former period, as the style of handling it appears to have been in vogue a few years back. An average picture that will register quite strongly in some districts and very weakly in others."[34] Of *Man and His Woman*, released toward the end of Blackton's association with Pathé, the *Motion Picture News* said it "resembles an old-time melodrama with all the favorite hokum intact." It is in "a class somewhat above mediocrity. But the story itself suffers from want of a well-defined plot. It resembles a hodge-podge of theatrical situations and tragic happenings. . . ."[35] Although Pathé reported in the spring of 1920 that Blackton's films were increasing in popularity, with each film doing better than the one before it,[36] Blackton and Pathé parted company after the October release of *The Forbidden Valley. Moving Picture World* helpfully suggested that exhibitors should exploit Blackton's name, still a marquee draw, and the names of the leading players, and "go light on the feud angle" that comprised *The Forbidden Valley*'s plot.[37] After an eighteen-month hiatus from film production, Blackton resumed independent production in 1922. By 1923 he was back with Vitagraph, where he spent most of the remainder of his career.[38]

One Pathé feature from the 1919–20 movie season that deserves mention is *The Little Café*, a French comedy with long-time Pathé Frères writer-director-comedian Max Linder. As noted earlier, Linder's comedies were quite popular in the United States at a time when other European films were being ostracized, and he was an important influence on American comedy, particularly that of Charlie Chaplin. Linder was seriously injured during the First World War and was left with chronic health problems thereafter. In 1917 he came to the United States and made a trio of short comedies for Essanay, which failed to make much of an impression, then went back to France to resume his career there. *The Little Café*, produced by Pathé Frères in 1919, was the third film he made after his return to France and was his first feature-length film. Although a box-office hit in France, the *Moving Picture World*'s comments on the film seem a bit nostalgic and poignant: "The reappearance of Max Linder on the American screen is certain to awaken fond memories in the minds of picture fans, for the time was when Max led them all as a comedian. . . . Max will still give a good account of himself."[39] *The Little Café* would be Linder's last film for more than a year. He returned to the United States in 1921 to make three features for his own company. Again, the films failed to make an impact on the box office, and again Linder returned home. There he made a few more films before committing suicide, with his wife, in 1925.[40]

"DIVERSITY, QUALITY, PEP, AND ORIGINALITY"

Pathé reported an unprecedented increase in business in early 1920.[41] The company made this type of claim so often during the Brunet years that it becomes a bit suspect after a while. However, tangible evidence of success may be found in the fact that it was able to build a new corporate headquarters building in New York City, permitting it to move out of two and one-half floors of leased space. The new building on West Forty-Fifth Street was twelve stories tall and featured a glass-covered studio for the art department on the top floor.[42] The publicity posters and print ads generated by this department were regularly praised by exhibitors.[43] The offices of Brunet and the other Pathé executives were located one floor below the art department. The tenth floor featured "a projection hall for the routine use of the film committee and for special showings."[44] As a final bonus the new building provided enough space to allow the *Pathé News* staff to move from an office in New Jersey to the corporate headquarters.[45]

As the *Pathé News* approached its tenth anniversary at the end of 1920, Pathé pointed with pride to its longevity and accomplishments.[46] The newsreel operation was so efficient that it even put out versions specifically tailored to individual localities, when film of a parade or other event in that city was available.[47] However, like so much of Pathé's product, the newsreel rarely ran in the most prestigious first-run venues, intact anyway. As an interesting example of the effort that was put into the presentation of films at the nation's largest theaters in the silent era, many theaters cobbled together their own newsreels from multiple sources. For instance, in 1920, Sid Grauman's Million Dollar Theater ran the *Grauman's Weekly*, a newsreel that was assembled from the *Gaumont Graphic*, Hearst's *International News*, the *Pathé News*, and the *Pathé Review*.[48]

By 1920 the twice-weekly *Pathé News* had two companion pieces: the aforementioned *Pathé Review* and *Topics of the Day*, both of which were issued weekly. Pathé described the *Review* as "the film magazine supreme, containing the incomparable Pathécolor, slow motion photography, nature pictures, science, art, etc."[49] The Pathécolor sections, which made up approximately one-third of the reel each week, appear to have mostly been travelogues made by Pathé Frères–affiliated producers throughout the world.[50] The slow-motion segments were primarily motion-analysis studies and were produced by the Navagraph Film Corporation. A presumably typical example of the *Pathé Review* was number 79, described in the *Moving Picture World* of November 27, 1920, as follows: "The tinted scenes from Brittany are very fine and the closeups of the children will set an audience in good humor at once. Following this are many good topics, including the manufacture of dolls, an Ollendorf dance picture, interpreted by Agnes Hunter, some queer animals at the Zoo, and tinted pictures of great religious processions taken in Japan. The number is exceptionally strong in interest."[51]

Topics of the Day was a very short film (one-third of a reel or approximately four minutes) produced by Timely Films, Inc. It was described as being "selected from the press of the world by the editors of The Literary Digest,"[52] containing "lively humor, keen satire and trenchant criticisms on the social, political and other foibles of the day."[53] "Comprised of the most pointed and humorous quotations assembled from newspapers and magazines,"[54] *Topics* was sold to theaters as "an irresistible laugh-maker for any audience."[55]

Serial production continued unabated in the early 1920s despite the loss of Pearl White, who decided to pursue a feature-film career at Fox in 1920.[56] The year that White left, Pathé had thirty serials behind it and eight in various stages of planning and production for the 1920–21 season.[57] The large number of older serials accumulating in Pathé's vaults prompted the company to promote a novel scheme to fight the industry's annual doldrums in the summer of 1920. The idea was to have theaters run an entire vintage fifteen-episode serial in a week's time at the rate of three episodes per night. How many theaters bought into this notion is unclear, but those that did reported success.[58]

The continuing success of the serial in 1920 seemed to be confirmed when Pathé announced a record number of first-run bookings[59] for *Ruth of the Rockies*, its latest serial starring its new serial queen, Ruth Roland.[60] However, there was trouble brewing for the serial as a form, trouble that Pathé sought to dispel in a 1921 trade-journal article. Pathé noted that some print articles "tend to create an impression that the picture chapter play has to rely chiefly on its interest for children. Pathé says that such impression is erroneous and alleges that many exhibitors in all parts of the country rely on one or more 'serial days' in the week for their largest and most profitable throngs, which means adults."[61] Yet when Ruth Roland made a personal appearance in Atlanta in April 1921 to promote *Ruth of the Rockies*, she was mobbed by scores of her biggest fans: children.[62] The fact was, by the early 1920s, serials were no longer considered the type of entertainment for adults that they had been in the days of *The Perils of Pauline*. Rather, they were rapidly becoming fodder for children's Saturday matinees, a status they would hold through the introduction of sound and all the way into the 1950s. This decline in the status of the serial carried with it a decline in the status of those who made them, including Pathé.

Despite the fact that the production of short films in the early 1920s was generally becoming stigmatized as the province of marginal producers, short films were considered part of a "balanced" program. Shorts were more important to small theaters, because in larger theaters part of the "balance" in the program, the entertainment offered in addition to the feature film, came in the form of live stage shows. These could become quite elaborate sometimes, with the feature film paused at a certain point to allow the actual actors from the movie to come on stage and reenact a scene.

As a typical example of a stage presentation from the last week of January 1920, New York City's Rialto Theatre opened its evening shows with the house orchestra playing selections from *Madame Butterfly*. This was followed by the *Rialto Magazine*, a newsreel made up of individual stories pulled from *International News*, *Kinograms*, *Gaumont Graphic*, and *Pathé News*. After the newsreel came the "Neapolitan Song," sung on stage by baritone Edoardo Albano, followed by the evening's feature picture *The Cinema Murder* starring Marion Davies. The program was rounded out by Charlie Chaplin's 1916 comedy *The Rink* and an organ solo. Small theaters didn't have the means to book talent for live shows, so in addition to newsreels and short comedies, they booked travelogues, cartoons, short dramas, and specialty shorts, such as Pathé's *Review* and *Topics of the Day*.[63]

Since short comedies were booked in both large and small theaters, Pathé was indeed fortunate in its association with comedy specialist Hal Roach. Roach's star, Harold Lloyd, was rapidly gaining in popularity in the years before 1920. Although he was still appearing as Lonesome Luke in the spring of 1917, Lloyd was included in J. A. Berst's "A list" that included Pearl White, Frederick Warde, and others "who have been established as 'box-office stars.'"[64] Later in 1917 Lloyd shed his Lonesome Luke persona, which had borne more than a passing resemblance to Charlie Chaplin's Little Tramp, and appeared instead as a glasses-wearing all-American youth. By the beginning of 1919 Pathé reported that the Lloyd comedies had shown an "unusual increase during the last few months, and exhibitor comment has been . . . highly favorable."[65] Later in the year the Lloyd films were expanded from one to two reels, and Lloyd's popularity exploded, giving both Hal Roach and Pathé a very valuable commodity. Among other things, this permitted Roach and Lloyd to spend extra time and money on a film, seeking a level of quality unusual for short-film series.[66]

Another series of the same period that at least had potential to develop into a major box-office draw was done under the guidance of Lucille Drew. Drew had been half of a writing-directing-starring team with her husband, Sidney, first at the Vitagraph studio, then for their own company. The comedies of Mr. and Mrs. Sidney Drew, as they were billed, eschewed slapstick comedy and centered instead on domestic situations, resulting in films that were more subtle and sophisticated than the general run of screen comedy at the time. The partnership came to an end when Sydney died in April 1919.[67] Lucille's first work following her husband's death was to adapt an Edna Ferber story into a screenplay for *The Gay Old Dog*, a feature produced and directed by Hobart Henley for Pathé release in November 1919.[68] She still billed herself as

"Mrs. Sidney Drew," and in a posed publicity shot that shows her conferring with Henley and the film's star, John Cumberland, she appears to be wearing mourning clothes.[69] The film was well received, with the *Motion Picture News* calling it "one of the most human pictures ever shown."

The success of *The Gay Old Dog* led to a contract for a series of eight to ten two-reel "specials," to be written, produced, and occasionally directed by Drew.[70] The series title was *After Thirty*, and by all appearances it was similar in tone to the comedies Drew had done with Sidney. The films featured *The Gay Old Dog* star John Cumberland and sported intriguing titles like *The Emotional Miss Vaughn* and *The Stimulating Mrs. Barton*. Although it was Drew's intent to refrain from appearing in the films, preferring instead to concentrate on writing and "supervising the direction," she reconsidered and costarred in the third and fourth installments.[71] Then, after the fourth entry, she terminated the series. By most accounts, she had lost interest in filmmaking when Sidney died. After leaving Pathé, Drew would direct a single feature for her old studio, Vitagraph, later in 1920, then would retire from films completely.

Dramatic feature-length pictures had risen steadily in popularity after 1910, while comedy had largely remained in the one-to-two-reel length. With the exception of serials, dramatic short films became increasingly rare by 1920. Believing that exhibitors would still book short dramas if they were available, Pathé decided to buck the trend.[72] Significantly, Pathé sensed that the demand for short dramas was the greatest in the western genre, a form that, like the serial, appealed mainly to children.[73]

While most of Pathé's short westerns from the period were two-reelers featuring "Young Buffalo," Tom Santschi, and Edgar Jones, one series that deserves note ran but a single reel per episode. The *Adventures of Bill and Bob* shorts were part contemporary western, part documentary, and part reality series, but they were classified by the trade journals as "educational." They featured the exploits of two American youths who, in their wanderings, discovered and learned about various animals named in each short's title: *The Mountain Lion*, *The Skunk*, *The Civet Cat*, etc. The stars were director R. N. Bradburry's real-life eleven-year-old twin sons, William and Robert.[74] Robert Bradburry would later change his name, and as Bob Steele he would become a star of "B" westerns, some directed by his father. Perhaps his most memorable role was not in a western, but in Hal Roach's 1940 drama *Of Mice and Men*, in which he plays the sadistic ranch foreman Curley.

In an effort to get more mileage out of old features, Pathé actually edited some of its past successes into short form and released them as Pathé Playlets.

While Pathé was not alone in this practice, it was one of the relatively few mainstream companies to do the editing in-house, rather than temporarily reassigning the distribution rights or selling its old films outright to marginal companies that specialized in this type of work. Pathé's stated incentive for the cut-downs was to accommodate the exhibitors' desire "to get a quicker turnover of audiences without sacrificing feature quality. . . . 'Pathé Playlets' will be three reels of compact action."[75] In a January 1922 ad, Pathé helpfully suggested the manner in which its Playlets could be combined with other Pathé short subjects to make up an entire program:

Pathé Playlet	3 reels
Pathé Serial	2 reels
Hal Roach Comedy	1 reel
Total	6 reels

Or

Pathé Playlet	3 reels
Santschi Western	2 reels
Pathé News	1 reel
Hal Roach Comedy	1 reel
Total	7 reels

The ad closed with the line "Try short subject programs with a Pathé Playlet as the feature; you'll have diversity, quality, pep and originality, and at prices at which you can make money."[76] On an earlier occasion Pathé had pointed to a program of all shorts and a musical at New York's Capitol Theater, headlined by a Harold Lloyd three-reeler, as evidence that such programs could be successful in even the largest venues.[77]

But of course the problem for Pathé was that it was suggesting an idea that had already been tried. In the not too distant past, the film industry had distributed nothing but short films. In head-to-head competition with all-shorts programs, the feature-length drama had proved itself, and there was no going back, no matter how much Pathé wanted it. By focusing more and more of its resources on being a short-film specialist, Pathé was charting a course that would take it ever farther from major-studio status.[78]

ASSOCIATED EXHIBITORS

When Charles Pathé reported during his spring 1919 visit to the United States that he saw no dangers of monopoly in the film industry, he was stating a minority opinion.[79] As 1919 drew to a close, Paul Brunet voiced the fear of many when he predicted that "1920 will develop the biggest struggle for supremacy since the inception of the cinema industry in the United States."[80] Practically everyone in the film business, particularly the theater-owning end of the business, feared the juggernaut that was Paramount–Famous Players–Lasky. At an exhibitors' convention in Cleveland, Ohio, in the summer of 1920, a series of eighteen resolutions was drawn up that reflected the concerns of theater operators. The very first resolution dealt with Paramount, denouncing "the Famous Players-Lasky Corporation [as] the most flagrant offender against the independent exhibitor movement, in as much as this corporation . . . has continued to extend its theatre activities in unfair competition with the independent exhibitor."[81] The resolution went on to urge "every independent exhibitor to protect himself by all lawful means from" Famous Players–Lasky until the latter furnished evidence that it would deal fairly with independent exhibitors.[82] The specific allegation made against Paramount was that it would approach independent theater owners and demand that they either sell their theaters to Paramount or sign long-term contracts for the entire Paramount line, which in 1920 was eight to ten features per month plus several short-film series. If the theater owners refused Paramount's demands, Paramount would threaten to build a competing theater in the same neighborhood to drive the independent house out of business. In addition to theater owners, producers and actors also had misgivings about Paramount's clout. Each group dealt with the threat by attempting to band together for the common good and starting film companies of their own to compete with Paramount. Some succeeded; the majority didn't.

The most successful of the new companies was United Artists. The first trade-press announcement of what was at first referred to as the "Big Five" combination came in January 1919. At that time it was reported that four of the industry's top actors, Mary Pickford, Charlie Chaplin, Douglas Fairbanks, and William S. Hart, would join together with director D. W. Griffith to distribute their own independently produced films. All but Chaplin were producing their own films but distributing them through Paramount subsidiary Artcraft. Chaplin was an independent producer as well, but he was distributing through Associated First National, a company to be discussed shortly. Hart would drop out of the negotiations early on, but the remaining four would establish United Artists.

From the outset it was apparent that the four partners would not produce enough films to keep the enterprise afloat, so United Artists soon began accepting the work of other independent producers. In this regard it actually somewhat followed Charles Pathé's "film publisher" notion and became a direct competitor with the Pathé Exchange for the product of top producers.

The company would struggle through the years; its business model of accepting independent work often made it difficult to plan movie seasons in advance the way other studios did, and sometimes, particularly in the early 1940s, the quality of the independent output fell far short of the "prestige" type of picture upon which United Artists was founded. However, through bad times and good, United Artists managed to adapt to changing industry conditions, surviving into the twenty-first century.

The other film companies established in reaction to Paramount's business strategy did not enjoy United Artists' longevity. Associated Producers, established in 1920 by producers and directors including King Vidor, Thomas Ince, Maurice Tourneur, Allan Dwan, and Mack Sennett, lasted but a single year.[83] United Theaters of America, started in 1918 by theater owners and headed by recently deposed Pathé vice president J. A. Berst,[84] eventually acquired the exchanges of the recently liquidated Triangle Film Corporation.[85] Taking over the Triangle distribution system pushed costs to a point beyond what United's theater-owning partners were willing to pay, and United Theaters of America would be gone by the end of 1920.

A far more successful alliance of theater operators was First National, formed in 1917. In an early trade-press ad, the company announced, "The First National Exhibitors Circuit stretches forth its arm of protection to every exhibitor against any manufacturer who tries to use 'Steamroller methods.'"[86] First National's first star was Charlie Chaplin, who had just entered independent production and needed a distributor. The contract called for Chaplin to make eight films, but Chaplin, working ever more slowly, didn't complete his First National obligation until 1923, meaning that he was unable to join his partners at United Artists until then.

In 1919 First National announced that "[t]he producing-distributing trust that two years ago threatened our very business existence is no longer in a dominating position. . . . Now a new and greater danger threatens. But we are aware of it—are watching it—and are at present engaged on plans to defeat it. . . . Our advice to exhibitors is: don't be bluffed into selling your theater. . . . Don't sign long term contracts for film service."[87] By the end of 1919 First National had formed two subsidiaries: Associated First National Theaters, Inc., and Associated First National Pictures, Inc.[88] This last corporation would move First National into the actual production of films, rather than merely acting as a distributor. First National Pictures would survive as a major studio until 1928, when a majority interest was bought by Warner Brothers. First National's Burbank, California, studio remains the home of Warner Brothers to this day.

Associated Exhibitors was yet another consortium of theaters, whose success lay somewhere between First National and United. The principal difference, though, was that this company was backed by Pathé. Once Associated was under way, Pathé would often characterize its relationship with the firm as one of simply handling the physical distribution of Associated's film prints in much the same manner as it had handled Hearst's International Film Service product in the decade before 1920. However, the connection between Pathé and Associated ran deeper than that. Paul Brunet, who held a seat on the board of directors of Associated, described the firm as a "community of interest," a partnership between Pathé and theater operators. He continued by affirming that Associated had "large amounts of ready money for the acquirement of the best of the feature productions, and Pathé is ready with its money to stand behind the plan to the utmost."[89]

In addition to making Pathé's money available to the new organization, Pathé would soon contribute its top talent as well. Fred Quimby, Pathé's sales manager, left Pathé in February 1920 to become Associated Exhibitors' general manager. He was succeeded by Elmer Pearson.[90] Quimby's employment with Associated would be short-lived. In October he left to briefly become an independent producer.[91] He would soon be back in film sales, ultimately working for Metro-Goldwyn-Mayer.

In May, Pathé reassigned distribution of the increasingly popular Harold Lloyd comedies to Associated.[92] Finally, in early 1921 Pathé turned its entire feature sales force of sixty-seven employees over to Associated, along with the sale of Pathé's three features per month. Pathé did retain its separate short subject and serial sales force of 125.[93] Brunet was joined on the board of directors by Elmer Pearson. Arthur S. Kane, who had recently been an independent producer through First National and who had once been general manager of Eclectic, became Associated's president.[94]

On the exhibition end of the business, the Capitol Theatre in New York City served as the flagship house.[95] At its peak, Associated claimed to have contracts with 250 first-run theaters and 8,000 smaller houses.[96] The pictures Associated released to these theaters were a mixed bag. Some of the films would likely have been released by Pathé anyway, while others seem to have been lured by the promise of more favorable terms and prestige from Associated. In the former camp were the films of Harold Lloyd and Associated's first release, *The Riddle: Woman*, which was opera diva Geraldine Ferrar's last film.[97] One production that probably would have gone to First National or somewhere else were it not for Associated Exhibitors was *The Devil*, a film produced in Fort Lee, which served as the screen debut of George Arliss.[98] These films earned Associated a reputation for "lavish magnificence"[99] and did quite well at the box office, with *The Devil* breaking house records at its first two venues, the Strand in New York City and the Criterion in Buffalo.[100]

In 1922 the relationship between Pathé and Associated Exhibitors became complicated, and, given the paucity of corporate records from the period, it is now difficult to untangle. Pathé reentered the feature film market by reassuming distribution of Harold Lloyd's films and by occasionally distributing other high-profile (and high-profit) features like *Nanook of the North* (1922) and Hal Roach's *Call of the Wild* (1923). Yet when Mack Sennett began distributing his short-film product through Pathé in mid-1923, he was obliged to release his Mabel Normand feature *The Extra Girl* through Associated Exhibitors.[101] Furthermore, Pathé appears to have relied on the Associated Exhibitors sales force to sell the few feature films it had begun to release under its own banner. Hence, the 1923 Harold Lloyd feature *Why Worry?* was advertised as a "Pathécomedy" for which Associated Exhibitors acted as "selling agents."[102] All that is clear is that Pathé continued to handle the physical distribution of Associated's films and to have seats on its board of directors. Associated Exhibitors would remain in the business of releasing independent productions until 1926, although by the end it was distributing low-budget westerns almost exclusively.

In 1921 Paramount's Adolph Zukor sought to answer his critics in a published open letter to exhibitors. In the letter he claimed that he had only begun to buy theaters as a reaction to the production inroads being made by First National. In the letter Zukor reminded exhibitors that he had been a theater operator himself before he got into production: "Famous Players-Lasky Corporation entered the exhibiting field only after certain exhibitors entered the field of producing and distributing pictures and put forth an organized effort to take from us our stars and directors. . . . The attacks upon me are an effort to make the exhibitors believe that we are attempting to drive them out of business. . . . I want every thinking exhibitor to know that we are primarily a producing and distributing organization and our only thought is to please the exhibitor. . . ."[103] By the end of the 1920s Paramount would control the largest chain of movie theaters in the United States.

On a related note, at the beginning of 1920 theater operator Marcus Loew bought a majority stake in the producing company Metro Pictures.[104] In the mid-1920s, Loew would also purchase the Goldwyn Picture Corporation and would bring in producer Louis B. Mayer to form Metro-Goldwyn-Mayer (MGM). Controlled by his theater chain, Loews, Inc., MGM would become a producer-distributor-exhibitor combine to rival Paramount Pictures. Combined companies like MGM and Paramount would dominate American filmmaking through the 1950s, and companies lacking the wherewithal to assemble such a combination would find themselves pushed to the fringes of the film industry.

As Zukor and Loew, along with William Fox and the Warner Brothers, climbed to the apex of the film industry, Pathé was merrily heading in the opposite direction. For one thing, it stuck with its policy of open booking. While open booking was extremely popular with exhibitors, it didn't work so well for producers and distributors. Open booking meant that only the cream of a company's product line would be shown and that the weaker films would be a total loss. United Artists, too, practiced open booking, often to its disadvantage, and it had a better class of films than Pathé.

Pathé did have a small incentive for an exhibitor to book blocks of its films; exhibitors who did so were entitled to lower "wholesale" rental rates.[105] However, to the chagrin of the exhibitor, the days of theaters paying a flat rental fee for a film were drawing to a close. Soon all film companies would charge theaters a percentage of the box-office take, with the rental fee being a guaranteed minimum that the theater was obliged to pay even if it didn't sell a single ticket.

Lacking the growing clout of Paramount and its top-tier competitors, Pathé began to focus its efforts on the small-town theater, actually depicting itself as protecting small theaters from "the opposing forces that struggle to gain control of the motion-picture market."[106] In article after article in the trade journals at the beginning of the 1920s, Pathé made assertions like "within the last fortnight, several hundred more small exhibitors have come under the wing of the Pathé Rooster, seeking assurance for a continued high class feature, short subjects and serial product."[107] The problem for Pathé was that while the costs associated with selling films, physically delivering film prints, and keeping accounting records for small theaters was the same as for big theaters, the financial returns were only a fraction of what the big houses brought. Thus Pathé's claims that Harold Lloyd's films were booked in six thousand theaters and the one-reel Rolin Comedies were booked in five thousand or that 65 percent of U.S. theaters ran the *Pathé News* and 75 percent ran Rolin Comedies were virtually meaningless, absent statistics on theater size.[108] At the height of the big-studio era, 15 percent of the theaters in the United States took in 75 percent of the industry's revenue. These were the biggest theaters in the largest cities. The small rural theaters that Pathé championed were toward the bottom of the remaining 85 percent.[109]

THE REFORMERS

Starting toward the end of 1920, a new threat to the motion picture pushed the controversy over Paramount's business practices off center stage. The religious-based groups that had succeeded in passing the prohibition of alcohol sales in the United States turned their attention toward the film industry.[110] Obtaining a blanket prohibition against the manufacture and exhibition of movies was too tall an order, so these groups pushed for two goals: having theaters close nationwide on Sunday and censoring the content of films.

Not surprisingly, the exhibition end of the film industry was more incensed over proposed Sunday closings than the threat of censorship. In this they were in good company, because the proposed "blue laws" at the federal level would require that not only movie theaters be closed on Sunday, but public libraries, art galleries, and sporting events as well. Additionally, the laws would ban the Sunday sale of newspapers and gasoline for touring, as opposed to emergency use. The backers of the blue-law movement claimed that every major religious denomination in the United States backed their efforts, except Roman Catholics, Unitarians, Seventh-day Adventists, and Jews, and the last two, it was asserted, didn't support the movement because they worshipped on Saturday and not Sunday.

The *Moving Picture World* borrowed a term from a Hearst newspaper editorial writer and dubbed the movement "Sour Sunday."[111] Speaking for Pathé, Paul Brunet said that he wouldn't go as far as one unnamed journalist who called blue laws a form of Bolshevism, but he did see a couple of practical problems. He noted that closing theaters and other forms of diversion on Sunday wouldn't automatically force people to go to church, and, in any case, most movie theaters didn't open until Sunday afternoon, well after morning services had concluded. He then used the rhetorical style of those pushing for blue laws by asking, "Is it not better that the young man and girl go to a moving picture on Sunday than be turned loose on the street with no place to go and let the Devil find work for idle hands to do?"[112]

The Catholic press came out strongly against national blue laws, calling them a form of "extremism." William McGinley, supreme secretary of the Knights of Columbus, said, "American common sense . . . will reject any program calling for organized and legalized unhappiness." The *Syracuse Sun*, a Catholic paper, wrote, "These people imagine they can force their fellow citizens to be good, and they imagine, too, that they can bring about the beneficent result by making Sunday a smileless day."[113] The Eastern Association of Congregational Churches issued a statement that "Christianity stands for freedom as well as righteousness."[114] With motion pictures, newspapers, and several other industries aligned against it, the national blue-law movement failed.

Film censorship was another matter. For one thing, the film industry was alone in fighting this one. For another, the Supreme Court of the United States had decided in 1915 in the case of *Mutual Film Corporation v. Industrial Commission of Ohio* that movies were a form of commerce not protected by First Amendment freedoms. Some cities and states already had their own local censorship boards with virtually unlimited power, although occasionally film companies could mount a successful challenge. In 1916 Pathé went to state court to reverse censor-ordered cuts from the feature *New York* and from the first two episodes of *The Iron Claw*, with the serial losing a total of nine hundred feet. Pathé argued that the cuts amounted to mutilation of the films and that "[e]xhibitors who had seen these reels before their mutilation were dissatisfied with the censored product and cancellations had resulted with consequent loss of money and prestige to the company." The chief censor complaint regarding *New York* was the repeated use of the word *wanton*. The judge hearing the case said that the word was acceptable in literature and that it should be no less so on the screen. The judge also ordered the reinstatement of much of the footage excised from *The Iron Claw*, although he did uphold the elimination of scenes in which the villain's hand is mutilated in a vise and a character is branded.[115] Just a few months after this victory, though, J. A. Berst asked for exhibitor aid in his push for national censorship. Berst saw a national board as the only protection from having footage removed from film prints at the order of local censors and often either not replaced properly or not replaced at all before the print went back to the exchange. The exchange would then be faced with the choice of ordering expensive and time-consuming reprints of the missing scenes or sending the print out to the next theater as it was.[116] Berst's opinion on the desirability of a national censor board was not widely shared in the industry, and he let the idea drop.

With the new threat of censorship in 1921, individual film companies in addition to the National Association of the Motion Picture Industry actually gave financial support to local groups fighting film censorship.[117] The anti-censorship movement suffered a setback in April 1921 when the State of New York, then the nation's most populous, passed a censorship law.[118] Pathé soon found itself at odds with the New York censors when they ordered scenes of women in swimsuits, photographed at a public carnival in Dallas, removed from the *Pathé News*.[119] One week later the same board ordered the deletion of a similar scene from another reel of *Pathé News*, prompting the *Moving*

Picture World to fume, "The politically appointed, politically constituted and now thoroughly absurd censorship commission of the state of New York went after Pathé again this week."[120] Absurd or not, the censors won this battle (in the short term, anyway), with the New York State Court of Appeals finding in May 1923 that newsreels, like all other films, had to be submitted to the censorship commission for "inspection and licensing."[121] In 1926 the New York legislature revisited the issue and revised the state's censorship law to exempt newsreels from review by the censorship commission.[122]

Even before the 1921 New York law was passed, Pathé apparently decided that discretion was the better part of valor and announced that it would only distribute wholesome films.[123] By the following year it used a new industry buzz term when describing its latest serial. *Go Get 'Em Hutch*, Pathé claimed, was "censor-proof."[124]

For their part, in March 1921 the reformers agreed to give the industry time to "set its house in order for a clean screen."[125] Then, Labor Day weekend brought with it a party at the St. Francis Hotel in San Francisco and the scandal that cost Roscoe "Fatty" Arbuckle his career, followed in February 1922 by director William Desmond Taylor's murder and its fallout that damaged the careers of Mabel Normand and Mary Miles Minter. With all of the negative publicity for the film industry, national censorship seemed to be even closer than ever. In a preemptive move the major Hollywood producers founded the Motion Picture Producers and Distributors of America, which would draw up a code of good practices for the production of films. The code was based in part on the censorship rules of the various local boards, and the idea was to "pre-censor" films. If a film were made in compliance with the code, it would likely avoid problems with the local boards.

In addition to the threats to Hollywood from overproduction, Paramount Pictures, and those pushing blue laws and national censorship, the summer of 1921 saw the United States slowly beginning to emerge from an eighteen-month economic depression. It was also a very hot summer, which meant that theater attendance slumped even more than usual, delaying economic recovery for the film industry.

Pathé was in the process of wrapping up the 1920–21 movie season. The year had been much like the one that preceded it, with an emphasis on serials and other shorts. Feature-length films had been released at the rate of three per month through January. In anticipation of switching its feature output to Associated Exhibitors, Pathé became practically an all-shorts distributor in February, although it did continue to release a single feature per month.

As it had done in the past, Pathé saved its biggest feature release of the year for summer. This year the film was *Without Benefit of Clergy*, based on the first ever screenplay by Rudyard Kipling from his story of the same name.[126] The July release was greeted by mixed reviews. P. F. Reniers of New York's *Evening Post* wrote, "It is so seldom that one can say that a written masterpiece transferred to the screen still remains a masterpiece. . . . Rudyard Kipling's 'Without Benefit of Clergy' . . . is the best example of a purely lyric film that has come out of an American studio."[127] The film was also warmly received by critics in Boston, Atlanta, and Cincinnati.[128] However, Edward Weitzel of the *Moving Picture World* complained that the actors lacked the depth to realize their characters fully and that the director "has permitted too much talking in several of the scenes." Long scenes of talking heads were considered poor form in silent movies. "Careful editing," Weitzel continued, "would make 'Without Benefit of Clergy' good screen entertainment."

However, the public reception of their big summer film was not foremost in the minds of Pathé staffers at the beginning of July 1921. The movie season that had run its course in oh-so-typical fashion ended with a bombshell. One day before the release of *Without Benefit of Clergy*, the trade journals reported word from Paris that Charles Pathé had sold a majority interest in the Pathé Exchange to Merrill Lynch.[129]

CHAPTER FOUR

BANKING INTERESTS

1921–26

In September 1920 Charles Pathé announced his retirement from the presidency of the Pathé Exchange. Paul Brunet became president, with Pathé's sales manager, Elmer Pearson, being promoted to general manager. Bernhard Benson of Merrill, Lynch and Company, a firm that had a presence on the Pathé Exchange's board of directors, was named vice president.[1]

A few years earlier Charles Pathé had begun a radical revision of his industrial holdings. In 1918 he split Pathé Frères into two companies. The first, which retained the name Pathé Frères, dealt solely with phonographs and recordings and was headed up by Pathé's brother Émile. The other company was Pathé-Cinema, which remained under the control of Charles. In 1919 Charles began the liquidation of his foreign subsidiaries, and in 1920 Pathé spun off all remaining film production and rental activities to a new firm, Pathé-Consortium-Cinéma, in which Pathé-Cinéma had seats on the board of directors. The primary businesses retained by Pathé-Cinéma were the manufacture and processing of film stock and the manufacture of film and equipment for the "sub-standard" motion-picture formats used by schools and amateurs.[2]

As noted earlier, Charles Merrill and Edmund Lynch, along with their (and Pathé's) attorney Paul Fuller, had been on the board of directors of the Pathé Exchange from the outset in 1915. Merrill had resigned from the board (but retained his stock) when he entered the army in 1917, but Lynch had stayed on.[3] According to Edmund Lynch's biographer, in 1921 Brunet and Pearson found themselves at odds with company policy being imposed by Charles Pathé and hit upon the idea of seeking out a U.S. buyer to free the Pathé Exchange from the dictates of Paris.[4] Pearson approached Merrill and

Lynch, and, with Paul Fuller's encouragement, Merrill, Lynch and Company bought a controlling interest in the Pathé Exchange.

This version of Merrill Lynch's takeover of the Pathé Exchange appears to have come largely from the recollections of Elmer Pearson, recorded nearly twenty years after the event. The story has at least three problems. First, it suggests that Merrill and Lynch were not already intimately connected with Pathé. Second, it presents a rift between Brunet and Charles Pathé. While that is certainly possible, it seems unlikely. As has been seen, Charles Pathé was quick to dismiss employees who disagreed with him or asserted their own independence. Paul Brunet not only continued as a board member of Pathé-Cinéma in France, he would eventually become its deputy director.[5] Finally, Charles Pathé was liquidating or spinning off his international subsidiaries, so it makes perfect sense that the Pathé Exchange would have been on the block during this period.

Lynch's biographer has him traveling to Paris, where he negotiated for three months with Charles Pathé. According to the *New York Herald Tribune*, Merrill, Lynch and Company got the Pathé Exchange for $7 million. Of this, only $350,000 was cash. For the rest, Merrill, Lynch and Company assumed Pathé's U.S. debts and gave Charles Pathé $2 million in preferred stock and a seat on the board of directors. Again as related by Elmer Pearson, upon returning to the United States, Lynch discovered that Pathé's inventory had only about half of the represented value. Pearson remembered that Lynch became enraged and alleged misrepresentation, ultimately demanding that Charles Pathé return half of the preferred stock he had received in payment.[6] In Pearson's account, Lynch believed that Paul Brunet had been an accomplice in the deception and eventually fired him. Paul Fuller became president of Pathé Exchange, and Lynch became chairman of the board. As a result, Merrill, Lynch and Company wound up owning and running a company that it had intended to buy only as an investment.[7] Pearson recollected that for the first several months after the purchase, Lynch occupied an office at Pathé and worked there full-time. After the initial period, he divided his time more evenly between Merrill Lynch and Pathé.[8]

In his book *Wall Street to Main Street: Charles Merrill and Middle-Class Investors* (1999), Edwin J. Perkins offers a slightly different take on Brunet's exit from Pathé, suggesting that over time Lynch began to suspect him of mismanagement, if not outright fraud.[9] This seems more plausible, since Brunet did not leave the company for a full fifteen months after the change in ownership.[10] As late as nine months following the transition, in April 1922, Brunet was still so highly regarded that 1,800 Pathé executives and employees, virtually the entire workforce, presented him with an autographed testimonial book commemorating his fourth year at the company's helm. The book had a bronze medallion portrait of Brunet on the cover, and the text and autographs were on pages of Japanese vellum. The inscription began, "We, the Pathé family, by this token of our hands express to you our Gratitude, Love and Esteem. . . ."[11] It concluded, "It is accordingly our pleasure to wish you many more years as president of Pathé Exchange, Inc., and to extend the assurance of our loyalty and best efforts that we may continue to merit the favor of your counsel and command."[12] Yet, six months later, Paul Brunet was gone.

When it announced Brunet's departure in October 1922, Pathé's board of directors declined to name a successor, stating,

> No action was taken on the election of a new president nor is any such action contemplated for some time to come, and in all probability will be deferred until our annual meeting some time next year.
>
> The Pathé executive organization as now composed has been functioning with splendid efficiency and with entire satisfaction to all concerned. We accordingly see no immediate need of rearrangement or change.
>
> Furthermore, the resignation of Mr. Brunet will in no way affect the policy of the company nor its management.[13]

Pathé's board of directors, on which Charles Pathé retained one seat, did indeed elect Paul Fuller as president in May 1923. Edwin Perkins describes Fuller as something of a figurehead, with Lynch acting both as the new chairman of the board and as unofficial chief executive officer.[14] In any event, most of the day-to-day operation of the company would continue to be handled by Elmer Pearson, the general manager who had been installed by Paul Brunet. (A late 1922 trade-journal article actually identified Pearson as the "head of Pathé.")[15]

A few days after the installation of the new officers, Hal Roach sent Pathé's New York office a telegram that was obviously intended for publication. It has all the sincerity of a torture-induced confession: "Congratulations to your very able president, Mr. Paul Fuller, and to Mr. Pearson, the most capable Vice President and General Manager Pathé has ever had; and to Mr. Lynch, whose name will add dignity and stability as Chairman of the Board of Directors. May Pathé, under the guidance of these executives, continue to be the efficient, honorable and progressive organization that has built up its reputation."[16] Decades later Roach vented his real feelings about the new Pathé management to his friend and biographer, author Richard Bann. Roach saw Brunet as an able administrator and said that after his departure "[t]he management was just disgraceful. I never saw a company do so many things wrong so fast."[17]

Roach's misgivings notwithstanding, the years under Merrill Lynch were fairly profitable ones for Pathé.[18] Some of this was due to the type of business savvy Charles Pathé had sought when he brought Merrill and Lynch into the firm in 1915. For example, Merrill and Lynch forecast a business recession in 1921–22 and instructed Elmer Pearson to introduce incentives to get as many contracts with theaters as far in advance as possible. To this end Pearson ordered film rental rates to be reduced to make them more attractive and awarded $40,000 in prizes to the top-performing members of Pathé's sales staff. At the same time, Pathé ordered a drastic cutback in film production. As Pearson remembered, and as seems to be borne out for the most part by the historical record, Lynch adopted a hands-off approach when it came to *Pathé News* but slashed the production of expensive features. Within months Pathé was able to repay its $2 million in outstanding loans.[19] When the recession arrived and hit the other studios hard, Pathé rode out the storm with binding exhibition contracts that kept the cash flowing in. As Pearson's account continued, Merrill and Lynch also accurately predicted the end of the recession and resumed full production in time to meet rising demand.[20] In December 1921, at the depth of the recession, Merrill and Lynch were able to raise Pathé's assets to 385 percent of its liabilities through a successful issue of bonds.[21] Successful though this strategy may have been in the short term, a bolder and more adventurous approach would be required if Pathé were ever truly to break into the ranks of the major studios.

Pathé's bottom line would soon be bolstered by a bit of intellectual property that seemed insignificant when it was included with the purchase of the Pathé Exchange from Pathé Frères: patents to a method for manufacturing raw motion-picture stock that did not infringe on the Eastman Kodak process.[22] In 1921 Kodak was successful in having a tariff on the importation of raw film stock placed into a general revision of U.S. tariff law.[23] This raised the price on imported film to the point that it effectively eliminated competition from Pathé Frères and other overseas manufacturers and gave Kodak a virtual monopoly in the U.S. market.[24] Possessing the patents but lacking the ability to actually manufacture film stock itself, Pathé approached E. I. du Pont de Nemours and Company, a chemical manufacturer that had tried and failed to develop its own process for manufacturing film.[25] Pathé agreed to allow du Pont to have a 51 percent controlling interest in the new venture,[26] and the DuPont-Pathé Film Manufacturing Corporation was born in November 1924.[27] With its manufacturing plant in Parlin, New Jersey, the

DuPont-Pathé Film Manufacturing Company turned a substantial profit, especially for Merrill and Lynch when they eventually sold their personal holdings in the company to du Pont.[28]

Part of the reason for the new company's success was a conspicuous silence from its major competitor. Eastman Kodak had come under the scrutiny of the Federal Trade Commission (FTC) in 1923. The FTC charged that Kodak had secretly backed two motion-picture processing laboratories and that these labs received Kodak's film and chemicals at such a deep discount that other labs could not compete. The FTC further alleged that Kodak sold raw stock on better terms to laboratories that used its film exclusively than it did to labs that bought film from multiple manufacturers. Although Eastman Kodak managed to avoid being broken up into its component parts, as the FTC had desired, it was in no position to impede the progress of a new film manufacturing company entering the market in 1924.[29] While most major studios would continue to feel more comfortable using the tried and tested, better-known Kodak film, DuPont-Pathé stock became a favorite of budget-minded filmmakers.

Pathé's problem, though, and part of the source of Hal Roach's ire toward the new managers, was that they were too much like the old ones (making Roach's anger somewhat ironic, given his kindly feelings toward Paul Brunet). Specifically, Edmund Lynch's approach to Pathé's business model was very conservative, staying the course set by his predecessor while disregarding significant changes in the industry around him. While this approach may have produced profits in the short term, it also set the stage for Pathé's ultimate failure. The company continued to function largely as a distributor of short films to rural and neighborhood theaters. The influx of new capital facilitated by Merrill Lynch was used to expand Pathé's short-subject offerings,[30] and the new owners proclaimed that "[t]he policy rigidly adhered to since its inception, that of remaining out of the field of theatre ownership, will continue to be implicitly followed by Pathé Exchange, Inc."[31] This policy continued to ignore the trend toward more consolidation into ever-larger companies at both the production and theatrical ends of the motion-picture industry. A company that distributed the work of independent producers to independent theaters, few of them prestigious first-run venues, was doomed to be a minor player in the emerging Hollywood landscape.

ZOWIE!, LUNA-CY, OUCH!

Elmer Pearson spent much of the mid-1920s repeating a familiar refrain: "Short subjects are of more importance today than they ever have been.

Conditions which have so hampered the production of true quality features have not affected the Pathé short subject product. That product is better today than it has ever been."[32] In the summer of 1923 he sounded much like one of his predecessors from the previous decade when he spoke with pride about the ever-increasing number of reels of film Pathé was pushing out the door weekly.[33] Beyond the difficulty of trying to sell theaters on a steady diet of short subjects, Pathé also suffered from a lack of stability in its release schedule. While it did have a base of reliable producers and series, it also had a penchant for accepting films from producers incapable of mounting a sustained series. These films may have been intriguing as one-of-a-kind offerings, but they were often of rather low quality and did nothing to either burnish Pathé's reputation or to fatten its bottom line.

There were so many of these one-time films and limited series that a discussion of all of them is impossible. However, a few stand out because of their uniqueness or potential. Many are no longer believed to exist, so the only chance for evaluation comes from their descriptions and trade reviews. One such film was produced by Harris Dickson, a Vicksburg, Mississippi, author who had found some success writing a series of stories, published in the *Saturday Evening Post*, about African American life during Reconstruction. By all accounts the film was not well received, and the proposed series was canceled, but the subject matter and the fact that it was filmed on location in Vicksburg in 1921 certainly makes it *sound* intriguing. Another one-of-a-kind Pathé release is something of a milestone in movie history. *The Ballad of Fisher's Boarding House* (1922) was the one-reel directing debut of legendary filmmaker Frank Capra. Laurence Reid, a critic for *Motion Picture News*, was enthusiastic: "The little drama is marked for its intensity of scene. . . . The picture is a masterpiece of realism, carrying dramatic value and a spiritual flavor."[34] Happily, this is one film that still exists.

Only slightly more successful in terms of the number of films produced was the three-film *Oregon Trail* series produced by the Kiser Studios. One film in particular seems to stand out as an early environmentalist tract. *The Price of Progress* (1922) is described as "[t]he drama of the big timber country of the Northwest where giants that have taken centuries to achieve their growth are felled wholesale."[35] A bit longer still was a series of four stereoscopic (three-dimensional) films produced by Ives-Leventhal Stereoscopiks. With titles like *Zowie!*, *Luna-cy* (filmed on thrill rides at Coney Island's Luna Park), *Ouch!* and *A Runaway Taxi*, they would be fun to rediscover.

Produced under the auspices of the Extension Department of Yale University, the *Chronicles of America* series covered momentous occasions in American history beginning with the voyage of Columbus. In December 1923, a few months into the series' run, Pathé reported that it had received a "great body of letters . . . from admirers of the Chronicles of America series." These are from people of "discriminating tastes and of the type that it would be well for motion picture exhibitors to make permanent members of their audiences," according to Pearson.[36] Perhaps a more objective view was offered by a number of exhibitors who complained that these were straight educational films and were useless as audience draws unless there was a tie-in with the local schools. Indeed, Richard Koszarski feels that the series' greatest success was "in legitimizing the educational film market and creating a viable production niche for instructional and informational media."[37]

Another group that sounds interesting is the *Famous Melody* series from 1926. These were a cross between audience sing-along films and travelogues, as each film explored the popular music of a foreign country. The films were shot on location, and Pathé provided musical cue sheets for theater musicians. What makes this series noteworthy is that it was produced by James A. FitzPatrick, who would later produce and narrate the long-running *TravelTalks* series for Metro-Goldwyn-Mayer (MGM). The *TravelTalks*, beautifully photographed in Technicolor, almost invariably ended with FitzPatrick cooing, "As the sun sets on the horizon, we bid a reluctant farewell to. . . ."[38]

The last odd lot of films to be considered here was undoubtedly the most successful. During the years 1918 and 1919, Charlie Chaplin produced a total of four short films. These were the first films he produced for his own company, as opposed to being an actor-for-hire starring in films owned by others, and, consequently, were the first films in his body of work that he actually owned. The first two, *A Dog's Life* and *Shoulder Arms*, were wildly successful and hailed as instant classics. The other two, *Sunnyside* and *A Day's Pleasure*, were widely regarded as career missteps and were only moderately successful. In 1925 Pathé bought reissue rights to the films from Chaplin. Using the films' price tag for publicity, Pathé boasted that it had paid $500,000 for the four films, the same amount their original distributor, First National, had paid when they were new.[39] Pathé emphasized the special nature of the films by asserting that this was the first time ever a group of films had not depreciated in value between the time of initial release and Pathé's reissue.[40] Pathé's advertising emphasized the classic nature of the four films, apparently hoping that exhibitors and the public wouldn't remember that two of the films actually hadn't been very popular.[41] Although it was not by design, getting the reissue rights to the four Chaplin films meant that at one time or another Pathé handled the films of practically every major comedian of the silent era except Buster Keaton.[42] Beginning with *A Dog's Life*, which was released in 1925 while Chaplin's masterpiece *The Gold Rush* was still in theaters, the quartet was doled out very slowly over a span of three years.

What stability existed on the Pathé schedule was provided by the company's staples: the informational films led by *Pathé News*, the Pathéserials, Paul Terry's *Aesop's Fables* cartoons (to be discussed shortly), and comedies from Hal Roach and, beginning in 1923, Mack Sennett. Even here Pathé sabotaged itself and its producers by continuing to offer its films on an individual basis, rather than forcing exhibitors to buy an entire series. Pearson's stated Pathé's policy thus: "We say to the exhibitor: 'Book one or more or all, according to your conviction regarding their value to you in each instance.'"[43] This may have been an open and honest way to conduct business, and it certainly did express supreme confidence in the quality of the Pathé product, but it was a policy that made it all too easy for Pathé's films to be squeezed off theater screens by films from producers who did insist that exhibitors take entire series and blocks of pictures.

PATHÉ NEWS

As before, the cornerstone of Pathé's short-subject program was the twice-weekly *Pathé News*, the leader in what, until the late 1920s, was a pretty uncrowded field.[44] The two most interesting developments involving *Pathé News* during the Merrill Lynch years involved censorship and publicity.

As noted earlier, Pathé fought and lost a battle over censorship of its newsreel in New York in the early 1920s. Before the final decision in that case, Pathé took on another censor and, this time, won. Evalyn F. Snow had been appointed to Ohio's censorship board in April 1921. In a July reorganization the censorship board was abolished, and Snow became Ohio's chief (and only) censor for a term set to expire in January 1923. During her first year in office, she incurred the wrath of many in the film community by banning the exhibition in Ohio of several high-profile films, including Erich von Stroheim's *Foolish Wives* (1922). At this point Lewis Innerarity Jr., Pathé's secretary who had vowed to fight the New York censor to the bitter end, laid a trap for Snow.[45]

Snow had been quoted as saying that "75 per cent of the people never think at all."[46] In an account sympathetic to Snow published in the procensorship *Catechism on Motion Pictures in Inter-state Commerce*, the actual conversation that led up to this quote started with Snow being asked if the public were incapable of acting as their own censors in choosing which movies to see. Snow answered with another question: "If so, why did the Legislature of Ohio enact a censorship law?" She then went on to quote a Dr. Goddard as saying that only 75 percent of the people were thinking people. According to the *Catechism*, the quote was both taken out of context and inverted, making it appear that Snow personally held a dim view of three-quarters of the population.[47]

At this point Innerarity sent a *Pathé News* crew to photograph Snow, with her consent, for inclusion in the newsreel. As it turned up in *Pathé News* number 25, the shot of Snow was preceded by the subtitle: "In the Limelight. Cincinnati, Ohio. Can Americans Think? Mrs. Evalyn F. Snow, Chief of Ohio Censorship Board, who is quoted as saying–'75 per cent of the people never think at all.' She says: 'The people are not fit to judge for themselves.' WHAT DO YOU THINK?"[48]

When the film was released on March 25, 1922, Snow ordered the scene of herself cut from Ohio prints, despite the fact that Pathé had obtained her permission to photograph her for the newsreel, even if it had not informed her of the context in which the film of her would be used. Pathé appealed her decision, saying that there was nothing "immoral or harmful" in the scene and that it should be restored. In June the state attorney general reversed Snow's decision, and the governor promptly fired her.[49]

The other development of note regarding *Pathé News* during this period was its effort to use the new medium of radio as a promotional tool. During 1925 Pathé sponsored a series of *Pathé Newsletters* to be broadcast twice weekly over a nationwide "tie-up" that eventually included twenty-four stations, spread coast to coast from Boston to Los Angeles and San Francisco.[50] The only true radio network capable of broadcasting live programs simultaneously to a group of stations in early 1925 was operated by American Telephone and Telegraph (AT&T), and it only had seven stations, none of which was on the West Coast. Without a "true" nationwide network available the *Pathé Newsletter* was likely distributed in script form via telegraph to be read by staff announcers at the stations airing the show. The programs were designed to "direct the attention of the radio listeners to the current news reel program as being actually shown at the theatres themselves." Additionally the *Pathé Newsletter* related "the actual experiences of the cameramen in securing the shots."[51]

Pathé's use of radio as a publicity tool did not end with the *Pathé Newsletter*. To kick off an industry-wide promotion of short comedies called Laugh Month in January 1926, Pathé comedy stars Harry Langdon, Charley Chase, and members of Our Gang joined short-comedy stars from other studios as part of a three-hour program broadcast on Saturday, January 2, on Los Angeles radio station KNX, "The Voice of Hollywood."[52] Recent Pathé comedy acquisitions Larry Semon and his wife and leading lady Dorothy Dwan had appeared on a similar program a week earlier.[53]

Pathé's interest in radio was not unique. All of the studios regarded radio with ambivalence, valuing it as a promotional tool while simultaneously fearing it as a rival to film as a source of entertainment. After all, the hours that the public spent in their homes listening to their radios were hours not spent sitting in theater seats. One film industry leader who proved masterful at using radio was theater impresario S. L. "Roxy" Rothafel, who in the mid-1920s was manager of the Capitol Theatre on Broadway. Rothafel had a weekly variety show on the fledgling AT&T radio network, and he delighted the Pathé publicity department in May 1925 when he used his program to proclaim Pathé's release of Hal Roach's western feature *Black Cyclone* "the best picture that I have ever seen in five years."[54]

Pathé News still had the companionship of the weekly series *Pathé Reviews* and *Topics of the Day* on the release schedule. The *Review* still contained segments in Pathécolor, but starting in 1923 recycled European color footage was pushed out of the reel by new material, mostly of a travelogue nature, shot in America and sent to France for coloring.[55] Pathé reported that "[c]ritics and exhibitors have commended [the Pathécolor scenes] highly for the valuable eye-resting effect it produces when introduced midway of a long screen program, as well as for its own particular entertainment value."[56] Pathé went on to claim that "[m]any big theatres book the *Pathé Review* because of Pathécolor alone. Pathécolor is still the finest color in motion pictures. It is always beautiful, always clear, always natural. The beauty spots of the world have been put into Pathécolor."[57] Once again the "naturalness" of this highly artificial color process was stressed, as was its superiority over a field that now included two-color Technicolor.

PATHÉSERIALS AND FABLES

Serials continued to be a mainstay of the Pathé program. Following the cutbacks during the financial crisis of 1921–22, serial production became standardized at ten episodes per series, with the release schedule timed so that the first episode of a new series would usually be released either the same week as, or one week following, the concluding episode of the preceding series. *The Way of a Man* (1923), starring Allene Ray and Harold Miller and directed by Pathéserial veteran George B. Seitz, stands out from the 1920s serial pack as significant for two reasons. First, it kicked off Pathé's "Better Serial Movement," a conscious effort to gear new serials toward an adult audience. In identifying it as a turning point a year after its release, a Pathé publicity statement said that *The Way of a Man* strove to develop more plausible themes and human characters than the "dime-novel" variety of the early serials. This had paid off, according to the company, by securing "bigger distribution than any serial ever released, even including the most successful of the old Pearl White serials of years gone by when serial distribution was thought to be at its zenith."[58] The second thing of note is that *The Way of a Man* was released simultaneously as both a serial and as a feature-length picture.[59] This strategy gave the feature version a chance to be shown in the sort of major metropolitan theaters that would never even consider running a Pathéserial, and Pathé would continue the practice with its more ambitious serials to the end of the silent era. The downside, obviously, was that the feature versions were rife with plot and continuity problems resulting from cutting a two-hundred-minute serial into a seventy-five-minute feature.

By the mid-1920s Pathé was once again producing many of its own serials rather than relying exclusively on independent producers. Pathé's serials were produced in rented studio space on both coasts. The company's New York City serial base was the Cosmopolitan Studio. Arch Heath, who directed several serials there including *The Masked Menace* starring a young Jean Arthur, actually claimed that his production costs were 30 percent below what they would be in California.[60] In Hollywood Pathé rented space in the Fine Arts Studio,[61] a facility previously known as the Reliance-Majestic Studio when it was used by D. W. Griffith for films like *Intolerance* (1916) and *Broken Blossoms* (1919).[62]

Despite the Better Serials Movement and the continuous statements in the trade press that serials (and short films generally) were garnering ever more respect among exhibitors and the moviegoing public, Pathé was forced to admit in 1927 that its serials were still not playing in the more prestigious (and lucrative) first-run urban venues. While boasting that its serials ran in 40 percent of American theaters, it acknowledged that those theaters were a mix of rural cinemas and second-run houses in the big cities.[63]

Animated cartoons became an important part of Pathé's program in the 1920s. Pathé had distributed the work of pioneering animator John R. Bray from 1913 until he shifted his output to Paramount Pictures at the beginning of 1916. After that, aside from seven cartoons from legendary newspaper cartoonist Rube Goldberg in 1916 and the animated films that came as part of the Hearst-International package of 1917 and 1918, Pathé stayed away from the genre after 1915. The company made a new commitment to animation in 1921 when it contracted to distribute the work of Paul Terry, a former newspaper cartoonist whose recent work in animation had included a stint with Bray.[64] For Pathé, Terry animated a series of contemporary retellings of familiar Aesop fables, complete with a moral at the end. As time went on and the series became more and more popular, the cartoons tended to stray from the fables premise, although the series title remained the same.

Most of Terry's *Aesop's Fables* cartoons seem to have survived, in part due to their extensive reissue in the nontheatrical 16-millimeter film market and, later, their repeated showings on television during its earliest days. One is struck by the sameness of the plots and the simplicity of the character design, demonstrating none of the imagination of the contemporary Felix the Cat series or Max and Dave Fleischer's Out of the Inkwell cartoons. This was partially due to Terry's hectic production schedule, turning out a film a week for eight years. Yet, *Aesop's Fables* was considered at the top of the form in the 1920s. *Moving Picture World*'s analysis of *One Good Turn* (1924) is entirely typical of the rave reviews the series got in both the trade and popular press: "Reviewing one of Paul Terry's *Aesop's Fable* cartoons is a matter requiring deliberation, simply because they maintain such a high standard of excellence that the reviewer fears repeating words of praise he has used before, and digs out the dictionary to learn how to praise again. . . ."[65]

A testament to the high esteem with which Terry's cartoons were held in the 1920s is demonstrated by their influence on the formative work of Walt Disney. In 1922, when Disney's young studio in Kansas City was working on its first Laugh-O-gram cartoons, he borrowed a print of an *Aesop's Fable* so that his animators could study the drawing and movement frame by frame.[66] In 1928, after he had relocated to California and as his leading character was transitioning from Oswald the Lucky Rabbit to a certain mouse, Disney was quoted as telling one of his animators, "Someday I'm going to make a cartoon as good as a *Fable*."[67] Disney would reiterate the sentiment a decade later, writing, "Even as late as 1930, my ambition was to be able to make a cartoon as good as the *Aesop's Fables* series."[68]

Despite his success Paul Terry did encounter a couple of bumps in the road. While he worked for John Bray in 1917, he had been introduced to the method of animation in which the artists drew on transparent sheets of cellophane rather than paper. This process allowed transparencies of the moving aspects of a scene to be overlaid onto a stationary background, eliminating the need for redrawing the background every time a character moved.[69] When Terry set up his own shop, he continued to use this system. The problem was that the process was protected by five patents, and it could not be legally used without paying royalties to patent holders John Bray and Earl Hurd. The Bray-Hurd Process Company sued all animation studios that used its system without permission, and, in 1926, Terry's Fables Pictures became the first studio to settle with Bray and Hurd and to be licensed by them to use their process.[70]

Terry's other problem was that he was the manager of Fables Pictures, not the owner. He was initially backed by Keith-Albee, a company that controlled a large chain of vaudeville/movie theaters and that would loom large in Pathé's future. Around 1928 Keith-Albee sold Fables Pictures to short-film producer Amadee J. Van Beuren. Terry departed Fables Pictures in 1929, by some accounts after a clash with Van Beuren over the approach to talking pictures.[71] Interestingly, the first *Aesop's Fable* with sound, *Dinner Time*, was released by Pathé in October 1928, a month before Walt Disney's *Steamboat Willie*. After leaving Fables, Terry set up his Terrytoons animation studio, whose cartoons were distributed first by short-film specialist Educational Pictures and later by Twentieth Century–Fox. As for Van Beuren, he continued to make cartoons for distribution though Pathé and its successor, RKO-Radio Pictures, until 1936, when Radio-Keith-Orpheum (RKO) contracted with another animation studio. With no outlet for his films and in failing health, Van Beuren closed up shop. His place on the RKO release schedule was taken by none other than Walt Disney, the man who had found so much inspiration in the *Aesop's Fables* a decade earlier.[72]

"FRIENDSHIP AND INTIMATE RELATIONS"

Even after handing its feature division over to Associated, Pathé continued to release the occasional feature film under its own banner. Its ambivalence toward features was clear in its advertising copy at the beginning of the 1922–23 movie season: "For the coming year Pathé announces no definite extended schedule of feature releases, as it does not specialize in this type of production. . . . Unhampered by the restrictions imposed by a regular feature release, Pathé offers a limited number of true Special Features. *Nanook of the North* and *The Isle of Zorda* illustrate their quality."[73] *Nanook of the North* was Robert J. Flaherty's landmark 1922 documentary about a family of Inuit Eskimos; *The Isle of Zorda* was a feature reedit of a 1921 French serial adapted from the Jules Verne story "Mathias Sandorf."[74] Both films generated substantial prestige and revenue for Pathé, but their success failed to spur Pathé into a greater commitment to features.[75] Pathé did show some interest in distributing additional feature-length documentaries, but these other films never replicated the success of *Nanook*.[76]

The producer that did the most to polish Pathé's feature reputation, ironically, was short-comedy specialist Hal Roach. Roach's feature contributions followed two distinctly different paths. First were the films of Harold Lloyd, whose popularity continued to skyrocket through the 1920s. Lloyd was still doing short comedies when Associated Exhibitors assumed the distribution of his films in May 1921. In December of that year Associated distributed Lloyd's *A Sailor-Made Man*, which barely qualified as a feature at four reels. In an advertisement, Associated Exhibitors happily reported that *A Sailor-Made Man* ran fifty consecutive days at the Symphony Theatre in Los Angeles and that box-office records were broken in thirty-two cities.[77] In a survey, forty exhibitors who ran *A Sailor-Made Man* rated it an average 87 percent for box-office and entertainment values.[78] This is an extraordinarily high rating, considering that Douglas Fairbanks' *The Three Musketeers* and Mary Pickford's *Little Lord Fauntleroy* each averaged a rating of 80 percent (at a time when they were the industry's top stars), and Cecil B. DeMille's *The Affairs of Anatol*, starring the popular Wallace Reid and rising star Gloria Swanson, averaged a rating of 72 percent.[79]

In September 1922 the five-reel *Grandma's Boy* became Lloyd's last film to be distributed by Associated. *Grandma's Boy* had its premiere at the Symphony, where its nineteen-week engagement was five weeks longer than any film had been held by a Los Angeles theater.[80] The long Los Angeles run emboldened Associated Exhibitors to demand that other first-run venues book *Grandma's Boy* no less than a two-week engagement. It also announced that it would not accept any bookings with combined vaudeville/movie theaters. The film would only play "straight picture houses. Mr. Lloyd himself was insistent upon this."[81] Of the film, the *Portland Telegram* newspaper wrote, "The success of *Grandma's Boy*, not only in Portland [Oregon], but in New York and Los Angeles, is a convincing argument that the American people, as a whole, still love the clean, the true, and the beautiful in life."[82] An exhibitor proclaimed that he "did better with this than any Chaplin I ever ran. Lloyd has Chaplin outdistanced in every way, here."[83]

In November 1922 Pathé resumed direct distribution of Harold Lloyd's films with the five-reel *Dr. Jack*. The *Moving Picture World* noted a "tidal wave of public appreciation of Harold Lloyd," saying that house records were being broken in San Francisco, Kansas City, and Tacoma, despite the fact that the last two had below-zero temperatures and a heavy rainstorm, respectively.[84] By February 1924, over a year after its premiere, *Dr. Jack* was still winding its way through the nation's exhibition system. Pathé crowed that the film would soon achieve the "long sought but heretofore unattained goal" of playing in every community in the United States with a theater.[85] Despite the film's unqualified success, some small-theater operators complained that the high rental rates being charged by Pathé resulted in their barely breaking even, despite drawing a large audience.[86] Charles Martin, manager of the Family Theater in Mt. Morris, New York, groused that he actually *lost* $75 running *Dr. Jack*.[87]

April Fools' Day 1923 brought yet another Lloyd triumph to the screen. *Safety Last* still stands as one of the comedian's best films and provided American popular culture with the iconic image of Lloyd hanging off the face of a giant clock on the side of a building high above the street below. At seven reels, *Safety Last* was also the longest comedy to date.[88] Pathé knew it had a winner and pulled out all the stops in publicizing it. Among ten different "novelties" that Pathé provided theater operators for a fee were red balloons with Lloyd's face printed on them and promotional slogans and handkerchiefs embossed with "Dry your tears of laughter when you cry for joy at Harold Lloyd in *Safety Last*." This slogan was accompanied by the name of the theater and the dates it would run the film. The Pathé promotional materials added, helpfully, "An important feature is that the ink of handkerchief easily washes out." At the high end, Pathé prepared two different forty-by-sixty-inch oil paintings of Lloyd in gold-colored frames.[89] A theater manager in Oklahoma City spoke for many when he wrote that *Safety Last* was "the last word in superb moving pictures. Lloyd in this unexcelled by any character ever appearing on the screen. It is one of the funniest and most entertaining pictures ever shown. . . ."[90]

In terms of popularity and prestige, both Pathé's feature-film and short-film product was at its zenith in 1923. When he issued his summary of "The Best Moving Pictures of 1922–23," influential critic Robert E. Sherwood led off his list of sixteen features with *Nanook of the North* and *Grandma's Boy*. *Safety Last* and *Dr. Jack* didn't make the list, but they received honorable mentions. The Hal Roach and Mack Sennett comedies made the best short-film list, and Sherwood declared *Aesop's Fables* "foremost among the animated cartoons."[91] However, there was a dark cloud on Pathé's feature horizon.

In addition to being a talented comedian, Harold Lloyd was a savvy businessman. Wanting to maximize the benefits of his success, Lloyd had begun to renegotiate his contract with Hal Roach as early as November 1921, when he reapportioned the split of the producer's share of his films' profits to 80 percent for him and 20 percent for Roach.[92] At the end of 1923, following completion of *Why Worry?*, Lloyd left Roach to set up his own production company.[93] After just three more features, ending with his masterpiece *The Freshman* (1925), Lloyd left Pathé as well and began distributing his films through the mighty Paramount Pictures.[94] Pathé took out an ad in the trade journals to bid him farewell:

> Not long since[,] Pathé publicly voiced appreciation for the splendid and most unusual spirit displayed by the Harold Lloyd Corporation in

> spending upon "THE FRESHMAN," their last picture under the Pathé contract, a sum far exceeding their contractual obligation. Now Pathé desires, in all sincerity, to voice equal appreciation of the fact that this picture, representing a cost far beyond the producer's obligation, represents also a supreme effort in feature comedy making, a really monumental achievement in mirth-creation. . . . Pathé is proud to present this supreme testimonial of the friendship and intimate relations enjoyed for eleven years with Harold Lloyd.[95]

Privately, Pathé knew it had suffered a serious blow. Hal Roach's New York representative wired the studio in October 1924 that he "ran into [Elmer] Pearson in front of the building today. . . . He hailed me . . . and said, 'Frank, we have lost Lloyd now, and I want you fellows to hurry up with Tryon and Stone.'"[96] Both Roach's and Pathé's hopes for Arthur Stone or Glenn Tryon to be the next Harold Lloyd would soon be dashed. After a conference with Pathé executives only a month later, W. B. Frank reported to the studio that "unless a much better grade of Stone pictures is made in the forthcoming releases he will be too dead to revive. . . . Tryon has possibilities," but only in short films, not features.[97]

Pathé didn't pin all of its hopes for a new comedy headliner on Hal Roach. Even before Lloyd left for Paramount, Pathé contracted with Thomas H. Ince for a new series of feature comedies starring Charles Ray. Ray had achieved some measure of success after 1915 and through the early 1920s, generally portraying a "country bumpkin" character,[98] but his career had stalled in 1923 when he produced and starred in a very expensive and very unsuccessful version of *The Courtship of Myles Standish*, distributed, coincidentally, by Associated Exhibitors. The Pathé features were billed as Ray's "comeback."[99] Unfortunately, producer Thomas Ince died after the completion of the second film, *Percy* (1925), and, given the poor reception of both films, the series ended.[100] Ray's career did revive briefly in the last years of the silent era, particularly during a stint at MGM, but his fortunes took a dive once again with the coming of sound. By the time of his death in 1943 he was reduced to playing unbilled bit roles.

A career path similar to Ray's was the fate of Larry Semon. Looking something like a gargoyle in pancake makeup, Semon had been fairly successful in a series of short comedies in the years since 1910. A pair of failed features in the mid-1920s, including a bizarre and somewhat reviled version of *The Wizard of Oz* (1925), left him looking for a comeback. Through his own independent production company, Semon produced two features for Pathé: *Stop, Look, and Listen* (1926) and *Spuds* (1927). The former film was based on a musical stage play, and for it Semon traded his baggy pants and clown makeup for more of a "straight comedy characterization."[101] George T. Pardy, a reviewer for *Motion Picture News*, found *Stop, Look, and Listen* to be a fast-paced and amusing combination of melodrama and comedy,[102] but neither it nor its successor was sufficient to reestablish Semon's career. He directed for a time at Mack Sennett's studio, then returned to acting in short comedies for an independent producer. A noteworthy supporting role in Josef von Sternberg's classic 1927 gangster feature *Underworld* seemed to hold great promise for the future, but Semon died the following year of tuberculosis.

A somewhat happier story is that of Monty Banks, an Italian comedian who had worked in short comedies in the United States since 1916. By 1922 he was producing and starring in his own short comedies, and by 1925 he felt ready to enter the feature market. His initial feature, *Keep Smiling*, was distributed by Associated Exhibitors. His next five features were released through Pathé. One of these was his best-known film, *Play Safe* (1927), whose spectacular runaway-train climax has been included in innumerable silent-comedy documentaries and compilations. Banks' films were reasonably successful, although nowhere near the stratospheric levels of Harold Lloyd's work. In 1928 he packed up and moved to Great Britain, where he continued his film career. He returned to the United States during the Second World War and had the dubious distinction of directing Stan Laurel and Oliver Hardy in *Great Guns* (1941), the first film of the unhappy Twentieth Century–Fox phase of their career.

Beyond the Lloyd comedies, the other track that Hal Roach's feature production took was in the realm of action-adventure and western films. Roach had a great fondness for the rugged outdoors, and his tastes were reflected in these films. His first undertaking in this genre was *Call of the Wild* (1923), based on the Jack London novel. The following year he produced *The King of Wild Horses*, the first in a series of four westerns released at the rate of one per year featuring "Rex, the Wonder Horse." The Rex films were extremely popular, with *The King of Wild Horses* and its sequel, *Black Cyclone* (1925), listed as among the top ten box-office attractions of their respective years.[103] The exhibitors' satisfaction average for *The King of Wild Horses* was 85 percent, putting it in the neighborhood of the Harold Lloyd films for popularity.[104]

HAL AND MACK

Despite occasional friction Hal Roach enjoyed something of a favored son status with Pathé in the early 1920s. This was undoubtedly due in no small part to the runaway success of the Harold Lloyd comedies. Pathé tossed extra work Roach's way from time to time, including having Monty Banks lease space at the Roach studio in 1926 and 1927.[105] When Pathé decided in 1925 to replace the static artwork of a rooster with a live, crowing cock for the logo that opened its films, it turned to Roach. Roach's staff soon discovered that getting a rooster to crow on cue was no easy task; they had to turn to a vaudevillian named Billy Knight, who had a troupe of performing roosters.[106]

Perhaps the most significant work Roach picked up along these lines was to house the production of a pair of Ruth Roland serials, *White Eagle* and *The Timber Queen*, both of which were released in 1922 and were directed by Fred Jackman, who would go on to direct *Call of the Wild* and all four of the Rex pictures. After Roland moved on to another studio upon completion of *The Timber Queen*, Roach produced one more serial. *Her Dangerous Path* (1923) was something of a return to the self-contained chapter play reminiscent of Pathé's earlier serials *Who Pays?* and *The Price of Folly*. *Her Dangerous Path* started life under the working title *What Should a Girl Do?*, and, while less dramatic, the working title is more descriptive of the series. As announced by Pathé, "The star is called upon to interpret several different types of heroine illustrating the various dangerous paths which fate may call upon a girl to pursue. Hal Roach is the author of the story. . . ."[107] In the opening installment, Connie Grant (played by Edna Murphy), has her fortune told. As the series progresses, she sees what her life will be like if she marries men in different walks of life: a politician, an artist, a scientist, a rancher, etc. Pathé pointed to this series as the genesis of its Better Serials Movement, saying that *Her Dangerous Path* "was widely booked by houses that never before presented a serial."[108]

Despite the success he enjoyed with dramatic shorts and features, the foundation of Hal Roach's business was the short comedy, and there was one particular business decision that Pathé made regarding Roach's bread and butter that earned Pathé his lasting enmity. In the spring of 1923 Pathé contracted to distribute the entire short-film output of Roach's principal rival, Mack Sennett. Pathé tried to mollify Roach by asserting that this would make Sennett less of a competitor and more of an ally; that with Sennett under the same roof as Roach, Pathé would have a line of comedy films second to none. Roach countered correctly, but unsuccessfully, that this arrangement would give Pathé over one hundred short comedies a year, far more than it could possibly sell.[109] Making the competitive situation even worse in the summer of 1923 was the announcement by Paramount that it would reissue twenty-five Sennett comedies that it had distributed between two-and-a-half and four years previously.[110] Unlike Pathé's policy of selling its pictures individually, Paramount was a firm believer in booking films by entire series. The twenty-five Sennett reissues would serve to block the new Sennett and Roach films from many theaters for several months.

The short-film series that was by far and away Roach's most successful of the early 1920s was Our Gang. Inaugurated in the fall of 1922, the series was an instant hit and remained quite popular through the late 1930s.[111] And although Roach never did find a "replacement" for Harold Lloyd (and it wasn't for want of trying), he did find a strong comedy star in the person of Charley Chase. Born Charles Parrott, a name he continued to use when he directed his own films and those of others, Chase had entered the movies as a comic at Mack Sennett's Keystone studio at almost exactly the same time as Charlie Chaplin in 1914. In fact he played supporting roles in a number of Chaplin's Keystone films. For the next several years Chase worked at various studios both as an actor and as a writer-director before landing a job with Roach in 1921. Chase initially served as supervising director, in overall creative control of the entire Roach output except for the films of Harold Lloyd. At the end of 1923 he decided to resume his acting career, appearing in a series of single-reel comedies playing a character named Jimmy Jump. From the beginning the Chase comedies were appreciated by critics, exhibitors, and audiences. Reviewing the Jimmy Jump comedy *All Wet*, Thomas C. Kennedy wrote, "When it comes to comedy of the clean-cut, theatrically effective sort, there is no surer hand in the realm of short subject specialists than Charles Parrott—he who has directed many of the most successful one and two reelers and who now plays on the screen under the name of Charles Chase. The Charlie [*sic*] Chase[112] comedies, produced for Pathé at the Hal Roach Studios, offer one of the most consistent single reel series ever given to the exhibitors."[113] Perhaps unbeknownst to Kennedy, Chase was not alone at this point in crafting his comedies. Future Academy Award winner Leo McCarey directed most of Chase's one-reel and early two-reel comedies.

Beyond Our Gang and Charley Chase, though, two-reel comedy production at the Roach studio in the mid-1920s was a revolving door of failed series. Snub Pollard and Stan Laurel were both promoted from one-reelers to two-reelers, only to have their series quickly canceled due to poor exhibitor response. The Spat Family series, a prototypical situation comedy featuring a married couple and the wife's live-in brother, hobbled through two seasons before being laid to rest. Even a series starring popular stage and newspaper humorist Will Rogers only lasted a year. Rogers had appeared in a number of films before his brief stint at Roach, and he would appear in a series of Pathé travelogues afterward, but the problem with most of his silent efforts was that his humor was primarily verbal, a real disadvantage in the silent-film medium. Rogers would not succeed in the movies until they had a voice.

Roach and his staff began to blame some of their films' poor performance on neglect by Pathé, particularly when it came to their product competing with Mack Sennett's. By the fall of 1924 Sennett had three comedy series: one featuring longtime Sennett star Ben Turpin, one with the up-and-coming Harry Langdon, and a series of "Star" comedies that were headlined by Sennett stock comedy players like Billy Bevan and Andy Clyde. Roach's series at this point were Our Gang, Glenn Tryon, Arthur Stone, the Spat Family, and the one-reel Charley Chase comedies. Confirmation that Sennett's comedies were outperforming Roach's came when Frank informed Doane in October that a Pathé executive had confided to him that "Sennett had a little advantage of the sales so far due to the fact that he had three known brands of comedy to start this year's selling as against two of ours, and that for this reason he was sure Sennett was ahead. . . ."[114] Just a month later that "little advantage" had exploded. Frank gave Doane the grim news. Shorts starring Sennett's two top comedians, Ben Turpin and newcomer Harry Langdon, were earning an average of $60,000 and $45,000, respectively, per film. Langdon's box-office take was expected to go up to $75,000 per film as his popularity skyrocketed. Sennett's weakest performer, his "Star Series," earned an average of $50,000 apiece. By comparison, of Roach's three underperforming series, the Spat Family was bringing in an average of $17,905 apiece, and both the Arthur Stone and Glenn Tryon comedies were earning in an average $22,641 each.[115]

The relationship between the Hal Roach Studios and Pathé became increasingly icy. In the midst of the troubled fall of 1924, Pathé's head of publicity, Ed Supple, made the impolitic remark that Roach's comedies were difficult to promote because they starred "nobodies." "The Pathé Publicity Dept. is certainly in a terrible condition," Doane wrote to Frank. He continued by saying that if Supple had stills of Mary Pickford and Douglas Fairbanks he would probably run one each in a low-grade newspaper and think he had done his job.[116] More than a year later Doane's grievance was about the quality of the release prints coming out of Pathé's lab. Going so far as to say that acceptable prints were produced only by accident, Doane opined that the problem lay in the fact that the laboratory used outdated methods and equipment because "Pathé are starving their print factory in the same method they are starving their whole business, including their producers, and the print factory probably having no independent resources can do nothing else than turn out a very cheap grade of print under the circumstances."[117]

At the same time, Doane complained that Pathé's poor release of the Roach product overseas caused Roach to have to reach the break-even point of $70,000 per short entirely from the U.S. market, while other comedy producers could get at least $20,000 of that from the foreign market. He continued on to say that Roach was actually losing U.S. bookings by having to charge exhibitors a higher price than the competition to make up for the lack of a good foreign market.[118]

Beyond complaining, the Roach organization took matters into its own hands. For the 1925–26 movie season it entered into a direct contract with the prestigious Keith-Albee vaudeville circuit to give Roach the exclusive rights to show its comedies in towns with a Keith-Albee theater. The arrangement got off to a promising start. Keith-Albee's Hippodrome Theatre in New York City arranged a live-on-stage prologue for the Our Gang short *Your Own Backyard* (1925). Six of the Hippodrome's chorines and two of Paul Whiteman's male musicians performed the 1899 song "Stay in Your Own Back Yard" in a cottage setting. The women sat on a fence "in country dress" and the men were on a bench as all joined in song.[119]

However, the landscape of the motion-picture industry as it concerned Roach and the other independent short-film producers would change completely in late 1925. In October of that year, industry giant Paramount Pictures announced its intention to reenter the field of short subjects, an area it had abandoned a few years earlier. There was little doubt that the industry's new number-two powerhouse, Loews, Inc. (the theater chain that owned MGM), would soon follow suit. By all appearances, both companies would immediately seek to distribute the work of existing short-film producers, at least until their own in-house production units could get up and running.

The Roach staff busily set about calculating the positive and negative impact any of the possible combinations would have on their business. It was known that Paramount was interested in luring Sennett (whose product it had distributed in the early 1920s) and/or Christie (another short-comedy specialist). Knowing that the Paramount theaters were often the most prestigious in any town in which they were located and that Paramount theaters would give priority to films released by Paramount Pictures, W. B. Frank came to the startling conclusion that Roach would be better off if Sennett stayed with Pathé: "If Sennett and Christie went with Paramount, Pathé would have a very difficult time selling all of the Paramount houses our product next year. . . . If Sennett remains with Pathé we will not have very much to worry about from the Paramount producing companies' product at least the first year because of the inferior quality of comedies they would no doubt make."[120]

It went without saying that the best outcome they could hope for would be if Roach won the prize of a distribution agreement with either Paramount or Loews. After lobbying hard but unsuccessfully with the former, the Hal Roach Studios signed a distribution contract with Loews-MGM in March 1926.[121] The deal couldn't take effect immediately because Roach's contract with Pathé ran until September 1930.[122] This would later be renegotiated to September 1927, at which time he would begin releasing through MGM. In return for being allowed out of the contract early, Roach produced twelve extra films in 1927 for distribution by Pathé during the 1927–28 movie season. These films were in direct competition for screen time with Roach's first films for MGM.[123]

Although it couldn't commence distribution of Hal Roach's short comedies until the end of the Pathé contract,[124] Loews now had a vested interest in promoting Roach's films in the run-up to September 1927. In April 1926 Frank reported that Nicholas Schenck, Marcus Loew's second-in-command, had instructed the company's theaters "to start immediately playing as many of our pictures as possible, second run, behind the Keith organization—that is, exclusive of the Gangs which he has been playing second run since last September. This will help a little bit."[125]

As for the other two comedy specialists that were in play when Hollywood's two biggest studios decided to return to the field of short comedy, it was Christie that seemingly won the grand prize by going with Paramount, leaving Sennett with Pathé. Like Roach, Christie had to extricate itself from an existing distribution contract, in this case with short-film producer-distributor Educational Pictures. Christie was unable to join Paramount until September 1927. As Frank had predicted, the Christie comedies were weak competition for the Roach-MGM product, and Paramount dropped them in 1930. Christie then returned to its former distributor, Educational Pictures.[126]

ASSOCIATED EXHIBITORS, AGAIN

The dance between Pathé and Associated Exhibitors continued through the mid-1920s. Under the presidency of Arthur S. Kane, the number of films handled by Associated grew steadily as the quality diminished from its initial offerings.[127] In 1923 the company took out an ad in *Motion Picture News* to publish a declaration of principles that would have made Charles Foster Kane proud:

> A Message to Producers, The open door for important pictures, whether you make one or four—that's the policy of Associated Exhibitors.
>
> We produce no pictures—we own no studios, no exchanges (but use 34 of them), no physical plants and properties with their heavy overheads. We devote our time exclusively to selling. From the biggest city to the smallest community, Associated men are everywhere in the never ending business of circulating product.
>
> Producers are best served when given adequate economical and successful distribution for money making attractions—that's the aim of Associated Exhibitors.[128]

The ad concluded by reminding exhibitors that Associated Exhibitors owned no theaters and that it still practiced open booking.

In a cost-cutting measure in August 1924, Pathé and Associated Exhibitors combined their publicity and exploitation staffs.[129] In November the reduced staff saw their workload increase. Associated acquired eighty features when Lewis J. Selznick, the father of *Gone with the Wind* producer David O. Selznick, liquidated his company.[130]

Nineteen twenty-five was a turbulent year for Associated Exhibitors. In March, Arthur Kane resigned to join Universal Pictures.[131] J. S. Woody was elected as Associated's new president and promised radical changes.[132] One of these changes was the end of the open-booking policy. Henceforth, Associated would join other distributors by practicing block booking, announcing that it would sell features in groups of not fewer than eight.[133]

The changes apparently weren't radical enough. By October, Woody was out, to be replaced by Oscar Price. The new chairman of the board was P. A. "Pat" Powers, a colorful, controversial, and somewhat failure-prone Irish-born businessman who rotated through multiple film companies from 1910 through the 1930s.[134] His Pat Powers Picture Plays had been one of the core components amalgamated into Universal Pictures in 1912, but within a few years he was edged out by Universal president Carl Laemmle.[135] In 1922 he was in charge of the Film Booking Office, a low-budget producer-distributor, but by the following year he was gone.[136] Now he had been tapped to run Associated Exhibitors by the "banking interests" that had bought control of the company from Pathé.[137]

The new management used articles in the trade press to assert the company's total independence from Pathé. While it still used Pathé's exchanges to distribute its product, it emphasized that it paid Pathé for this service. It installed a new staff of film bookers at all of the Pathé exchanges.[138] At the beginning of 1926 Powers announced his intention for Associated Exhibitors to purchase a studio and begin producing its own films.[139] Yet by that summer Associated was very clearly in trouble again. The new ownership group, headed by the Phillips-Jones Corporation, a manufacturer of shirt collars, brought Lewis J. Selznick in to replace the "retiring" Oscar Price as president. According to a report in *Motion Picture News*, Price, "who has kept the company going through a difficult period of financial reorganization, expressed himself as pleased with the outcome of the negotiations." Powers stayed on as chairman of the board.[140]

The impending demise of Associated Exhibitors was clearly signaled in October 1926, when the trade journals carried the announcement that Pathé had hired all of Associated's branch managers and sales force to create a new Pathé feature sales department.[141] William A. Johnston of *Motion Picture News* optimistically saw it as the beginning of a new chapter, writing, "Associated Exhibitors has been rehabilitated under the wing of Pathé Exchange."[142] But it was really the end. The bulk of Associated Exhibitors' releases during its final months of operation were low-budget westerns, a product line Pathé would continue to sponsor after Associated's collapse. Associated Exhibitors' last release was *Bad Man's Bluff* starring Jay Wilsey, an actor who billed himself as Buffalo Bill Jr.[143] It was released New Year's Day 1927.[144]

BLAIR & COMPANY

In the mid-1920s *Moving Picture World* presented a series of caricatures of "Distinguished Picture People" drawn by the artist Covarrubias. The text that accompanied the caricature of Elmer Pearson in April 1926 started, "The manly art of selling motion pictures owes much to Elmer R. Pearson. A man without flaw in his personal or business character, in a firm without flaw in its commercial integrity or stain upon its business shield, he is held in singular affection and esteem throughout this entire industry."[145] On the surface, the praise of both Pearson and Pathé seemed entirely warranted. Pathé was able to report a net income for 1925 of $1,431,757, an increase of $119,148 over 1924's earnings. While Pathé had grossed $4.2 million in 1916, its 1925 grosses were over $18 million. Further, both grosses and nets had grown every year since 1923.[146]

In reality, Pathé's future prospects were not so rosy. It was about to pay the price for years of neglect. While pursuing its "stay the course" policy of distributing independently produced films, most of them short subjects, to second-run and rural theaters, the industry around it had changed. Paramount, Loews-MGM, and First National had all evolved into complex producer-distributor-exhibitors, owning first-run theaters situated in prime locations. William Fox and the Warner Brothers were amassing theater chains of their own; additionally, the Warner Brothers had just significantly enhanced their production and distribution capacity by buying the venerable Vitagraph studio. Not counting Pathé, Vitagraph had been the last surviving member of the Motion Picture Patents Company.[147]

In the summer of 1926 Pearson convinced Merrill Lynch that Pathé would have to either become more active in the production of feature-length films *and* acquire a theater chain, or go out of business.[148] It was too late. The estimated cost of acquiring theaters alone was $150 million. This would have pulled Merrill and Lynch completely into the movie business and away from their other endeavors. Charles Merrill concluded that the challenge of starting from scratch to compete with the already established production-exhibition chains was too great; it would require so much outside financing that Merrill Lynch's control over Pathé would be unacceptably diluted.[149]

Faced with limited prospects, Merrill and Lynch chose an option not foreseen by Elmer Pearson. In the fall of 1926 they sold their controlling interest in Pathé to another financial investment firm, Blair & Company, headed by Elisha Walker.[150]

Ferdinand Zecca (*left*) and Charles Pathé in 1920. © Corbis.

Pathé's Bound Brook processing lab.

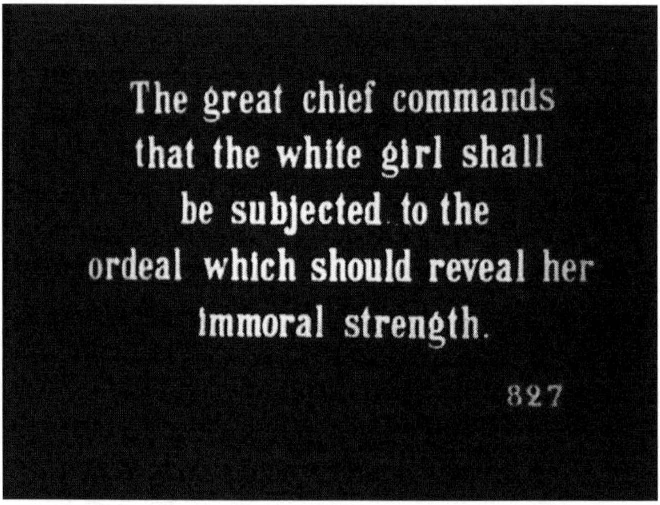

Pearl White, understandably alarmed at the chief's plans for her as expressed in the typographically challenged subtitle. From *The Perils of Pauline* (1914).

Warner Oland meeting Warner Oland in the serial *The Third Eye* (1920).

Ivan Mozzhukhin brooding and his friends being amused in the Russian Art Film *The Queen of Spades* (1916).

The omniscient *Pathé News.*

The steely glare of one of Pathé's top cowboy stars of the 1920s. This photo was one in a series of movie-star cards distributed with children's caramel candy.

The Thomas Ince Studio in Culver City, California, which was home to Pathé in the late 1920s and early 1930s. This image would later be immortalized as the Selznick International Pictures logo that opened *Gone with the Wind*.

Joseph P. Kennedy setting sail for Europe aboard the *Ile de France* in 1928. His face seems to reflect the collapse of his efforts to take over First National. © Corbis.

Constance Bennett (*center*) in one of Pathé's "A" pictures from 1929, *Rich People*.

Eleven performers and production crew members perished when flames ravaged Pathé's Manhattan Studios on December 10, 1929. © Corbis.

Pathé's starring lineup immediately before the merger with RKO, December 1930.

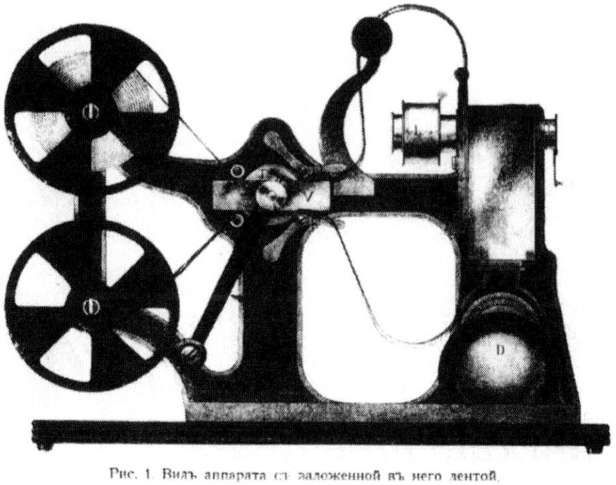

The Pathé KOK 28-millimeter home-movie projector, in an image taken from a Russian instruction manual.

Pathé's 9.5-millimeter home-movie system making its U.S. debut in time for Christmas 1925.

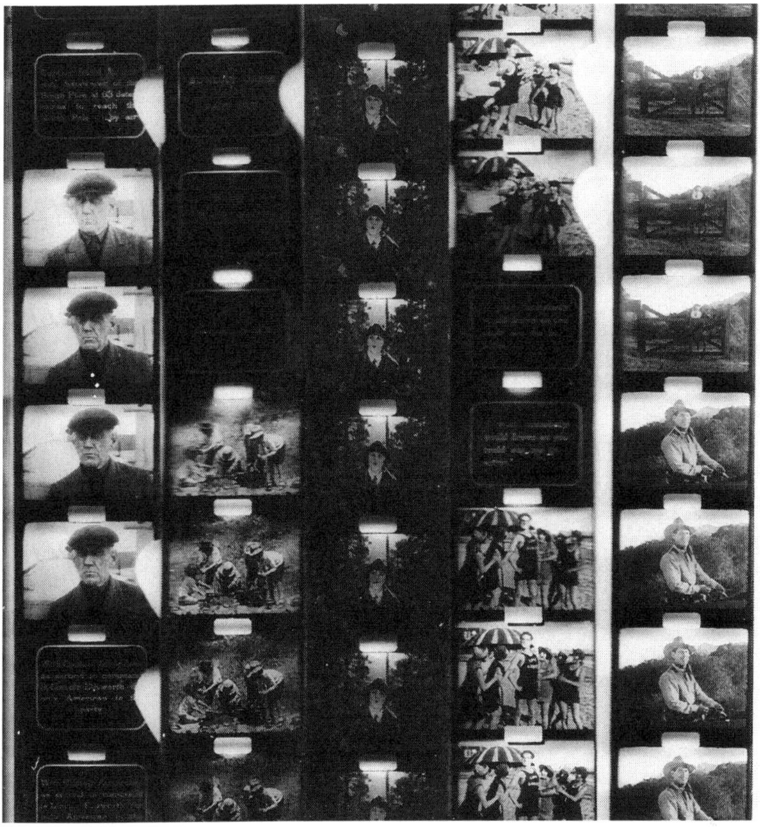

Five strips of Pathex 9.5-millimeter film. The notches on the first frames of strips 1 and 2 would automatically stop projection on the following frame for a freeze-frame (strip 1) or a title card (strip 2). Strip 4 has a freeze-frame followed by a title card.

Pictoreels box art before (*left*) and after the company's acquisition by Pathé Industries.

Leo Carrillo (*second from right*) explaining his latest scheme in PRC's *Crime, Inc.* (1945).

Pathé's last stand: the motion-picture processing plant in Hollywood. Courtesy of the Robert S. Birchard Collection.

CHAPTER FIVE

"TRYING TO FIGURE WHETHER PRODUCERS BOUGHT PATHÉ OR PATHÉ, PRODUCERS"

1926–28

Approximately one year before Blair's purchase of Pathé, two other film companies were undergoing transformations that would have a dramatic impact on Pathé in the near future. One, the Film Booking Offices of America, will be discussed shortly. The other was under the creative guidance of Paramount's (and possibly Hollywood's) premiere filmmaker, Cecil B. DeMille.[1] After a string of successes from 1910 through the early 1920s, DeMille found himself increasingly at odds with Paramount management over issues of budget and creative control, and he left the studio in 1925. With the help of financier Jeremiah Milbank, DeMille bought the Thomas Ince Studio in Culver City, California (recently vacated due to the sudden death of its founder) and set up Cecil B. DeMille Pictures. DeMille's association with Milbank extended beyond financing. Milbank acquired the failing distribution company of W. W. Hodkinson, the former Paramount executive turned independent distributor. With Hodkinson gone from his namesake company, Milbank rechristened the firm Producers Distributing Corporation (PDC). Under the arrangement between Milbank and DeMille, DeMille Pictures would produce a full annual slate of "program" pictures with modest budgets, and DeMille would personally direct one or two "special" big-budget films per year. These pictures would be distributed by PDC, supplemented by films shot at PDC's Metropolitan Pictures studio at Selma and Las Palmas in Hollywood and a few features from short-comedy producer Al Christie. DeMille Pictures, PDC, and Metropolitan were all controlled by a holding company, jointly owned by DeMille and Milbank, called the Cinema Corporation of America (CCA).[2]

The new venture experienced problems from the outset. PDC fared little better than its predecessor even with DeMille's prestige. Like W. W. Hodkinson, Inc., it remained a weak distributor and encountered difficulties placing its product in major markets.[3] On the production side DeMille Pictures struggled with its annual output of programmers. During its first year, it produced only ten program films, and in its second year it made fifteen, both numbers well below expectations.[4] The company lacked actors and actresses of any real marquee value. Furthermore, DeMille quickly tired of the day-to-day headaches of studio administration and appointed William Sistrom as general manager of both DeMille Pictures and Metropolitan. Sistrom's responsibilities apparently extended beyond administration, as the main title card of several of the company's films of the period begins with "William Sistrom Presents . . ." Both Sistrom and another PDC executive named John Flinn would soon become part of the Pathé saga.[5]

In late summer 1926 Cecil B. DeMille embarked on what would be his most successful independent production, a retelling of the Christ story called *The King of Kings*. An all-out DeMille epic, the film cost $2.3 million according to studio records, although Robert S. Birchard in *Cecil B. DeMille's Hollywood* asserts that the figure was actually closer to $1.2 million.[6] Regardless of the correct figure, money was becoming extremely tight at DeMille Pictures and PDC even before production commenced on *King of Kings*. In an effort to improve cash flow DeMille and Milbank sold 50 percent interest in PDC to the Keith and Orpheum vaudeville theater circuits in May 1926. Although it would soon change, in May 1926 Keith and Orpheum were the "affiliated" but corporately separate operators of fifty Keith-Albee theaters and forty-seven Orpheum houses in the United States. These were among the last vaudeville theaters not affiliated with a movie studio, and, at least in the editorial opinion of the *Moving Picture World*, their affiliation with PDC would be as transformative to the industry as Marcus Loew's acquisition of Metro Pictures and the subsequent formation of Metro-Goldwyn-Mayer (MGM). *Moving Picture World*'s opinion was not far off the mark, although more mergers and "divorcements" would be involved before Radio-Keith-Orpheum (RKO) Pictures would come out on the other side.[7]

During its first nine months under Blair, Pathé continued to release the same diet of short films and low-budget westerns as had been its wont in recent times. This was to be expected, since the 1926–27 movie season was already well under way when Pathé changed hands. Blair would chart a new course for the company beginning with the 1927–28 season. In the short term, though, the decision by Hollywood's two most powerful studios to reenter the short-subject market would affect more than Pathé's lineup of comedies. Paramount and MGM announced their intention to start their own newsreels.[8] Paramount went so far as to hire the editor of Pathé's newsreel, Emanuel Cohen, to head up its new short-subject department.[9] Pathé sought to reassure its customers that as the industry's "pioneer news reel," it had earned the public's trust.[10] Pathé took out a two-page ad in the trades warning theater operators of the dangers of substituting one of the new reels, asking, "'Something Just As Good?' Try and Get the Public to Believe It!"[11] Pathé was also quick to point out the fact that 70 percent of the editorial staff[12] and 80 percent of the camera staff were still with Pathé.[13]

Paramount took the opposite tack in its promotion of its newsreel, embracing its newness by proclaiming it the "eyes of a new world. This swift world demands faster, better new mediums. Air mail supplants rail mail. Trans-Atlantic telephones outstrip cables. So in the news reel field—Paramount News."[14] By late 1927 Pathé was forced to take a new approach in the marketing of its newsreel. Its timeworn slogan, "Sees All—Knows All," was replaced with "First on the Scene—First on the Screen."[15]

ONE OF THE BIG FIVE

Blair & Company's plans for their new acquisition became apparent on April 17, 1927, when a merger, which had been rumored for over a month, was officially confirmed. The Keith-Albee and Orpheum vaudeville theater circuits would "merge" with Pathé, DeMille Pictures, and PDC. The new combination, which would keep the venerable Pathé name, would join Paramount-Famous-Lasky, Loews-MGM, Stanley–First National–West Coast Theatres, and Fox Film and Theaters as one of the "Big Five" film companies that dominated the industry. Since it continued to be partnered with DuPont, the new Pathé could now boast that it was the only studio that controlled the entire filmmaking process, from the manufacture of raw film stock to exhibition in the Keith-Albee and Orpheum theaters. J. J. Murdock, general manager of the B. F. Keith Corporation, would become Pathé's president and chairman of the board, a board that included E. F. Albee, Cecil B. DeMille, Jeremiah Milbank, and, incredibly, company founder Charles Pathé.[16]

While the combination of Pathé, DeMille Pictures, and PDC as a single production-distribution entity was a true merger, the theatrical side of the operation was more of a contractual affiliation with interlocking directorates. At least one contemporary observer described it as a "15-year tie-up," in which the Pathé interests would gain the same preferential access to Keith-Albee and Orpheum theaters as had PDC. However loose the affiliation between the new Pathé and the Keith-Albee and Orpheum theaters, it was a relationship that gave the exhibition side a large measure of control over Pathé, shared only by Blair & Company. This would prove critical within a year.[17]

During its first year as a "major" studio, the operations of the various Pathé components continued in many ways as they had before. Pathé just added the DeMille films to its release schedule of shorts and westerns, most of which were produced by independent contractors. Cecil B. DeMille remained production chief at the Culver City studio, which managed to turn out a total of twenty-two films including the DeMille-directed *The Godless Girl* (1928) and the DeMille-supervised *Chicago* (1927). DeMille's epic *The King of Kings* had premiered as the debut attraction of Grauman's Chinese Theatre in May 1927,[18] and it toured major U.S. cities for the next few months as a road-show attraction distributed by PDC. Its general nationwide release in 1928, however, was handled by Pathé.[19]

DeMille's authority had its limits, set out by the five-year contract he signed with Pathé in April 1927. He served at the pleasure of Pathé's new board of directors, and the board's expectations of him were written into his contract. He was to personally direct one to three features per year with budgets of $450,000 each, and he was to supervise the production of an additional fifteen to thirty pictures each year with a combined budget of $3 million, regardless of the number made. He needed the approval of either Pathé's president or its chairman of the board before he could buy film stories or make a personal service contract for longer than one year or more than $2,500 per week. In exchange for his services, Pathé would pay DeMille a salary of $2,500 per week and would pay DeMille Productions, Inc., $5,000 a week. Additionally DeMille Pictures received a percentage of the gross box-office receipts, starting at 5 percent for "personally directed" films and 1¼ percent for supervised films, then rising to 15 percent and 4 percent, respectively, after Pathé had recouped its costs for each film's negative, prints, and advertising.[20]

DeMille still sounded very much like the man in charge when he addressed a banquet attended by employees of PDC and Pathé in June 1927: "Don't spend your time trying to figure whether Producers bought Pathé or Pathé, Producers. It doesn't matter. The great thing is that we are one institution." He continued, "Our principal is for the independence of the artist. We are not a factory. We are making works of art and that is why Mr. James Cruze is with us."[21]

Unfortunately, Mr. James Cruze would not live up to DeMille's expectations. Like DeMille, Cruze was an émigré from Paramount, best known for the epics *The Covered Wagon* (1923) and *Old Ironsides* (1926). Pathé announced that Cruze would continue making films in the same vein, directing two "epic" road-show pictures and supervising an additional three "regular" releases.[22] While the addition of Cruze to the Pathé roster may have appeared as confirmation of the studio's new status, in truth it was an acquisition that the company could ill afford. For the most part Cruze had already peaked as a filmmaker and was beginning a long, slow downhill slide. Of six pictures scheduled to come from James Cruze, Inc., for the 1927–28 movie season, only three were completed. Two were directed by Cruze and the third by journeyman director Walter Lang. For the most part the films featured players drawn from the DeMille and Metropolitan stock company, and none of the three Cruze pictures rose above the quality of the average PDC "regular" release. The remaining three pictures called for under the contract were canceled, but story and preproduction costs on these, plus a film story that was bought but never even got as far as preproduction, cost Pathé an additional $37,500. The DeMille-Cruze relationship ended in accounting quarrels, with DeMille Pictures auditing Cruze for cost overruns, and Cruze accusing DeMille of excessive administrative and overhead charges. The situation became so acrimonious that Cecil B. DeMille Productions briefly seized the equipment of James Cruze, Inc., holding it at the Metropolitan Pictures studio until accounts could be settled.[23]

An interesting metamorphosis that demonstrates the power struggle between DeMille and his new bosses occurred in Pathé's advertising during the run-up to the August start of the 1927–28 movie season. An ad in *Motion Picture News*, July 29, 1927, promoted the 1927–28 Pathé-DeMille program, but the way the companies are listed at the bottom makes it appear that DeMille Studio Pictures is the producer and Pathé is the distributor. Under DeMille Studio Pictures, in smaller print, are *Pathé News*, Pathécomedies, Pathéserials, and Pathépictures. By August 26, 1927, the company billing in advertising copy was changed to Pathé Exchange, Inc., over a small-print list that includes DeMille Studio Pictures, *Pathé News*, Pathé westerns, Pathéserials, and Pathécomedies. The actual film credits underwent a similar change. The main title card of an October 30, 1927, program comedy starring Marie Prevost and Harrison Ford (no relation to the later actor of the same name) reads, "William Sistrom Presents, *The Girl in the Pullman*." A later full-screen title in the opening credits identifies the film as "An Erle C. Kenton Production." Only after Kenton's credit is the audience informed that the film is "[d]istributed by Pathé." This is the only mention of Pathé during the entire film, which closes with the "Cecil B. DeMille Pictures" logo of a knight in armor on the back of a white steed. By the February 19, 1928, release of a Rod

La Rocque–Lupe Velez swashbuckler, it is "Pathé Presents, *Stand and Deliver*" with DeMille Pictures Corporation credited at the bottom of the screen.

The first DeMille Pictures production to be distributed by Pathé was *The Country Doctor*, directed by Rupert Julian. The film opened to good reviews and happy exhibitors.[24] Unfortunately, the income for the remainder of the year for Pathé's program was hit or miss. J. J. Murdock and the bankers who now controlled DeMille Pictures blamed it on what they saw as DeMille's unreasonable extravagance and refusal to cut costs in response to their urgent pleas. DeMille blamed poor marketing by Pathé. Both perspectives were partially correct.

DeMille's films were hobbled to a certain degree by a lack of big-name box-office stars. The program pictures featured actors like by Ford, Prevost, Franklin Pangborn, Phyllis Haver, and the father and son duo of Rudolph and Joseph Schildkraut. All were competent, but none had marquee name value, and most were actually nearing the end of their careers. Two other actors, Alan Hale (Sr.) and Robert Armstrong, would develop into bankable character actors after the advent of sound, Hale as sidekick to Errol Flynn in *The Adventures of Robin Hood* and other films and Armstrong as Carl Denham in the original *King Kong* (1933) and its successors, but they had little drawing power when they were under contract with DeMille.

DeMille's "special" films, those whose bigger budgets and presumably greater audience pulling power demanded higher theatrical rental rates, were anchored mostly by Rod La Rocque and William Boyd, the latter often teamed with Hale and/or Armstrong. La Rocque had been a rising star at Paramount, playing the "bad" son in DeMille's *The Ten Commandments* (1923), and had followed DeMille into independent production, but by the mid-to-late 1920s his career had peaked. He had the dubious distinction of playing second male lead in *One Romantic Night* (1930), the disastrous talking-picture debut of the great silent-film actress Lillian Gish. While La Rocque would continue to work through the 1930s, his roles dwindled to supporting parts in studio productions and the occasional lead in poverty-row films.

Unlike Rod La Rocque, William Boyd still had the best years of his career ahead of him, but they would not be spent with DeMille or Pathé. Boyd had established himself as a solid supporting player at Paramount and elsewhere in the early 1920s before he was given one of the lead roles in DeMille's independent production of *The Road to Yesterday* (1925). He would become firmly established as one of DeMille's most promising leading men the following year in *The Volga Boatman*. Yet his screen persona rapidly became one of a rather arrogant and irascible character in a series of "buddy" films that featured him either as a construction worker (*Skyscraper* and *Power*) or in the military (*Dress Parade*, *The Leatherneck*, and *His First Command*). It would not be until his career hit its low ebb in the mid-1930s that he landed the role that would earn him a permanent place in film history. In 1935 he played the title role in the low-budget Paramount western *Hop-a-long Cassidy*. He would be almost exclusively identified with the character of Hopalong Cassidy for the twenty years remaining in his career, becoming in the process one of the most beloved cowboy heroes of matinee westerns and early television.

The problems that DeMille's films were experiencing at the box office, as DeMille saw it, had nothing to do with the quality of either his films or his actors. It was that Pathé was as ineffective in marketing his studio's output as PDC had been. Although Pathé certainly had a longer and more successful history than PDC, its product, especially in the mid-1920s, had been geared toward the smaller independent and rural theaters. The films coming from DeMille's operation, regardless of their merits, were designed to go head to head with the output of Paramount and MGM. It was clear to DeMille that Pathé was not going to be able to routinely book his films in the type of venues they needed for success. Even the agreement with the Keith and Orpheum theaters gave them the right to reject any film they wished.[25] And Pathé's regular clientele, the small theaters of Middle America, resented having to pay what they considered outrageous prices for what they and their small-town patronage believed to be substandard pictures. As examples of what these theater managers had to say about the DeMille productions, while most had a favorable attitude toward *Dress Parade* (1927), William Boyd's West Point drama, one exhibitor complained that it was not a "special" feature and had little drawing power. Similar sentiments were expressed for the Rod La Rocque–Phyllis Haver costume adventure *The Fighting Eagle* (1927), with one exhibitor commenting that "[t]he DeMille's of late have been falling down on their so-called specials." An exhibitor review of *Girl in the Pullman* (1927) liked the film, but noted that the new print it had received was "very bad." About the Marie Prevost–Harrison Ford program comedy *The Rush Hour* (1928), one exhibitor cracked, "Another reason why the radio is so popular." For the Rudolph Schildkraut comedy *Turkish Delight* (1927), an exhibitor warned his brethren, "Terrible. By all means, boys, be sure to shelf [*sic*] this one."[26]

It wasn't that Pathé hadn't tried to prove that it was ready for the big time. In October 1927 a sales promotion called "Pathé Week on Broadway" was able to get a record number of Broadway movie houses to play Pathé films. A wildly enthusiastic, and possibly compensated, editorial appeared in the October 10, 1927, issue of *Moving Picture World*:

THEY DON'T LIKE 'EM—NOT MUCH!

No, they don't like the Pathé product. Not much!

Only sufficiently to book Pathé-De Mille feature pictures into every Broadway film theatre in the "roaring forties!"

During the week of October 29, every individual who clamors for motion picture entertainment between Fortieth and Fiftieth streets, must perforce see a Pathé production.

That's all there is. There isn't any more!

At the "Roxy," which shows a pardonable partiality for Fox Films, Pathé's "The Main Event" will make the elastic house record tremble.

At the "Paramount," where "Jesse L. Lasky presents" more often than not, Pathé's "The Forbidden Woman" will have a long queue of box-office Johnnies awaiting her.

First National yields its place in the sun at the "Strand" to Pathé's "Dress Parade," and Joe Plunkett will grin as he stands in the lobby and counts the crowds of customers.

Uncle Carl Laemmle's "colony" theatre plays Pathé's "The Angel of Broadway." And it's sure to prove some box-office angel—or it wouldn't be given precedence over Universal product.

Pathé's "The Wise Wife" proves the wisdom of the booker for the "Cameo." With the world to pick from, the "Cameo" chooses to play a Pathé.

The big "Hippodrome" gives Pathé a ride with "The Girl in the Pullman"—a non-stop express straight from the pay window to the bank.

Down where the dress suit belt begins, the "Broadway" plans to clean up enough with Pathé's "A Harp in Hock" to pay off the mortgage on the farm.

And as the Kohinoor in the Pathé crown of accomplishment, that mighty, magnificent miracle of achievement, "The King of Kings" will continue to thrill and awe multitudes as it has through seven stupendous months.

What a record! Eight features in seven days on ten blocks! And that isn't all. Just to make it unanimous, or something, there will be Pathé News, Pathé comedies, Pathé Fables, Pathé Topics of the Day, on the programs with the Pathé features.

Can you beat it? Why, you can't even tie it! If the nation's showmen don't see the light—they'd better consult oculists.

The public doesn't like Pathé pictures. Not much![27]

The following week, another *Moving Picture World* article that summarized the success of "Pathé's Week on Broadway" added three more theaters to the list, although the three simply ran Pathé shorts as part of an otherwise non-Pathé program. The MGM-affiliated Loew's State ran a Pathé–Mack Sennett comedy, the Capitol ran *Pathé News*, and the Palace ran *Pathé News* and *Aesop's Fables*. Claiming that the total attendance for all of the theaters showing Pathé films for the week was 750,000, the article concluded that since the announcement of Pathé week, "the film atmosphere has been charged with a current of excitement and brings to the entire film-loving public the realization that Pathé under its new regime, with Cecil B. De Mille in direct charge of production of all pictures and J. J. Murdock at the business helm, has started out to do the big things this ambitious organization has promised."[28]

Even before "Pathé's Week on Broadway," the investment bankers who controlled the company's fate were having strong misgivings about its future. A June 1927 offering of debentures had been unsuccessful, and, according to Cari Beauchamp, Pathé "stock was slumping. Bankruptcy was a possibility . . ." and while the bankers still hoped to turn the company around, they also had a contingency plan for a "gradual liquidation of the company." Elisha Walker's Blair & Company had already invested $6 million in the company, and he was willing to advance another $2 million, but only if Pathé would hire a fellow banker from New England who had enjoyed seemingly phenomenal success in the film industry.[29]

"THE WIDENING INFLUENCE OF MR. JOSEPH P. KENNEDY"

Joseph P. Kennedy, the father of the future U.S. president, took the film industry by surprise when he purchased a controlling interest in Film Booking Offices of America in February 1926.[30] The thirty-seven-year-old Harvard graduate had achieved some early notoriety by becoming the "youngest bank president in America" at age twenty-five.[31] He left banking during the First World War to become assistant general manager of Bethlehem's Fore River Ship Building Corporation. While at Fore he made the acquaintance of future U.S. president Franklin D. Roosevelt, who was then secretary of the navy.[32] Following the war Kennedy returned to the world of finance by taking a job with a banking and brokerage firm, but he branched out and made his own investments as well. One of these ventures was the formation of a New England franchise for the distribution of movies made by a weak West Coast producing and distributing firm called Robertson-Cole.[33]

Robertson-Cole had started out as a British importer/exporter that dealt primarily in automobiles and, as a side venture, in film. In 1919 the firm decided to become more active in film. It set up a distribution system, and in 1921 it built a production studio on the corner of Gower and Melrose in Hollywood. Next to the new Robertson-Cole studio was a rental facility called United Studios. In 1926 United Studios was purchased by Paramount, and that location remains Paramount's primary studio today.[34]

In 1922 Robertson-Cole changed the name of its distribution system to Film Booking Offices of America, or FBO, although the corporate name of the production side of the business would officially remain Robertson-Cole Pictures Corporation through the mid-1920s. As mentioned earlier, Pat Powers and some other investors bought into FBO in 1922, and Powers functioned briefly as the studio's production chief.[35] The majority stake in the company was still controlled by British interests, and they fired Powers after only a single year, replacing him with an Englishman, Major H. C. S. Thomson.[36] Throughout the early 1920s FBO was known primarily as a producer-distributor of low-budget action films, mainly westerns. Like Pathé, it catered to the rural, independent-theater market. Unlike Pathé, it lacked the occasional "prestige" feature and the strong lineup of short films. It was among the most marginal of independent film studios.

When Joseph Kennedy bought control of FBO, its thirty-five distribution exchanges, and its Robertson-Cole Pictures Corporation subsidiary from the British, he continued the same basic product line while slashing the already thin budgets.[37] Kennedy became actively engaged in FBO's operation. He quickly replaced Major Thomson with a new vice president in charge of production, former Paramount associate producer William LeBaron.[38] As treasurer, he selected Edward B. Derr, an associate from his days at Fore River.[39] Two years after taking over, Kennedy explained his approach to the studio in a letter to Guy W. Currier, a business associate in the East:

> [W]e have a very definite niche in the film business of this country. For producers who own the high class theaters there is a satisfactory outlet for their pictures. For producers who make high class pictures without a theatre outlet it is a very unsatisfactory condition. For the producer who makes a middle class product there is no outlet whereby he can get his cost back. This may seem strange and yet very elucidating. . . .
>
> We go into none of these classes at all. We make what we call the low cost productions; i.e. our average negative cost is approximately fifty odd thousand dollars, consisting of twelve to fourteen Western pictures averaging sixteen thousand dollars; a series of dog pictures, and another series of outdoor pictures, twelve in all, averaging twenty thousand dollars. The balance of our program is made up of features, some of which cost as

high as seventy five thousand dollars. On this type of product there is a very definite market. Even assuming that we cannot get the so-called first runs, by our wide distribution we are able to maintain a very satisfactory gross. It is in this field that Fox and Universal, who had absolute control of this type of business, made their reputations and their fortunes. They have subsequently moved out of this field. Fox is now entirely making high class productions to satisfy his large theaters, and Universal is still strattling [*sic*] the fence; i.e. trying to make both classes of product. . . .[40]

In conclusion Kennedy noted that while FBO's previous owners had lost seven million dollars, the end of his first year at the helm had seen an income of nine million.

What astonished film-industry insiders about Kennedy's success at FBO was his lack of any previous show-business experience, beyond his almost casual involvement with distribution and exhibition in New England. Then as now, those within the film industry almost prided themselves on the quirky nature of their business, a business whose eccentricities are almost impenetrable to the standard business-school graduate. After the initial shock of this outsider being able to turn around a company that seemed doomed to failure, the trade publications that acted as the official voice of the motion-picture business hailed Kennedy as little short of a miracle worker. Typical was an editorial from the combined *Exhibitor's Herald & Moving Picture World* that commemorated Kennedy's affiliation with Pathé in spring 1928:

> Additional evidence of the widening influence of Mr. Joseph P. Kennedy in the motion picture industry is seen in the recent announcement that he has become associated in an advisory capacity with Pathé Exchange, Inc.
>
> The swift and certain progress of Mr. Kennedy, and the interests with which he is associated, should be a matter of no surprise. In entering the motion picture business only a little more than two years ago, he brought to [this] new connection a keen and experienced intellect, together with a personality that was bound to count importantly in this business of personalities. At no time since the industry attained its present proportions has any executive come into it from another field of activity and so quickly introduced himself into a position of industry-wide influence and respect as has Mr. Kennedy.
>
> The industry is fortunate in having won the interest and association of Mr. Kennedy. His influence thus far has been wholesome and constructive and those who know him and his record best are convinced that he will continue to figure more importantly in the industry.[41]

I'M READY FOR YOUR FADE-OUT, MR. DEMILLE

It was against this background that Elisha Walker approached Kennedy about taking over the management of Pathé in fall 1927. Kennedy agreed, with two stipulations: he did not want his participation in the company announced until February 1928, and he wanted the announcement to say that he was becoming involved with Pathé in an unpaid position, doing it strictly as a favor to Walker. In *Joseph P. Kennedy Presents His Hollywood Years*, Cari Beauchamp says that behind the scenes, Kennedy was to receive a fee of at least $500,000 in the form of Pathé stock.[42] Additionally, Keith-Albee-Orpheum invested $1 million in Kennedy's FBO to interlock the organizations.[43] By May 1928 the "unpaid special advisor" was receiving a $2,000 per week salary, retroactive to February.[44]

Meeting with Pathé president and board chairman J. J. Murdock, Kennedy learned about two of the company's most pressing problems. First, while it had been anticipated that the combined Pathé and PDC would save money by combining their distribution networks, after the merger it was discovered that "many of the exchange offices had long leases and the high-priced executives had multi-year contracts."[45] This situation meant that Pathé would be stuck with a duplication of resources for the foreseeable future. And then, of course, there was the matter of Cecil B. DeMille.

Shortly after his conference with Murdock, Kennedy boarded a train headed west to confront DeMille. He already knew that Elisha Walker wanted DeMille out; it was just a matter of how to do it with minimal cost to the company, either from a monetary or a public-relations standpoint.[46] When he met DeMille, Kennedy explained that the Pathé board had decided to liquidate the studio and, as such, needed to terminate the contract between Pathé, Cecil B. DeMille Productions, and DeMille personally. DeMille's reaction, predictably, was less than positive. He complained that he had repeatedly warned Elmer Pearson and other Pathé officers of impending financial collapse, only to be reassured that the company was financially sound. To add insult, numerous press reports had blamed him and his production methods, DeMille noted, for the company's financial quagmire. First and foremost in any settlement, DeMille concluded, would have to be an official statement to the press that he was not responsible for Pathé's difficulties.[47]

Convinced that Pathé was headed for liquidation whether he stayed or not, DeMille accepted the buyout of his contract.[48] He left Pathé and signed a three-picture directing contract with MGM. He returned to a financially battered and somewhat humbled Paramount in 1932 and never left again.

Once the matter with DeMille was settled, Kennedy turned to the real housecleaning at Pathé, canceling the distribution contracts for all of Pathé's independent producers.[49] This would affect all of Pathé's western series, but perhaps most significant was its impact on the "King of Comedy" Mack Sennett, an impact that underscored Hal Roach's incredibly good timing in getting away from Pathé when he did.

For Sennett the timing could not have been worse. He had already lost most of his best-known comedians and was trying to cultivate new talent, including Eddie Quillan, Carol Lombard (who had not yet added the *e* to the end of her first name), and Australian Daphne Pollard. Sennett was also in the midst of an expensive upgrade to the "look" of his productions. During the 1927–28 season he had included Technicolor sequences in his "Sennett Girls" comedies, something none of his rivals had done with any of their short-comedy series. At the same time, he built a new studio in an undeveloped section of the San Fernando Valley that would eventually be known as Studio City. Finally, with the film industry beginning to convert to the production of talking pictures, Sennett signed a contract with the Radio Corporation of America (RCA) to use Photophone, Pathé's preferred sound system. Photophone will be discussed shortly.

So it was that in April 1928 as Sennett was preparing to vacate the somewhat ramshackle studio in the Edendale section of Los Angeles that had been his studio's home for more than a decade and to move into his state-of-the-art facility in the "valley," he signed a final contract with Pathé that called for the delivery of three new comedy series. Initially the agreement called for twelve two-reelers to be produced for each series, but ultimately the number was reduced to six of each, for a total of eighteen shorts. Similarly, the initially proposed term of the contract was halved, from two years to one.[50] The films were the very first to be produced at Sennett's new studio, and they were among the cheapest comedies Sennett had made in quite some time. In *Mack Sennett's Fun Factory*, Brent Walker notes that while Sennett's films of 1927 had been allowed shooting schedules of as much as four to six weeks, the shorts produced for the 1928–29 season were made in five days each. All eighteen of the films were shot between May and July 1928, and all were silent. These comedies were combined with Sennett's backlog of twenty unreleased shorts, also silent, to create his 1928–29 Pathé release schedule.[51]

Left with a heavy debt burden, no distributor, and few options, Sennett signed a distribution agreement with Educational Pictures. At Educational, an organization that itself would soon be crushed by competition from the short subjects being released by the major studios, Sennett's income was severely curtailed from what it had been with Pathé. As if to add salt to the wound,

Pathé even hired Eddie Quillan, Carol Lombard, and Daphne Pollard away from him. The first two would star in Pathé features, with Lombard going on to screen immortality, and Pollard would become a featured player in Pathé's new in-house short-comedy production unit. In what initially seemed a stroke of good fortune, Sennett signed a distribution agreement with Paramount for the 1932–33 movie season. However, Paramount almost immediately went into receivership and did not renew Sennett's contract for 1933–34.[52] Unable to find another distributor, Sennett closed his new studio and went bankrupt. The studio would become home to Republic Pictures from the mid-1930s to the mid-1950s. It was then bought by the Columbia Broadcasting System (CBS) and was renamed CBS Studio City. It continues to operate as a CBS production facility to this day.

Even before Joseph Kennedy began handing out pink slips, Pathé's release schedule started reflecting the atmosphere of uncertainty that permeated the company. The results were interesting, and in some ways harkened back to Pathé's earlier more eclectic days. In addition to the films from DeMille's studio, the westerns, and the usual short subjects, Pathé released a pair of Scandinavian features at the end of January 1928. At the same time it released a film produced and shelved in 1925; *What Price Beauty?* had been supervised by Natacha Rambova while she was still married to Rudolph Valentino and starred Rambova and Nita Naldi.[53] Other "special" feature releases from the period included the British-made *Passion Island* and a version of *Alice through the Looking Glass*. Pathé also began throwing science two-reelers into the schedule, with tantalizing titles like *Boats and Fishermen of the Arctic and Tropics* and *How Man Suits His Life to His Surroundings*. By February Pathé's situation was so uncertain that it did not even publish its March release schedule until the end of the month. When it was published, the very first title on the list was *Chicago*. Codirected by Frank Urson and an uncredited Cecil B. DeMille,[54] it was based on the same Maurine Dallas Watkins play about the fictitious Roxie Hart that was turned into a stage musical by Bob Fosse and Fred Ebb and subsequently produced as a film in 2002.[55]

THE PALLOPHOTOPHONE

In 1922 Charles A. Hoxie, an employee of General Electric (GE), developed a machine that recorded sound as light patterns on motion-picture film. Dubbed "Pallophotophone," the initial intent for the device was to record sound for radio broadcasts, not for movies. The radio industry was not interested, and the device was shelved.[56] When Warner Brothers released the feature *Don Juan* in 1926 with recorded music and sound effects using Western Electric's

Vitaphone sound-on-disc system, interest in sound films was renewed among inventors and film producers alike, although there was some debate as to whether this would lead to full-talking films or to films that were essentially silent with prerecorded music tracks but no dialogue.

By 1927 Western Electric was promoting two motion-picture sound systems: Vitaphone and the sound-on-film Movietone. GE dusted off Pallophotophone, this time as a sound-on-film system, and rechristened it "Kinegraphone," before finally shortening the original name to "Photophone."[57] Unfortunately for GE, the Vitaphone and Movietone were ready for installation by mid-1927. While GE was trying to work the bugs out of its system, according to Donald Crafton, the Western Electric subsidiary Electrical Research Products, Inc., was putting together "a package so sweet" that no producer or theater owner would think of going with GE.[58]

By fall 1927 Western Electric's two sound systems were threatening to shut GE's Photophone system out of Hollywood completely. Marketing and sales of Photophone fell to RCA, a jointly owned subsidiary of GE and Westinghouse. In October David Sarnoff, RCA's head, met with Joseph Kennedy to try to sell Photophone to FBO. In exchange for RCA buying a $500,000 interest in FBO, 11 percent of the company's stock, Kennedy became the first studio head to agree to use Photophone.[59] When Kennedy assumed management of Pathé, it was a given that Photophone would follow.

Despite the fact that Photophone was embraced by very few producers in the beginning, a refined successor to the process would command almost as much market share as its competitors by the mid-1930s and would ultimately become the industry standard.[60] Before that could happen, a few problems had to be fixed. First, despite repeated assurances from RCA, Photophone equipment was not available until well into 1928. Even so, Pathé managed to keep apace of the other studios in its adaptation to sound films. Its first sound venture, a shortened[61] "general release" version of *King of Kings* with music and sound effects, went into theaters on September 30, 1928. Pathé's first full talking feature, *Strange Cargo*, debuted on March 31, 1929.

One embarrassing incident involving sound had occurred with *Pathé News* in May 1927, months before either Kennedy or Sarnoff entered the scene. When Charles A. Lindbergh took off from Roosevelt Field on his historic nonstop flight to Paris, a number of newsreel cameras were present including a Fox Movietone sound camera and a conventional Pathé silent camera. Though the sound recorded by Fox was nothing more than the noise from Lindbergh's engine and the crowd of onlookers, the Fox newsreel was a sensation. When Lindbergh returned from France and received the Distinguished Flying Cross from President Calvin Coolidge, Movietone and Pathé cameras were there again. Not wishing to be bested by Fox, Pathé, at least in some areas, released a Lindbergh newsreel accompanied by a phonograph recording of Lindbergh's speech accepting his medal, with instructions suggesting that the recording could be synchronized somehow with the film. An Oklahoma theater manager complained that the reel was "nothing like Pathé said it was. There is no place in it to play the victrola [*sic*] with his speech as they claimed. . . . I'd say it's bunk."[62] Unfortunately, this was just a harbinger of what was to come as *Pathé News* attempted to buy very expensive portable sound-recording equipment to compete with the better-financed newsreels of the major studios.

Another problem with Photophone regarded its compatibility with the Movietone system. Western Electric had realized that some sort of standardization of its sound systems might be desirable and had fixed the running speed for both Vitaphone and Movietone films at twenty-four frames per second. Although it was thinking more of competition than cooperation, GE used the same speed for its sound films. Also, despite the fact that the two types of sound track were recorded using radically different approaches, variable area tracks for Photophone and variable density tracks for Movietone, they were close enough in principle that they could both be played back by the same type of sound reader. However, GE did choose to make its soundtrack slightly wider than a Movietone soundtrack, one hundred mils as opposed to eighty. This difference improved the quality of Photophone's sound when played on a Photophone sound reader, but it also meant that the sound would not properly reproduce on the Western Electric sound readers found in most theaters. Played on Western Electric equipment, the Photophone track sounded distorted and muffled.

David Sarnoff had been willing to do a certain amount of pro bono work for FBO and Pathé using Photophone. After all, GE and RCA were desperate to showcase their process and prove that it could hold its own with Movietone. The problem was that it soon began to appear that Kennedy wanted virtually *everything* done gratis.[63] Additionally, the incompatibility of Photophone's track with Movietone's readers needed to be resolved.

In July 1928 Sarnoff ordered a halt to all ongoing sound work for Pathé and FBO, and he requested a meeting with Elisha Walker in New York City. Joseph Kennedy was on the West Coast and unable to attend. They discussed the work under way and the conditions that would be required before any other work would be done. *King of Kings* had been scored and recorded on a hundred-mil track at a cost to Photophone of $14,286. *The Godless Girl* had been scored but not yet recorded at a cost of $15,000. For FBO, *The Perfect*

Crime (1928) had been scored and recorded on a hundred-mil track at a cost of $6,200, and *The Hit of the Show* (1928) had been scored but not yet recorded for $7,500. Additionally, for reasons that will be explained shortly, a pair of First National productions entered into the conversation. *Lilac Time* (1928) had been scored and recorded on a hundred-mil track for $24,860, and some work had been done on *The Good-Bye Kiss* (1928) for $3,500 before Photophone work on that project was canceled. The upshot was that Photophone had spent $71,346 without receiving one penny of reimbursement, a situation that was particularly galling to Sarnoff since the sound versions of *King of Kings* and *Lilac Time* were currently playing in some large theaters that had Photophone equipment, and they were generating revenue for their producing companies.[64]

After the meeting Walker and Sarnoff agreed that no further Photophone work would be done until an upcoming test to determine if an eighty-mil Photophone track could be played successfully on a Movietone sound reader. In the meantime, to the extent that *King of Kings* and *Lilac Time* were being shown with their original hundred-mil tracks in Photophone theaters, Pathé and First National would pay Photophone "proportionally to the benefits they receive."[65] If the test of the eighty-mil Photophone track was successful (which it was, and Photophone was standardized at eighty mils.),[66] Photophone would record eighty-mil sound tracks for *The Godless Girl*, *Hit of the Show*, and would rerecord *The Perfect Crime* on an eighty-mil track, all at Photophone's expense, provided the cost did not exceed a total of $30,000 for all three. Pathé and FBO agreed to pick up any costs over $30,000. Also, if testing was successful, Photophone would rerecord *King of Kings* on an eighty-mil track, but at Pathé's expense. As First National had announced that they were not going to use Photophone for their sound system, there was no discussion of rerecording the work done on *Lilac Time*. This was another source of the friction between Sarnoff and Kennedy. First National was far closer to being a truly major studio than Pathé or FBO, and Kennedy had indicated that he could "deliver it" to Sarnoff. As it turned out, virtually all of the money Photophone had spent on its two projects for First National was a lost investment.[67]

Two final issues were ironed out in the meeting. Pathé had decided that it wanted to shoot two talking sequences for *The Godless Girl* in addition to the music and sound-effects track already under way. It was quite common during the transition to sound that completed silent films would have one or two talking sequences added, permitting them to be advertised as "talking." Films that had dialogue throughout had to be distinguished in advertising as "all-talking," and movie audiences soon learned that a film that was promoted as either "sound" or "synchronized sound" would likely be a silent film with music and sound effects added.[68] Because the new scenes for *The Godless Girl* would be shot at Pathé's Culver City studio, Sarnoff made clear that Pathé would be expected to pay for the transportation and installation of sound recorders in California, in addition to the salaries of the Photophone sound engineers involved.[69] Pathé agreed to the terms, and the two talking sequences were produced under the direction of Fritz Feld, since DeMille had already left Pathé by that time.[70]

The last item in the minutes of the meeting between Sarnoff and Walker is rather cryptic: "Mr. Sarnoff stated that during the period while negotiations for the proposed merger of certain companies are under way, Photophone is willing to synchronize pictures for F.B.O. and Pathé on the same basis of royalty and copyright fees as charged by Western Electric to its customers."[71] The change that loomed on Hollywood's horizon in the summer of 1928 extended beyond the "talkie revolution," although the expense attendant to equipping studios and theaters with sound equipment might have been at least partially responsible. The film community was abuzz with stories about mergers and consolidations among the major studios. Most of these were strictly rumor, but a few did happen. In 1925 Warner Brothers had purchased Vitagraph, the last "living" member of the Motion Picture Patents Company aside from Pathé. When Marcus Loew, founder of Loews Theatres and architect of its production subsidiary combine MGM, died in 1927, his empire seemed up for grabs. For a time it would be bought and controlled by William Fox, before the stock-market crash and Fox's serious injury in an auto accident cost him not only Loews-MGM but his own Fox Film Corporation. Fox Film would be merged in 1935 with a new company, Twentieth Century Pictures, to form the Twentieth Century–Fox Film Corporation. Had the Fox-MGM combination stood, a Paramount–Warner Brothers merger was waiting in the wings. And, of course, 1927 had seen the merger of Pathé and DeMille with Keith-Albee-Orpheum.

The big story for the summer of 1928, though, was a spectacular merger described in a dispatch from the Boston News Bureau.

> Bankers are working on a fourth large moving picture combination, to be probably formed out of group of independent companies including Stanley, Co., First National Pictures, Pathé Exchange, Keith-Albee-Orpheum, Inc., Film Booking Offices, known as F.B.O, headed by Joseph Kennedy, and Warner Bros. Pictures. Universal Pictures is also a possibility. . . .
>
> Change in banking management of Stanley immediately was followed by an agreement with other theater chains which were large First National

> stockholders to pool their interests with Stanley, thus giving Stanley a working control of that film producing company. Pres. Rossheim of Stanley Co. has been elected president of First National Pictures, and a contract has been made with Joseph Kennedy, who will act as special advisor to the management.

The story went on to explain that if the merger were to occur, the combined company would join Paramount, Loews, and Fox as one of the major studios.[72]

Some of the companies mentioned in the Boston News Bureau did indeed merge, although into multiple entities rather than a single one. The merger alluded to by David Sarnoff resulted in one of these entities. In October 1928 RCA bought a controlling interest in FBO, and the following month merged it with Keith-Albee-Orpheum to form Radio-Keith-Orpheum, or RKO.[73]

CHAPTER SIX

"I HAVEN'T ANY HI-FALUTING THEORIES ABOUT PRODUCTION"

1928–31

The program announcement of the Film Booking Offices of America (FBO) for 1928–29, the last season before it became the production arm of Radio-Keith-Orpheum (RKO), touted the accomplishments of its chairman. Under a large portrait of Joseph Kennedy was an equally large caption that proclaimed him "[t]he Man of the Hour."[1] Indeed, in the summer of 1928 it truly appeared that Kennedy's time had come. In addition to his work at FBO and Pathé, and the fact that in May he was named president of Keith-Albee-Orpheum, Kennedy had become a silent partner in Gloria Productions, the independent production company of film star Gloria Swanson, and he had just been named special advisor to First National, which had recently been hobbled by infighting among the theater chains that controlled it.[2] It was widely assumed that Kennedy would merge all of his interests, with one trade paper reporting a plan that would see First National producing "specials," FBO making program pictures, and Pathé turning out shorts. Then Kennedy's movie empire began to unravel.

To please Swanson and to establish himself as a top-notch producer capable of turning out a film of the highest artistic caliber, Kennedy hired Hollywood's enfant terrible Eric von Stroheim to write and direct Swanson's next feature, *Queen Kelly*. In Kevin Brownlow and David Gill's wonderful television documentary series *Hollywood*, director Byron Haskin gives an amusing assessment of von Stroheim's approach to his employers in the 1920s: "He was always against the management, wherever he was. It didn't matter. And he was going to wreck 'em. If they thought they had suffered before, he was going to show them real suffering."[3] Von Stroheim's usual tactic was to write a script that was too long, too complicated, and never quite finished when production began. He would then commence to shoot film for days, then weeks, then months until the producer stepped in and took the camera away from him. Strangely enough, this usually worked fairly well, as attested by von Stroheim's *The Wedding March* (1928), the last film he completed before *Queen Kelly*. His film for Kennedy and Swanson, however, would go down in Hollywood annals as a fascinating disaster, and it would spell the end of his directing career. Von Stroheim was fired from the project before it was even close to being finished, and the directors who were hired to try to wrap it up were never able to satisfactorily complete the task. While a patched-together version of the film was released in Europe and South America in the early 1930s, with very few exceptions *Queen Kelly* did not see the light of day in the United States until a 1985 home-video restoration. One of the exceptions was a brief and brilliantly ironic moment in Billy Wilder's *Sunset Boulevard* (1950). Gloria Swanson, playing faded silent-film star Norma Desmond, sits in her private screening room and watches one of the films of her youth. It is a scene from *Queen Kelly*, and the man in the projection booth running the film is her former husband and screen director, who is now reduced to the role of butler. The character is named Max von Mayerling, and he is played by Erich von Stroheim.

In the summer of 1928 Joseph Kennedy was still blissfully ignorant of the trouble that lay in store for him with *Queen Kelly*. His only grievance at that point was that von Stroheim seemed to be taking an inordinately long time to finish the script.[4] That was a trifling irritation compared to the problems he was facing at First National. Kennedy had approached First National, as he had FBO and Pathé, with the assumption that the studio's difficulties were the result of a poor organizational structure and fiscal sloppiness. It followed that if he eliminated what he saw as wasteful production practices and introduced a more businesslike atmosphere, he would achieve the same sort of "miracle turnaround" for which Hollywood had lionized him. This time it didn't work. Kennedy had failed to take into account the fact that while FBO and Pathé had been fairly impoverished outfits with spotty track records when he found them, First National was a proud organization capable of producing truly first-rate pictures starring a line of top contract actors including Richard Barthelmess, Mary Astor, Milton Sills, and an actress who consistently ranked at the top of popularity polls in the late 1920s, Colleen Moore. Kennedy's efforts at First National demoralized the staff and earned him some real enemies on the First National board of directors. Kennedy ruffled even more feathers on the board when he attempted to annul First

National's contract to use the Western Electric sound system and replace it with Photophone.[5] In July the First National board demanded that Kennedy abandon his efforts to sign the company with the Radio Corporation of America (RCA), a move that infuriated Sarnoff and directly precipitated his cancellation of all work for FBO and Pathé until definite terms of payment could be worked out with Elisha Walker.[6] The final straw came in August, when the board refused to agree to any plan that would merge First National and Kennedy's other film interests. Kennedy resigned from First National and began the secret negotiations with Sarnoff that would lead to RCA's acquisition of FBO in October.[7]

Before he sold his FBO stock to Sarnoff, Kennedy found himself facing an insurrection at Keith-Albee-Orpheum. In a scenario similar to what had happened at First National, the shareholders complained of Kennedy's drastic cuts, the board was unhappy with reports of low morale, and the company was under threat of a hostile takeover by Warner Brothers, which was in the process of acquiring First National. Threatened with the termination of his contract if the situation did not improve, Kennedy instead resigned as president of Keith-Albee-Orpheum and sold his stock in that organization to RCA as well. Donald Crafton reports that a "later audit would reveal that KAO-FBO had lost $1,064,278 during the eight months ending 31 August 1928. But after less than three years in the film business, Kennedy was some $5 million richer."[8] By the end of 1928 Joseph Kennedy's influence in the film industry had shrunk to only his involvement in Gloria Productions and Pathé. Nevertheless, he felt that a merger of some sort would be in his best interests.

GLORIA PRODUCTIONS

Like most independent producers, Gloria Swanson's company owned no studio facilities. It had to rent space where it could. From the time Kennedy became involved with Gloria Productions until October 1928, Swanson had worked at the FBO studios. When he sold FBO, Kennedy moved Gloria Productions to Pathé. By that time von Stroheim had been fired from *Queen Kelly*, and Edmund Goulding had been brought in to try to finish it. In early 1929 production on *Queen Kelly* was suspended, and Goulding began work on what was to be Swanson's first talking picture, *The Trespasser* (1929). Work would eventually resume on *Queen Kelly*, this time directed by Richard Boleslavsky, before it was abandoned completely.[9] Gloria Productions would complete one more film at Pathé, *What a Widow!*, directed by Alan Dwan.

Although Swanson was working at the Pathé studio, she could not release her films through Pathé due to a distribution contract with United Artists.

Because of her close ties to Joseph Kennedy, many assumed that Swanson was receiving preferential treatment and reduced rates for the use of Pathé's facilities.[10] Actually, the reverse was true.

For the use of most facilities Gloria Productions was charged the same rate as Pathé's in-house pictures. The rate for soundstage use was $700 per day and $300 per night. However, since Swanson's films didn't start shooting until between one and three in the afternoon, most production days straddled the day/night divide and were billed a full $1,000 per day. Gloria Productions argued in vain that the "day" should be shifted to begin in midafternoon and that the going rate charged to independent producers by the other studios was only $750 for a twenty-four-hour day. Gloria Productions was even unhappier to discover that the use of Pathé's recording facilities had cost the company almost twice per picture what it cost for the average Pathé in-house production.[11]

The fact was that Gloria Productions was actually supporting Pathé, rather than the other way around. In the summer of 1930 Pathé's auditor wrote a memo to the studio manager to disabuse him of any notion that Gloria had gotten a free ride:

> My understanding of the deal with Gloria was that their occupancy of the studio would assist Pathé in absorbing some of [Pathé's] general studio overhead . . . and also to help the prestige of the company. . . . I have attempted to show all of the items that may be questioned by anyone not familiar with them. I have done this for the reason that gossip and hearsay has linked Gloria Productions with Pathé and some of the remarks overheard were to the effect that concessions were being allowed to Gloria at the expense of Pathé. This gossip, however, has not come from anyone in a position to know the facts.[12]

William Sistrom would go even further, calling Gloria Productions "a lifesaver for the studio."[13] In the spring of 1930 Pathé's finances were in such bad shape that the studio had to cease all new feature production for a time. Gloria Productions' *What a Widow!* was the only picture shooting on the lot and was single-handedly paying studio overhead. Yet the situation as depicted in Pathé press releases was that Swanson's production was extravagant and excessive, taking up eleven of Pathé's thirteen stages and making it impossible for Pathé to do any other work.[14]

When Pathé tried to tack on an additional $150,000 in charges in the summer of 1930, Gloria Productions commissioned an independent audit by Price Waterhouse. Pat Scollard, one of Pathé's New York executives, frantically wired his Culver City counterpart, "DO NOT LET PRICE WATERHOUSE IN UNTIL YOU HEAR FURTHER FROM ME."[15] When Price Waterhouse was allowed in, the auditors discovered some irregularities in the billing, but not as many as Gloria had hoped for. Chief among the disputed charges that were reversed after the audit was more than $20,000 for personnel for whom Gloria Productions had already paid. An $18,000 charge for constructing and furnishing a bungalow for Swanson, remodeling and refurnishing a dressing room, and remodeling offices was reversed since the bungalow and the remodeled rooms remained at Pathé and were still in use by others. Some of the disputed charges, though, were for equipment and facility use that Pathé management at the time had indicated would be provided for free. Price Waterhouse determined that Pathé was not contractually obligated to cancel the billing strictly on the basis of verbal assurances by Culver City executives who no longer worked there.[16]

The finding of the audit was that Gloria Productions did owe Pathé another $80,000. Gloria Productions was able to whittle that amount down a bit by successfully pointing out that it should not have to shoulder the entire costs of the construction of some of the sets, since they had been used subsequently by other Pathé productions, in some cases violating a studio policy against using sets until at least six months after the release of the film for which they were built. Resigned to pay the remainder, C. J. Dunphy wrote Pathé's board that the proposed Price Waterhouse settlement was "very, very bad for Gloria Productions." One of Gloria Productions' creditors was none other than Joseph Kennedy, who held outstanding notes totaling $700,000. Dunphy informed Pathé that the Price Waterhouse settlement meant that Gloria would never be able to repay Kennedy more than a "negligible fraction" of that figure. "Despite all this, Gloria Productions, feeling that it should not in any way embarrass Mr. Kennedy in his relations with Pathé," would pay the remaining amount being billed by Pathé's Culver City management, "who, after investigation, and certainly not with a very friendly attitude, decided that this settlement was best for all concerned."[17]

Gloria Productions was finished. Swanson would star in only four more films in the 1930s after *What a Widow!* and one in the 1940s before *Sunset Boulevard* in 1950.

BEHIND THE LINES

The 1928–29 movie season was Pathé's first as a fully integrated studio, with what had formerly been the DeMille interests combined with Pathé's. Curiously, considering that the United States was not engaged in any armed conflict at the time, Pathé's announcement for the season's product line was full of military analogies. Calling the Culver City facility "the Gibraltar of Studios," the announcement praised its production organization as its "strength back of the first trenches." The Pathé army was led by the triumvirate of general manager William Sistrom and associate producers Ralph Block and Hector Turnbull, all of whom had worked for DeMille. The announced lineup of feature films must have given pause to anyone with an interest in Pathé. Only the two features that Cecil B. DeMille completed before his departure, *The King of Kings* (which still had not gone into general nationwide release) and *The Godless Girl*, were mentioned by name. Beyond that, Pathé promised "11 Specials, with casts headed by Pathé's popular marquee names, each with a box office title, and made to order for elaborate exploitation" and "16 Super Features, varied in subject matter, woven around the best in original story material and widely known books and plays, and sure-fire in entertainment qualities."[18] It is hard to imagine a press release written in more vague terms. Pathé sounded as if it had a better handle on its bread-and-butter matinee westerns, listing the names of four series, but these were all series that were made by independent producers who had their contracts canceled by Kennedy the previous spring. The only westerns Pathé would release in 1928–29 were simply leftover films from the previous year.

In a similar vein, but rising to the level of cruelty since it had a hand in ruining his career, Pathé devoted a full page to the "new" comedies being produced by Mack Sennett, complete with a photo spread of the new studio that he would only use for a few years. Pathé actually had the nerve to imply that it had somehow contributed to the construction of the new Sennett plant, saying that the studio was recently completed *for* Mack Sennett, rather than *by* Mack Sennett.[19] The other short-subject offerings for the season, aside from Pathé's final five serials, were either produced by *Pathé News* or Amadee J. Van Beuren. Van Beuren had long produced *Aesop's Fables* and most of the other entertainment one-reelers, but starting with the 1928–29 season he began producing the popular Grantland Rice Sportlights series as well.

Two names stand out in Pathé's trade announcement, one for its absence. Gone was Pathé's long-time general manager Elmer Pearson. Rumors of his imminent departure had begun to swirl at the time of Kennedy's appointment as special advisor, but he managed to hang on to both his vice presidency and his board seat until June.[20] The other name was that of Terry Ramsaye, a journalist turned publicist and nonfiction film writer and producer. In 1928 Ramsaye was well known in the film industry not only for his work in the field but also for having been the author of one of the very first published histories of the American cinema, *A Million and One Nights* (1926). Ramsaye had joined Pathé in spring 1928 as the new editor of the *Pathé Review*, but soon he was editor in chief of the newsreel as well.[21] The *Pathé Review* for 1928–29 promised to incorporate "new and modern ideas" since it was now "under the guidance of Terry Ramsaye, historian of the motion picture industry."[22] Over the next few years Ramsaye would become the vital East Coast "eyes and ears" of the executives in Culver City.

A name that did not become publicized until months after Kennedy assumed control of Pathé was that of thirty-six-year-old E. B. Derr. Derr had left his position at FBO and began active fiscal oversight, if not creative control, of Pathé's Culver City studio, which became the company's only West Coast production facility when its lease at the Metropolitan Studios expired in August 1928.[23] In Culver City, according to a contemporary newspaper profile, Derr "fired right and left. He let the Pathé stock company go. . . . He was tearing down to rebuild. He tore down policies as well as individuals."[24] "There's more waste in the movies than a sane person can stand," Derr told the reporter.[25]

In June 1928 Derr wrote a reassuring letter to studio manager Sistrom. Referring to a letter in which Sistrom had outlined the difficulties of editing the short version of *King of Kings*, Derr said that in a brief time he had developed a "very strong friendly feeling" toward Sistrom and that Sistrom should never be afraid "to state your case." He acknowledged that the reorganization Pathé was undergoing at that moment had produced "hysteria," especially due to the fact that the reorganization was occurring exactly when studios needed to develop and announce their program for the upcoming season. Nevertheless, he told Sistrom that he felt that the reorganization of Pathé was going fairly well, compared to others he had seen.

Derr went on to inform Sistrom that as part of operating policy moving forward, Mr. Kennedy must have a budget airmailed to him on the East Coast for each picture. Kennedy also required a weekly production report that listed titles in production, the original budget on each title, the cost up to the end of the previous week, the estimated cost to complete, the cash already received by the studio applicable to that picture, and a division of the overhead applicable to that picture. He told Sistrom that Charles Sullivan, his second in command at Culver City, could show him a copy of this sort of report as used by FBO. Derr closed by saying that Pathé could not reasonably expect a return on a film budgeted at over $100,000, and any pictures budgeted above that mark must be offset by films whose budgets were substantially below $100,000. Further, the less expensive films must be made *before* production could commence on the more expensive ones.[26] The $100,000 figure was just over one-half of the average budget of $188,000 per picture during DeMille's last year.[27]

In September FBO production chief, William LeBaron, gave Kennedy a somewhat hopeful assessment of Pathé's condition. Speaking of the studio's feature releases for 1928–29, he wrote, "Of the ten pictures still to be made, 'Geraldine,' 'Noisy Neighbors, 'The Getaway,' 'Square Shoulders' and 'Listen Baby' will be fair. 'The Leatherneck' looks like their best picture of the year. The other Boyds will be Okay and 'The Elevator Girl' and 'Office Scandal' should work out pretty well. 'Ned McCobb's Daughter' and 'The Spieler' are very good."[28] Addressing the issue of sound technology, LeBaron reported, "It is going to take a long time to get the same efficiency in shooting sound pictures that we have in silent ones and, of course, all the work that is being done up to date is experimental. However, our Photophone engineers seem to have demonstrated one very important thing and that is the way they can shoot talking sequences at night on our regular stages without sound-proofing."[29] Apparently, cutting all possible corners was the order of the day.

LeBaron closed his assessment with the warning that

> [o]f course, the most important necessity for both F B O and Pathé is preparation of next year's programs. If we are going to make thirty pictures for F B O and approximately thirty for Pathé, that means that we must find or have written sixty stories in the next few months and time is getting awfully short. . . . There is a lot to be decided in the way of policy before we can get very definite in selecting material and this must be gone into very seriously at the earliest possible moment.[30]

The turmoil surrounding the introduction of the new management team resulted in the films for the 1928–29 season being largely the production schedule put in place by DeMille before his departure. Kennedy and Derr's influence would not become apparent until the 1929–30 season. In fact, surviving Pathé records identify the 1928–29 films as "Fourth Year Productions," continuing a numbering system set up by DeMille.[31]

Regardless of whose personality was stamped on the pictures, Pathé's 1928–29 feature output found rough sledding in the marketplace. Part of this was the legacy of the Keith-Albee-Orpheum–DeMille merger. On the surface it had appeared advantageous for Pathé to have a twenty-year franchise to run in Keith's theaters, which were concentrated in metropolitan New York, Boston, Cleveland, Rochester, and Syracuse. The downside that soon became apparent was that the Keith theaters only wanted expensive "Class A" pictures, and they were free to reject any film that did not live up to their standards. As a later internal report lamented,

> This obligated Pathé to produce expensive pictures for a very limited distribution. With the exception of the spots shown above Pathé had to sell its pictures to independent operators who could not pay first run rentals. Therefore, Pathé was obligated to produce expensive pictures under this franchise and with the exception of the towns covered by the franchise had to take rentals comparable with small companies producing $75,000 to $100,000 negatives. The other companies producing at a negative cost comparable to Pathé either had their own theaters in the large cities or else had franchises with other first-run houses as a result of trading playing time in other cities. Pathé having no theaters had no playing time to trade. The above created an impossible situation.[32]

Pathé's situation in the Keith theaters only became worse after the October 1928 creation of RKO and the simultaneous rift between the "Radio" group and Kennedy's interests. In a memo to Kennedy, Colvin Brown noted that the Keith-Pathé contract gave an "absolute advantage" to Orpheum "without compensating advantages to Pathé." It "would so cripple Pathé's possibilities of first run revenue in so many important money points that Pathé's future is seriously handicapped. . . . Keith obviously has lost sight entirely of the principle that if it is to get a better class of picture for its weekly change theatres, it must give a preponderance of support to a distributor which can supply that class of product to Orpheum in all of Orpheum's situations and not spread its support promiscuously to half a dozen distributors."[33]

A "WHIMSICAL POINT OF VIEW"

In the summer of 1928 Joseph Kennedy leased a studio at the corner of Park Avenue and 134th Street in New York City that had been used by Pathé in its earliest days. Remodeling it to accommodate the production of sound films and renaming it the Manhattan Studios, the facility was shared by FBO and Pathé through a jointly owned subsidiary, Sound Studios, Inc.[34] During the transition to sound, several of the major film companies set up or rehabilitated studios for the production of talking shorts featuring Broadway talent. For FBO and Pathé there was an added reason. New York City was much closer to Photophone's engineering staff in the event they were needed to keep the equipment working. And in the early days, they were.

FBO and Pathé's silent films destined to be released with music and effects tracks were scored and recorded at the Manhattan Studios, including *The King of Kings*. All were supervised by FBO and Pathé's shared musical director, Josiah Zuro. The Johnny Mack Brown silent feature *Annapolis* (1928) was not only scored at the Manhattan Studios, an unrelated, all-talking prologue of stage acts was shot there as well. Fashioned after the prologues for *Don Juan* (1926) and other early Warner Brothers sound efforts, *Annapolis* was the only Pathé film to be outfitted with all-talking opening acts.[35] What was to have been FBO's first all-talking picture, *Stepping Out*, starring popular tenor Morton Downey,[36] was shot in the Manhattan Studios. By the time it was released in March 1929, the film had been retitled *Syncopation*, and it became the first release from the new RKO. The absorption of FBO into RKO left Pathé as the sole tenant of the Manhattan Studios and the sole employer of Josiah Zuro, who would continue as Pathé's musical director until his death in an automobile accident in 1930.

Although it had already begun the production of all-talking features on the West Coast by early 1929, Pathé shot two cheaply made and poorly received musical features in New York, both starring Morton Downey. Among the complaints was that the films had a cramped and claustrophobic atmosphere, the direct result of the cramped and claustrophobic conditions of the Manhattan Studios. After the two Downey features the facility was used mainly for the production of sound short subjects, including the music and narration tracks recorded for the sound versions of both *Pathé News* and *Pathé Review*.

When he took over the *Review* in spring 1928, Terry Ramsaye had announced, "The Pathé Review becomes up-to-date, somewhat sophisticated, turning away from the bees, the birds and the flowers to the modernism of man, and not forgetting the ladies."[37] Despite the abandonment of the nature scenes that had usually been a showcase for Pathécolor, colored scenes continued to appear in the *Review* through the introduction of sound. At the end of 1928 the "Pathécolor" name was replaced by "Pathéchrome," but that seems to have just reflected a very minor refinement and rebranding of the earlier process.[38] According to a trade-paper story on Pathéchrome, a "section of each issue of Pathé Review is sent to Pathé Cinema laboratories in Vincennes, outside of Paris, where color experts with special training apply the process and return the film for American distribution. . . ."[39] The very first use of Pathéchrome in the sound version of the review, the *Pathé Audio Review*, was, logically enough, Pathé's crowing-rooster logo.[40] The combined *Exhibitors Herald and Moving Picture World* noted that being able to hear the rooster would be a "novelty in the line of trademarks" but then curiously added that Metro-Goldwyn-Mayer (MGM) might experience some difficulty producing a sound version of its roaring-lion logo.[41]

By the late 1920s the *Pathé Review* was increasingly abandoning the beloved Pathécolor (and its successor) and replacing it in segments still identified as "Pathécolor" with the much cheaper coloring method of tinting and toning. Used by filmmakers for almost as long as hand coloring, tinting was a process that shaded all of the lighter areas of the frame with a single color, while toning colored the darker areas of the image. Tinting and toning could be used separately, or they could be used in concert to produce a two-color effect. This was a very inexact approach to film color, since all of the light areas, whether people, walls, or the sky, would be tinted in the same hue, and all of the darker areas would be similarly toned in the second color.

Of known surviving original *Pathé Review* prints from the late 1920s with their color segments intact, noted film preservationist Anthony L'Abbate describes one in the collection of the George Eastman House from 1927 as featuring scenes with lavender, amber, pink, and yellow tints and green tones but no actual stencil coloring.[42] On the other hand, another Pathécolor *Review* segment identified as being from 1927 and housed in the holdings of British Pathé is entirely in stencil color.[43] A reel of "Pathécolor" clips also held by British Pathé and dated at approximately 1928 features both stencil-color and tinted scenes, as well as one scene identified by a title card as "Pathéchrome" but actually is in black and white.[44]

In the absence of film prints, contemporary trade-journal reviews provide some insight into the point at which the Pathéchrome process was nudged out completely by tinting and toning. Unfortunately, since the reviews for short films were extremely brief themselves, usually running but a single paragraph, the absence of any mention of color in a review is not absolute proof that the film did not have a color sequence. The last mention of a process that certainly sounds like Pathéchrome was in a March 29, 1930, critique of *Pathé Audio Review #13*.[45] After that the reviewers are pretty clear that the series used tinted stock exclusively, except for three or four more shorts, released almost monthly between June and September, which may have used Pathé's Coloratura process to be mentioned shortly.[46] The shift away from Pathécolor/Pathéchrome in the late 1920s was undoubtedly due to financial considerations, but an even more compelling reason to abandon it completely would soon arise.

Still in the process of downsizing his company, Charles Pathé incrementally merged his film manufacturing interests, including the plant in Vincennes, into Eastman Kodak between 1927 and 1929 to form Kodak-Pathé.[47] The exact date that the Vincennes facility ceased producing Pathéchrome prints is hard to pin down. Paul Read asserts that the coloring studio was closed in 1928,[48] yet the British all-star revue film *Elstree Calling*, released in early 1930, contains several scenes that are attributed to the Pathé process and clearly *are* in stencil color. As will be noted shortly, Pathé's Culver City staff discussed the use of Pathéchrome in a series of comedies as late as April

1930. And, as already mentioned, the *Review* appears to have used it through March 1930.

In early 1930 Pathé proclaimed that its newsreel would henceforth feature color segments as well. This time it was not to be in the form of stencil-color or tinted stock, but actual photographic color. Pathé's Coloratura process supposedly used a special DuPont-Pathé film stock and did not require the use of special filters or prisms, as did Technicolor.[49] The process used standard cameras and generated two black and white negatives, one of which captured the blue-green part of the color spectrum and the other, the red-orange end. The final color film, it was claimed, could be on the screen a mere three hours after it was photographed.[50] With great fanfare the first subject was announced as a story on the Mardi Gras celebration in New Orleans. Beyond that the process was shrouded in mystery. It was suggested that Terry Ramsaye had a hand in the development of Coloratura, having benefited from his association some years earlier with Charles Urban, the financial backer (but not inventor) of Kinemacolor, the first moderately successful color motion-picture process.

In fact, Pathé Coloratura was essentially another variation of a two-color process that had originally been known as Prizma and had been around in the years before 1920 but with very little use since then by the Hollywood film industry. In 1930 the system was generally marketed as Multicolor, and by the mid-1930s, under the name Cinecolor, it would finally be embraced by low-budget producers as an economical, if inferior, alternative to Technicolor.[51] The system did indeed use standard cameras, which were slightly modified and outfitted with magazines that would accommodate two rolls of film rather than one. One of the rolls was orthochromatic film, which was sensitive to the blue-green end of the light spectrum, and the other was panchromatic stock, which was normally sensitive to the entire color spectrum. The two rolls were exposed together in the camera's gate, with the orthochromatic film on top of the panchromatic. A special filter coating on the orthochromatic stock prevented the blue-green light from passing through to the panchromatic stock, so the latter only registered the red-orange end of the spectrum. As with Technicolor, the black and white negative "records" were then used with a dye process to produce film prints that reconstituted the original colors of the photographed scene.[52]

Despite the hype Pathé Coloratura flopped after a few trials. Responding in March 1930 to E. B. Derr's inquiry about the availability of Coloratura prints for Los Angeles theaters, Ramsaye admitted that the color promotions were little more than a way to get publicity: "We haven't the machinery to do much but samples."[53] It appears that the process made a timid debut in the handful of *Pathé Audio Reviews* mentioned earlier. The trade-journal critique of a July *Review* does not actually mention Coloratura, but rather complains of "blurred" color effects. A Coloratura makeup demonstration from September is described as featuring a woman's face that is so bleached out photographically that the rouge disappeared as it was applied. Unfortunately, the surviving archival copy of a critique of a June *Review* release is incomplete and simply stops after mentioning that the short has a Coloratura segment. A second *Review* from September is described as having two ice skaters in a "colored and effective" routine, but there is no mention of the color process.[54]

Another photographic process that was developed by Pathé's partner in the film manufacturing business had more real impact and drew more attention than Coloratura. DuPont's "Hyper-Sensitized Panchromatic" film could be exposed under much lower lighting conditions than most other film stocks of the day. Its use in *Pathé Audio Review #8*, a film essay on New York City at night, drew high praise from the critics.[55]

When the new *Pathé Audio Review* was announced, Pathé promised that it would reflect Terry Ramsaye's "whimsical point of view and expression." Ramsaye's "daring, saucy, impish humor" must have been something of an acquired taste, or perhaps it just spoke to the times. Of his approach to the *Audio Review* Ramsaye wrote, "I've let D. W. Griffith, Von Stroheim and Herbert Brenon strut their stuff long enough. My forbearance is at an end. I'm going to produce Pathé Audio Review to provide ear and eye entertainment for the theatres and audiences of true discrimination. It is to be seen on the screens where superior pictures play. It will be smart and modern. It will tell who's who and what is what. It will brook no competition nor acknowledge any."[56] Presumably, Ramsaye did not mention DeMille in the pantheon of top directors because of his unhappy association with Pathé. One wonders if he was aware of Joseph Kennedy's problems with von Stroheim.

Beyond Ramsaye's reels, the Manhattan Studios were primarily used for the production of two-reel comedies and musicals for most of 1929. During the 1928–29 season Pathé distributed the last of its Mack Sennett shorts as well as the short-lived silent two-reel *Smitty* comedy series produced by Amadee J. Van Beuren. The theatrical market for two-reel shorts had become increasingly difficult during that period due to the entry of Paramount and MGM into the field, as well as the fact that many of the larger metropolitan theaters were eliminating two-reelers in favor of live stage shows.[57] Nevertheless, Pathé decided to produce seven series of full-talking two-reelers under the brand names *George LeMaire Comedies* (after its star), *Manhattan Comedies*,

Variety Comedies, *Melody Comedies*, *Follies Comedies*, *Checker Comedies*, and *Golden Rooster Comedies*. Many of these series attempted, as did competing series from Pathé's rival studios, to bring Broadway-styled entertainment to "the masses" by means of the talking picture.[58] Beyond the New York–based productions, a series of *Buck and Bubbles* two-reel comedies with sound for the 1929–30 season was independently produced in Hollywood by Monte Brice and starred the African American team of Ford Washington Lee and John William Sublett.

The Pathé-produced series had their occasional high points. George LeMaire's first few films were given critical plaudits for originality. William Frawley, who was just beginning a transition from stage to screen acting, appeared in one *Checker* and one *Follies* comedy. Frawley's Pathé shorts would inaugurate a long film career as a character actor that would climax more than twenty years later with the role of Fred Mertz on *I Love Lucy*. The husband and wife writing and performing duo James and Lucile Gleason appeared in a pair of *Golden Rooster Comedies*. James Gleason would go on to become one of Pathé's, and then Hollywood's, busiest character actors from the 1930s through the 1950s. The most significant future star to appear in Pathé's New York comedies was Ginger Rogers, who made her second-ever screen appearance headlining a *Melody Comedy* titled *A Night in a Dormitory* (1930). Unfortunately, these films were the exception. Far more typical series entries drew extraordinarily harsh critical rebukes: "The less said about it the better," "Weak in every department," and "Inexcusable."[59] Bad films, though, would soon prove to be the least of Pathé's problems at the Manhattan Studios.

"HOLDING TOGETHER THE REMNANTS"

At around 10 A.M. on Tuesday, December 10, 1929, shortly before the last day of shooting was to commence at the Manhattan Studios on a *Melody Comedy* titled *The Black and White Revue*, a large spotlight was placed too close to the black velvet curtain that served as a stage backdrop. What happened next was described by the Associated Press:

> The stage was set in the rear of the first floor of the building, preparatory to filming a miniature review, titled the "Black and White Revue." The orchestra leader and his fourteen musicians were waiting for the signal to start playing. The cameras were ready.
>
> On the floor above about thirty chorus girls, many of them not yet dressed in their scanty stage clothes, were waiting their calls.
>
> There was a flash from the backdrop and flames and black smoke rolled across the stage.

> Immediately all was in confusion. Men and women fought to escape from the flames, which were sweeping through the whole building. . . .
>
> For more than an hour the fire raged and then, as the flames died down, the ten bodies were found, most of them just inside the 134th Street entrance to the building, having died but a step or two from safety. Although several of the bodies were badly burned, most of them had died from suffocation. Two priests from a nearby church administered the last rites.[60]

Ten people died at the scene, and an eleventh died later in a hospital.[61] Any grief or shock felt by the Pathé management was tempered by the necessity of continuing to turn out pictures. In a telegram sent to Derr the day of the fire, Ramsaye focused on business: "CAN YOU HAVE ABOUT THREE AUDIO REVIEW STORIES PRODUCED THERE [in Culver City] BY MCELWAINE [to] MEET PRODUCTION EMERGENCY HERE?"[62]

By the end of the week Ramsaye wrote to Derr, thanking him and Kennedy for having been in constant touch during "this trying week." He commended the Pathé management at the Manhattan Studios, particularly John Flinn and Fred Lalley (the facility's production head and studio manager, respectively), for having maintained their poise since the fire. In closing, Ramsaye noted that he had spent the week "pulling together a music library and holding together the remnants of the machinery, both mechanical and human."[63]

As it happened, Flinn and Lalley would soon need all of the composure they could muster. New York City district attorney Thomas Crain brought numerous charges against both men ranging from improper storage of highly flammable nitrate film stock to manslaughter in the second degree for each of the eleven fire casualties. Subsequent investigations revealed first and foremost a pattern of lax inspections and enforçement by the city's Fire Prevention Bureau and Board of Standards and Appeals. On an inspection one month prior to the fire, Inspector John Lynch estimated that between forty thousand and fifty thousand feet of film were stored (the number was later found to be closer to 250,000 feet[64]). The building had been permitted in 1917 to store film, but the permit had expired in 1921 and had never been renewed. Nevertheless, under normal circumstances, even without a permit, up to two hundred thousand feet of stored film were permitted in buildings with a sprinkler system, and only five thousand feet in buildings without a sprinkler system. The Manhattan Studios had no sprinkler system, a situation that, as lessee, was the responsibility of Pathé and its management to rectify. However, Pathé had appealed the May 1929 order to install automatic sprinklers and was awaiting the outcome of that appeal at the time of the fire.[65] The depth of the lax fire-code enforcement became apparent when it was revealed that the Manhattan Studios building had been ordered to install sprinklers as early as 1919.[66] Beyond the absence of sprinklers, the Manhattan Studios had eight fire hydrants, but only three were actually equipped with hoses. Finally, the inside of the studio was covered with "ozite," a highly flammable type of sound insulation that was illegal in theaters but unregulated in film studios.[67]

The grand jury considering manslaughter charges against Flinn and Lalley in the deaths of two of the studio's dancers declined to indict either man, noting that both had started working at the studio a mere six weeks before the fire and that neither was aware of the fire-code violations.[68] However, in a concurrent review of the fire, chief city magistrate William McAdoo stated that he believed that Pathé was guilty of "maintaining a nuisance" and that manslaughter charges were justified. He went on to criticize various city fire agencies and appealed to city leaders to reorganize a clearly dysfunctional system.[69] The very next day, District Attorney Crain brought manslaughter charges in the deaths of two more dancers before a new grand jury. This time the grand jury chose to indict.[70] The exact wording of the indictments, Crain announced, would be "patterned on those returned against two men in the fire in the Triangle Building in University Place in 1911."[71] The earlier fire had cost 150 lives and had become a rallying point for workers' rights, particularly the right to safe working conditions.

There was considerable irony in Crain's evoking the Triangle Shirtwaist Factory fire, irony that partially explains his tenacity in prosecuting Flinn and Lalley, even while ignoring the culpability of the fire inspectors, the building's owner, and the Pathé and FBO management at the Manhattan Studios prior to October 1929. Crain had actually been the judge who presided over the Triangle fire case. His instructions to the jury, that the defendants could be found guilty only if it had been proven that they knew an escape door was locked, led to acquittal and outrage.[72] Now, nearly twenty years later, Crain was comfortably installed as district attorney under flamboyant and controversial mayor Jimmy Walker. Walker's administration, and the Tammany Hall machine that had put him in office, were under increasing public scrutiny and needed neither a repeat of the Triangle fallout nor an investigation into the city's fire-prevention bureaucracy that might reveal cronyism, incompetence, and corruption.

If this was indeed the reason for Crain's zealous prosecution of the Pathé case, it misfired. In the spring of 1931, almost exactly one year after the new indictments were handed down against Flinn and Lalley, New York's City Club, an organization founded to promote effective and honest government, began public hearings investigating the district attorney's office. The first two items for examination were charges that Crain's office routinely disregarded complaints of racketeering at the Fulton Fish Market and an allegation that Crain had "ignored evidence of criminality against Tammany officeholders" in the Pathé fire.[73] The City Club's Crain hearings were only part of a broader investigation into widespread corruption within Jimmy Walker's administration. In September 1932 Walker resigned as mayor of New York City and fled to Europe to avoid criminal prosecution.

As for Flinn and Lalley, they were ultimately cleared of virtually all of the charges against them. The only guilty verdict was for improper storage of film on the studio premises, resulting in each having to pay a fine of $500. While Flinn and Lalley certainly were guilty of that charge, it should be noted that the stored film neither started nor contributed to the fatal fire. All of the film survived the fire intact. Not so much as a single reel of the highly volatile nitrate film burned during the blaze that consumed the studio.[74]

THE COMEDY VILLAGE

At the time of the fire Pathé still had around twenty two-reelers to produce to fill out its release schedule for 1929–30. It moved its short-comedy production units to rented space at the Metropolitan Studios in Fort Lee, New Jersey.[75] Scrambling to complete its release commitments as best it could, Pathé actually took the film that had been shot for the ill-fated *Black and White Revue* and filmed new material to finish it out, releasing it as *Sixteen Sweeties* in April 1930. The grim fact was that four of the "sweeties" had perished in the fire.[76] Production in Fort Lee had been under way for less than a month when Pathé experienced another blow that would spell the end for its East Coast short-comedy production. George LeMaire, who had starred in one series and produced comedies for the others, suffered a fatal heart attack at the age of forty-five on January 20, 1930.[77]

After LeMaire's death Derr decided to relocate all of Pathé's short-comedy production to Culver City, leaving only Ramsaye's reels and the independently produced Van Beuren films in metropolitan New York. Knowing that it would take some time to gear up a new unit, Derr arrived at a stopgap measure by purchasing the U.S. distribution rights to six two-reel comedies produced in Great Britain. The films were all directed by former Pathé comedy star Monty Banks, who had moved to the United Kingdom after completing his last silent feature, *A Perfect Gentleman* (1928). Banks' shorts were inserted into Pathé's various comedy series as needed, with one even being released as the last George LeMaire comedy. Not only did the films provide welcome relief to Pathé's comedy production units as they rebuilt in Culver City, they had the added benefit of "counting" in Pathé's favor when it came to getting its own films played in United Kingdom cinemas under Great Britain's quota laws.[78]

E. B. Derr widely promoted Pathé's new West Coast comedy unit as the Comedy Village, a production complex that would be "larger than the facilities of Roach or Sennett."[79] Although the name "Comedy Village" summons up the wonderful image of an autonomous colony of comic artists free to practice their craft at what would have truly been the zaniest place on earth, in fact it was only two stages and a few permanent exterior sets at Pathé's Culver City lot.

The announced output from the Comedy Village for the 1930–31 season was to be organized in nine series, with an average of six shorts per series. Some of the series names were continued from the previous year: *Checker*, *Manhattan* (although now made in Culver City), *Melody*, and *Follies*. Added to these were *Capital Comedies*, *Campus Comedies*, *Whoopee Comedies*, *Rodeo Comedies*, and *Rainbow Comedies*.[80] Because of its name, someone in Pathé's advertising department had the logical but mistaken assumption that the *Rainbow Comedies* were to be shot in color, much to the consternation of Pathé executives who knew otherwise. Fearing a bad reaction from exhibitors who had booked the *Rainbow Comedies* believing them to be in color, E. B. Derr and Pat Scollard exchanged telegrams in April 1930 in which they considered the idea of sending the completed *Rainbow* shorts to France for the Pathéchrome treatment. Ultimately they decided that the high cost of Pathéchrome would not be worth the exhibitor goodwill it might generate. Absent from this discussion was any consideration of actually shooting the films in color, either using Coloratura or the similar Multicolor process that Pathé had used for color segments in some of its 1929–30 features.[81] By June the decidedly black and white *Rainbow Comedies* were advertised as being "designed for colorful settings," a promotional phrase that did little to appease either theater owners or their patrons who had expected color.[82]

The primary stars of the series produced at the Comedy Village were Franklin Pangborn, Daphne Pollard, and Edgar Kennedy. Pangborn had been a supporting player in several of DeMille's Metropolitan feature comedies, and Pollard and Kennedy had recently come to Pathé from Mack Sennett and Hal Roach, respectively. As had been the case with the New York comedies, the stars were not wedded to individual series. Instead, their short comedies were spread virtually across Pathé's entire line. As an example, Daphne Pollard starred in at least one short in every series except *Manhattan*, *Rodeo*, and *Campus*. Other familiar comedy players who turned up in one or more Pathé shorts included James Finlayson (Laurel and Hardy's favorite comic foil), Mack Sennett alumni Billy Bevan and Harry Gribbon, frequent early Roscoe Arbuckle and Buster Keaton collaborator Al St. John, and Arthur Housman (Laurel and Hardy's favorite comic "drunk"). Some interesting one-shot casting included Mildred Harris (Charlie Chaplin's first wife) in a *Rodeo Comedy*, the film debut of vaudeville legend Al Shean in a *Melody Comedy*, and Bing Crosby as one of the "Rhythm Boys" in the first *Campus Comedy*. One reviewer of the Crosby film commented, "No students in any college looked as dumb and amateurish as those selected for this short."[83] A later *Checker Comedy* titled *One Nutty Night* drew the harshest criticism yet from the short-film reviewer at *Motion Picture News*: "This is such a crack-brained attempt at comedy that your audiences will probably rush for the doors holding their noses. In all departments it is an insult to theatre-goers."[84] The poor reception of so many of its short comedies may explain why Pathé spread proven laugh-getters like Pangborn, Pollard, and Kennedy across so many different series. Short subjects were sold to theaters by series, not individual titles. A theater would play as many series as it was willing to buy. Having its top comics appear in at least one film of each series may have been Pathé's attempt to ensure that any theater booking one of its comedy series would get at least one good short in the batch. If this was the strategy, it didn't work. In August 1930 the New York office told Derr that not only were exhibitors unhappy, Pathé's own sales force was complaining that the comedy shorts were simply no good.[85]

One final group of short subjects announced for 1930–31 didn't get much past the planning stage: a return to the serial field after a one-year hiatus. Among the titles mentioned for what would have been Pathé's first slate of sound serials were a western titled *Pardon My Gun* and a remake of *The Perils of Pauline*. At the time of the announcement, *Pardon My Gun* was actually in production with George Duryea and Sally Starr in the leads. It was released in June not as a serial but as one of the strangest western features ever produced. There is virtually no plot, and approximately one-third of the film's one-hour running time is spent on a parade of vaudeville acts that are supposedly providing entertainment at a barn dance. Don Ashbaugh summarized the film beautifully in his review for the *Motion Picture News*:

> There's about everything in "Pardon My Gun" except a trained seal and a baby elephant. Perhaps they can add those before the film is released for general theatre consumption. It is one of the weirdest westerns ever conceived—looking very much like what a bookkeeper's conception of a motion picture should be. . . . Maybe the picture was supposed to be a satire on sound. Maybe it's to be a straight western, but whatever it is don't bank on anybody tearing down the doors to get in. Kids are your best bet.[86]

The release of *Pardon My Gun* as a jerry-built feature was almost certainly a desperation move arising from Pathé's critical shortage of feature product in the summer of 1930 that will be discussed shortly. Pathé reaffirmed its serial intentions in September, stating that it would soon commence production on not only *The New Perils of Pauline* but *The New Exploits of Elaine* and *The New Poison Pen* as well.[87] The serials would be sixteen chapters each, an increase from the ten-chapter serials that had been the norm in the late 1920s. Once again, though, the serial program was stillborn. In November 1930, as Pathé entered the worst financial crisis of its history, it announced that it was abandoning the project.[88] Films titled *The Perils of Pauline* would indeed grace the big screen again, but none of them would be made by Pathé. In 1933 Universal Pictures revisited *Pauline* in a twelve-chapter serial, and the title would reappear in 1947 and 1967 feature-length parodies of the silent-serial form. Beyond the theatrical reworkings of Pauline's perils, "The Perils of Pauline" has been used as the title of individual episodes in several television series. Apparently alliteration never goes out of style.

"HE WOULD NOT TALK WITH ANYBODY"

As noted earlier, the 1929–30 movie season was the first to reflect the change in management from DeMille to Kennedy's team. DeMille star William Boyd continued to receive starring roles, while the contracts of Marie Prevost and Phyllis Haver were not renewed. New faces who had begun to turn up in Pathé features during the 1928–29 season were Mack Sennett émigrés Eddie Quillan and Carol Lombard. Quillan quickly became one of Pathé's most popular male stars in a string of light comedies, but Lombard was largely wasted in a series of bland romantic screen pairings with the likes of William Boyd and Robert Armstrong. When Pathé instituted budget cuts in the wake of the October 1929 stock-market crash, Lombard was dropped from its roster. It was then that she added the *e* to the end of her first name and went on to become a Hollywood legend.

As part of the same late-1929 housecleaning, Alan Hale and Robert Armstrong had their contracts terminated. While Hale would prove to be better suited as a supporting actor than as a lead, as his long subsequent career at Warner Brothers would indicate, cutting Armstrong was a costly mistake for Pathé. His fast-talking wise-guy persona was perfectly suited to talking pictures, and the last films he did at Pathé before being dropped, *Oh, Yeah?* and *The Racketeer*, had been among Pathé's most profitable of late 1929. He went on to freelance at other studios, including a costarring role in RKO's wide-screen railroading epic *Danger Lights* (1930), directed by Pathé serial veteran George

B. Seitz. By the time Pathé managers realized their mistake and rehired him, he demanded and received a salary of $1,750 per week, nearly twice what he had made before being fired.[89] The last to go in the purge of late 1929 were studio manager William Sistrom and associate producer Ralph Block. Despite the fact that Sistrom would continue to find ready employment as an associate producer or producer at other studios until his retirement in the late 1940s, he remained bitter at being ousted from Pathé for quite some time, a fact that did not help Pathé when he was interviewed by the auditors investigating the Gloria Productions charges. Sistrom was replaced by E. B. Derr, who became actively and publicly engaged in the studio's operation. Derr would not only stamp his personality on Pathé's films for 1930, he stamped his name on them as well. Practically all of Pathé feature films for that year are identified as "Produced by E. B. Derr," and the Comedy Village shorts are headlined "E. B. Derr Presents." The day-to-day management of the Culver City facility fell largely to Charles Sullivan, another member of Kennedy's inner circle.[90]

Going into the 1929–30 season Pathé's managers were apparently satisfied with their male leads, although they would drop Hale and Armstrong midyear. The studio's lineup of leading actresses was another matter. Failing to realize the potential of Carol Lombard, Pathé looked outside of the studio to recruit new talent. Pathé signed Ann Harding, a stage actress who made her film debut at Pathé; Helen Twelvetrees, another stage actress who had recently done three films for Fox; and Constance Bennett, a silent-film actress who had taken a break from the screen in 1926 to marry the second of her five husbands.[91] All three actresses proved to be good hires. Their films would be among Pathé's most popular of the early sound era, and they were valuable as loan-out "properties" to other studios during downtime between pictures in Culver City. While Twelvetrees' success was short-lived and she was out of the movies by the end of the 1930s, Bennett and Harding would go on to long and successful screen careers.

One actress who almost worked for Pathé was the enigmatic Louise Brooks. Having run her course as a Paramount supporting player, she agreed in early 1929 to sign with Pathé for the paltry salary of $450 per week. As a contract stipulation Pathé insisted that she attend an acting school in New York. After verbally consenting to the deal but before the contract was signed, Brooks received an offer from a German film studio for $1,000 per week with a thirty-week guarantee. She accepted and sailed off into film immortality to star in *Pandora's Box* and *Diary of a Lost Girl*.[92] The films, both masterworks directed by G. W. Pabst, were the defining moments in Brooks' otherwise lackluster movie career.

The program announcement for Pathé's 1929–30 feature releases was the exact opposite of the one from the previous year. This time Pathé overstated its lineup, including titles that management may well have known would never be made. "Pathé's first musical production," the ad promised, would be "elaborate and spectacular."[93] *The Treasure Girl*, as it was to be called, would feature a score by George Gershwin. Another musical *The Greenwich Village Follies* would be photographed entirely in color. Neither film would ever go into production. Another all-color effort mentioned in this fever dream of a product announcement was a William Boyd western titled *The Painted Desert* that was to be released, appropriately enough, entirely painted in the Pathéchrome process![94] *The Painted Desert* actually was shot and released, although not until January 1931. Extant copies of the film are 100 percent black and white, and it is almost certain that moviegoers saw it that way in 1931.[95] *The Painted Desert* is probably best known for the appearance of a very young Clark Gable who is billed fifth in the cast as the villain. The film is now in the public domain in the United States, and the DVD (digital video disc) cover art used by most of the bargain-bin video labels that distribute it features a large photo of Gable, rather than William Boyd, and give Gable top billing. Caveat emptor!

The 1929–30 product announcement stated, "Every Pathé picture of the coming season will carry color."[96] While this was a significant overstatement, it actually was true that at least three of Pathé's feature films for 1929–30 did contain a few scenes photographed in color. Evidence for which color process was used is vague, but contemporary reviewers were under the impression that it was Multicolor. Of the three films, *His First Command* (1930), starring William Boyd, is widely available, but only in a black and white version. The Constance Bennett picture *This Thing Called Love* (1929) is not readily accessible, and for *Red Hot Rhythm* (1929), Alan Hale's last starring film for Pathé, it appears that a color musical number is all that survives. Film credits, usually a source of valuable information, are of no help either. The opening credits of *His First Command* make no mention of color, perhaps indicating that only a few prints with the color sequences were struck for the more prestigious metropolitan theaters.[97]

As noted earlier, Pathé underwent a major sea change at the end of 1929. Joseph Kennedy had been elected as Pathé's board chairman the previous May.[98] Although it took a while for the stock-market crash to affect the overall film industry, Pathé's shaky finances and the fact that it still routinely ran in the red caused it to take an immediate hit. At the time of the mass firings in Culver City, Kennedy announced that Pathé would be remodeled after United Artists, producing fewer films of higher quality. Under the new "Kennedy formula" Pathé would only attempt to produce ten feature films for the remainder of the 1929–30 season, although the schedule for short-subject production would not be affected.[99]

In early January 1930, not long after he officially became Pathé's Culver City production chief, E. B. Derr wrote a letter to Terry Ramsaye in which he confided his hopes and frustrations about the quantity and quality of the studio's product:

> I am sure we have found the solution to the production problem out here, but no conversation nor faith will prove that until I send in the first five pictures. There is every indication that we will have four or five pictures in production within three weeks and each one of these pictures has a story of entertainment rather than problem plays. . . . If we make artistic triumphs or great problem plays, we are satisfying twenty-five percent of the audiences, but if we can get into a picture some romance, music, comedy, and one big dramatic moment or one thrill, then I am sure that is entertainment for seventy-five per cent of the people.
>
> I haven't any hi-faluting theories about production except that I know I am going to try to make the kind of pictures we always hoped each one would be when we sat in a projection room in New York to see the latest thing from Hollywood.[100]

Despite assurances that the promise of higher budgets for fewer films was more than just a publicity promise, in February Derr was appalled to learn that the New York office had spent much of his production budget to make a payment on the studio's mortgage. In an incredibly run-on telegram, Derr could barely contain himself. He informed New York that he was "horribly disappointed that our production cash was used to pay mortgage and it might just as well be known now that my budget provided consumption of entire cash without considering mortgage obligation and it's up to you get that cash back in till for production purposes and I don't want it to be considered as an aid to us when they return us the mortgage money."[101]

Despite the funding setback Derr was able to commence production on the first film under the new program, a Helen Twelvetrees circus extravaganza titled *Swing High*.[102] The new policy appeared to pay off, with the reviewer for the *Motion Picture News* proclaiming it "undoubtedly the best box-office attraction that has come off the Pathé lot in many months."[103] By the summer of 1930, however, the news was not so rosy, with the *Motion Picture News* reporting that in Los Angeles, "One of the worst performances at local first runs in many weeks was . . . Pathé's 'Swing High,' which grossed only $7,500 for a full seven-day period at the Orpheum. The exploitation was heavy, but not effective despite the big dough spent on a circus ballyhoo and other stunts."[104]

Even more ominous was an increase in the trade press of stories speculating about a merger between Pathé and RKO. The stories had begun around the time of Kennedy's sale of FBO to RCA in 1928, but their frequency increased dramatically after the layoffs of December 1929. All of the parties involved, including Derr, denied that any merger was in the works; Derr may have been alone in actually believing what he told the press was true.[105] He appears to have been genuinely committed to making Pathé succeed, but he probably didn't realize what he was up against. It must have been quite a jolt in April 1930 when he asked for Kennedy's assistance in straightening out the financial and other crises he was facing in Culver City. Instead of getting a response from Kennedy himself, the reply came by wire from Kennedy assistant Eddie Moore: "HE [Kennedy] TOLD ME TO TELL YOU AND TO TELL YOU IN NO UNCERTAIN TERMS THAT YOU TWO WERE RUNNING THINGS THERE AND THIS WAS ONE OF THE PROBLEMS THAT YOU WOULD HAVE TO STRAIGHTEN OUT YOURSELVES FOR HE WOULD NOT TALK WITH ANYBODY ANY MORE ABOUT IT."[106] Clearly, Derr and Charles Sullivan were no longer part of Kennedy's inner circle, and by distancing himself from them he sent an unmistakable message that either they, Pathé, or both had little time left.

Derr and Sullivan carried on as best they could, but in the absence of production funding they were only able to release one feature per month from June through November 1930. While the first of these was the slapdash *Pardon My Gun* and two others were modestly budgeted Eddie Quillan comedies, the remaining three proved that Pathé could turn out top features if given a chance.[107] The July release *Holiday* actually received Academy Award nominations for best actress in a leading role (Ann Harding) and best adapted screenplay (Horace Jackson). But by the time that Harding and Jackson learned they had lost to Marie Dressler (*Min and Bill*) and Howard Estabrook (*Cimarron*) at the Fourth Academy Awards ceremony in November 1931, Pathé no longer existed as an independent film-production company.

"TOO MANY LAWYERS AND NOT ENOUGH CHAIRS"

Once again, in the fall of 1930, Pathé announced that it was cutting back on production so that it could concentrate on fewer but better pictures. Derr told the *Motion Picture News* that he "would rather have stars and featured players on his payroll than at work on productions of doubtful quality."[108] The same article, though, reported that Pathé's stars, particularly Harding and Bennett, were not idle at all but were busy at other studios as "loan outs." Since the common practice was to have the studio that "borrowed" another studio's star actually pay the second studio a price higher than the star's normal salary, Pathé received much-needed income from the loan outs without having to risk production money.

To those outside of the film industry, it appeared that Pathé was finally turning a corner. Hearing a lawsuit brought by a Pathé creditor, a chancery judge in Trenton, New Jersey, felt that the company was actually "bettering" its condition. He noted that it had only lost $66,431 during the first quarter of 1930, compared to a $4,566,000 loss during the previous four years. The judge concluded that "insolvency is far from inevitable."[109]

What did seem inevitable to the denizens of Hollywood was that Pathé would merge with RKO. If nothing else, a merger would free RKO's theaters from the long-term contract requiring them to play a certain percentage of Pathé short-film and feature product. Also, while most of the big studios had established newsreel departments, the still-new RKO had not. Merging with Pathé would not only provide RKO with a newsreel, it would be a newsreel with stature and name recognition.[110] When Joseph Kennedy announced in late spring of 1930 that he was retiring from active management of Pathé, although not as Pathé's board chairman, the move was seen as yet another indication that a merger was imminent.[111]

By October of 1930 the involved parties were no longer denying that a merger was in the works. It became increasingly apparent that this would be no merger of two equals. RKO was going to purchase a controlling interest in Pathé's film production and distribution operations, although it promised that Pathé's studio operation would continue to function semi-autonomously and would still produce films under the Pathé name.[112] One issue for negotiation, which would continue through December, was the determination of exactly which of Pathé's assets RKO wanted to buy. It was understood that RKO did not want some of Pathé's holdings, including the Bound Brook film processing facility in New Jersey and Pathé's 49 percent stake in the DuPont-Pathé Film Manufacturing Company. These would remain the property of the Pathé Exchange, Inc.

By December the last details were ironed out. RKO was willing to pay $4,630,780 for Pathé's production and distribution entities. As chairman of the board, Kennedy sent a letter to Pathé stockholders that explained why the sale to RKO was a fiscal necessity. It noted that

Pathé's position as an independent in the industry, without theatres and with limited resources, has become increasingly difficult. . . . Pathé, as an independent, must constantly be able to make better pictures than other companies with much greater resources, in order to get adequate exhibition contracts.

Pathé had for many years the only important news-reel, which was played in most theaters and represented a very substantial sourcc of profit. Now each of the large producing companies has developed its own news-reel, with resulting competition, lack of adequate playing time for our news-reel, and rapidly lessening receipts.

In addition, the universal demand for talking pictures and resulting complications, such as differences of language, have greatly increased the cost of making pictures, and therefore, the amount of working capital required by picture companies. The outstanding indebtedness of Pathé, amounting to $7,301,503, as shown by the last annual statement of December 28, 1929, is disproportionately large compared with stock capitalization, and makes it extremely difficult for Pathé to borrow the money which it must have to produce pictures.

For all these reasons the Board of Directors is convinced that the carrying out of the agreement with R-K-O is much more advantageous than would be an attempt to continue in business under the present conditions. . . . Your Directors are convinced that the transaction will relieve Pathé from its difficult position as an independent producer, and will leave it with a 49% interest in DuPont-Pathé Film Manufacturing Company, which should grow with the industry, but which is not sensitive to the difficulties peculiar to Pathé, or seriously affected by the rise and fall of any of the production and exhibition units. Your Directors, therefore, urge you to take immediate advantage of the present opportunity.[113]

Anticipating no difficulties with ratification of the sale at a Pathé stockholders' meeting called for January 6, 1931, Kennedy wrote a letter to "All Home Office Employees" on December 9, 1930:

As you have learned from the papers in the last few days, Pathé has entered into a contract, whereby R-K-O will likely take over our picture producing and distributing business, in something like two months from the present. It is R-K-O's plan and desire to continue Pathé as a separate unit, and they have already made official announcement to that effect.

They will therefore need the services of our entire present staff, insofar as they find the staff efficient. If you are doing your work intelligently and faithfully, you need have no concern as to the day they take over the reins of management.

You may be sure that I am appreciative of your efforts.

Joseph P. Kennedy[114]

As it turned out, some of Pathé's investors were convinced that the terms of the sale were designed to enrich the board of directors at the expense of the shareholders. A group of stockholders filed suit to stop the sale, stating that the purchase price was less than one-half of what Pathé was worth; that Pathé's board, many of whom also sat on RKO's board, had fraudulently understated Pathé's earnings to induce stockholders to agree to the sale; and that RKO was, in effect, a weak company buying out its stronger competition.[115] The *New York Times* described the January 6, 1931, stockholder conclave as "a boisterous meeting, at which heavily armed private detectives were unable to preserve order, although they did succeed in preventing physical violence." Joseph Kennedy was greeted with epithets when he entered and jeers when he spoke. Nevertheless, stockholders approved the sale by a vote of 668,545 to 9,002.[116] The outvoted stockholders asked the U.S. Justice Department to investigate the merger as a violation of the Sherman Antitrust Act and briefly obtained a court order to stop the transfer of Pathé assets to RKO. By the end of January the regulators were satisfied, and the sale went through.[117]

Out in Culver City, E. B. Derr and Charles Sullivan awaited word on whether or not they would be included in the new RKO-Pathé combine. The already strained relationship between Kennedy and Derr had completely snapped in the fall, when Kennedy ordered Derr to suspend operations due to the impending RKO deal. Derr's reply, as a member of Pathé's board of directors, was to demand a meeting so that the full board could vote on whether or not to continue production.[118] When a reporter asked for his feelings about the RKO takeover, Derr responded with the peculiar detachment of a somnambulist: "New alignments and readjustments have solidified the entire business structure, while production has kept pace with the new demands made by the advent of sound and the resultant enhanced discrimination of the entertainment public."[119] By the end of January 1931 Derr and Sullivan were out of Culver City, replaced by Lee Marcus. The pair went to work briefly for Howard Hughes' Caddo Company,[120] and Derr would reemerge in 1936 as a producer of low-budget features, a livelihood he would pursue until he left the industry in 1943.

Despite its humble origins as the lowly FBO, RKO's alignment with the mighty RCA and RCA's two subsidiary national radio networks of the National Broadcasting Company, NBC Red and NBC Blue, emboldened RKO to proclaim itself in trade-paper ads as the new "titan" of the film industry. Writing in the *Motion Picture Herald* not long after the takeover of Pathé, Terry Ramsaye gave an elegiac account of his employer's last hours as a film production company:

> Twenty-six years have passed since Pathé brought a snappy red rooster over from France to scratch and peck and crow in the American film garden. The beginning was that summer day in 1905 when a blond and belligerent Frenchman, Mr. J. A. Berst, dropped a suitcase full of films on the floor of a tiny office looking out on Madison Square and declared Pathé Frères in business in the United States. But the end came in the night, just as unostentatiously, but, in its way, dramatically, with the brittle drama of anti-climax. A great, famous and once powerful corporation arrived at a fadeout between midnight and dawn.[121]

As Pathé executives waited in the company's New York City office for the final documents to be delivered, "[o]ver at RKO a phalanx of lawyers, barristers and solicitors was dictating, reading and revising the astonishingly big array of contracts, leases and releases that pertain to taking a mess of movie assets out of one pocket and putting them into another."[122] When the contracts finally arrived,

> there were plenty of papers, too many lawyers and not enough chairs. There were lawyers for two film concerns, assorted banking houses and sundry related concerns. . . . Gentlemen ordinarily immaculately ordered in the manner of movieland offices had wilted collars and tousled hair. A tough bird to get on paper, that rooster. There were more and more documents. The end was near. At 2:05 A.M. Eastern Standard Time the RKO-Pathé deal had become a fact—as of midnight. So we come to the end of the lovely story of how the great big titan caught the little red rooster. It was the dawn of a new day and they lived happily ever after. Pax vobiscum.[123]

CHAPTER SEVEN

THE BELLIGERENT GALLIC GAMECOCK

1931–PRESENT

But the bird wasn't quite cooked yet. Pathé soldiered on in two guises: RKO Pathé and the Pathé Exchange, Inc.,[1] which continued to own those Pathé assets that RKO (Radio-Keith-Orpheum) did not purchase. As the mascot of the newly created RKO Pathé, "the little red rooster" became in trade advertisements "the old fightin' cock," a phrase that clearly sought to summon up the comfortable familiarity of a scrappy independent survivor in an industry dominated by a handful of major companies. The RKO Pathé logo that preceded the opening title sequences of the company's features was surely one of the oddest in film history. RKO's Radio Pictures logo of a radio transmitting tower sitting atop planet Earth, spreading its signals throughout the universe was modified by removing the radio tower and replacing it with Pathé's crowing cock. The image of a gargantuan rooster perched atop the globe was made even stranger by the fact that while the Earth turned, the bird supposedly standing on top of it remained stationary.

RKO did attempt to make good on its pledge to operate RKO Pathé as a semi-autonomous company, at least for the short term. Only three of the Pathé Exchange's completed-but-not-released features were included in the sale to RKO: *Sin Takes a Holiday*, *The Painted Desert*, and *Beyond Victory*.[2] The rest remained the property of the Pathé Exchange, to be distributed theatrically by RKO Pathé. Box-office receipts on these films went to the Pathé Exchange after RKO Pathé had deducted a discounted distribution fee. Only getting three Pathé Exchange features outright left the new firm with a critical shortage of features to sell to theaters, resulting in a serious cash-flow problem from the outset. In June 1931 RKO Pathé found itself having to borrow $6 million from the Chemical National Bank "to be applied to new production and immediate cash requirements."[3]

RKO Pathé's money woes were compounded by the fact that its parent company was having major financial difficulties of its own. Despite the fact that it outwardly maintained its image as a "depression-proof" business, the film industry had felt the effects of the stock-market crash of October 1929 almost immediately, with a slump in the value of studio stocks in late 1929 and a downturn in theater attendance in spring 1930.[4] By 1933 all of the studios would feel the crushing weight of the Great Depression. RKO became the first of the major studios to go into receivership, in January 1933, followed shortly thereafter by Paramount and Fox. As a newcomer to the field, RKO had already been on shaky financial ground before the crash. The 1930 box-office drop, coupled with what proved to be an ill-timed binge of theater acquisition in an attempt to achieve parity with the established major studios, was disastrous for the company's bottom line.[5] And it soon became apparent that its acquisition of Pathé Exchange assets was a serious blunder.

Cari Beauchamp asserts that in order to make Pathé look profitable, Joseph Kennedy had made it appear that most of the monetary losses had occurred before he got there and that they stopped when he arrived: "Film properties were moved between Pathé Sound Pictures, Inc. and Pathé Exchange, Inc. and money was shifted among Bank of America, Bancamerica-Blair, and Jeremiah Milbank so that it was close to impossible for an outsider to get a real picture. . . . The fact was that Pathé had no cash reserves, nothing to mortgage, and a negative earnings record." The company was "in the red by $1 million for the first three quarters of 1930."[6] In a more contemporaneous account of Pathé's last years, 1934's *Other People's Money*, John Flynn notes that "[b]eginning with Kennedy, sales increased very little, but costs rose very rapidly. In the three years before the coming of the wizard, the company's sales exceeded costs every year. . . . Under his brilliant management the common stock ceased to earn anything and the earnings for preferred stock were more than cut in half."[7]

In 1933, as part of an investigation into the motion-picture industry, New York congressman William I. Sirovich singled out the RKO–Pathé Exchange deal as a prime example of the type of backroom dealing that was all too common in Hollywood. As related by Betty Lasky in her history *RKO: The Biggest Little Major of Them All*, "Sirovich stated that 'a group was loaded down with a very substantial block' of Pathé stock quoted at about thirty dollars. 'As soon as the merger was announced, this inside group pushed Pathé up to about eighty dollars' and 'unloaded [it] on the public, making millions of dollars. The purchase [by RKO] at levels not warranted by any values possessed by Pathé' ('the only property RKO obtained that it did not have was a news-reel service,' he said) 'practically emptied the RKO treasury.'" Sirovich's investigation was ultimately halted by Franklin D. Roosevelt at the request of his friend Joseph P. Kennedy.[8]

For the second half of the 1930–31 season and all of the 1931–32 season, the RKO Pathé feature-release schedule continued to headline actors who had been the stars of the Pathé Exchange roster: Constance Bennett, Helen Twelvetrees, Ann Harding, William Boyd, Eddie Quillan, Robert Armstrong, and James Gleason. During the 1931–32 season these features were supplemented by something of a throwback to Pathé's 1920s heritage: a series of one-hour westerns aimed at the children's matinee and rural markets. The westerns starred George Duryea, the actor who had assumed the stage name Tom Keene immediately following his starring role in Pathé's bizarre and disastrous serial-turned-feature *Pardon My Gun*.

RKO Pathé's short-film schedule largely followed the pattern set by the Pathé Exchange. The newsreels maintained their twice-weekly release schedule, but initial assumptions that Terry Ramsaye would stay on in some capacity were dashed when he accepted the job as editor of the *Motion Picture Herald*. Ramsaye's personal stamp had been so strong on the *Pathé Review* that management decided to discontinue the reel upon his departure.

What had come to be marketed as "the Van Beuren group," the one-reel short subjects produced by Amadee J. Van Beuren's studio, mostly continued as before. These included the popular *Aesop's Fables* cartoons, which lost their creative leader in 1930 when Paul Terry left to set up his own Terrytoons studio and the Grantland Rice Sportlights. The two-reelers continued to roll out of the Comedy Village, including one series produced by the Hollywood Masquers Club. John Flinn and Fred Lalley, who had been placed in charge of West Coast short-film production not long after the Manhattan Studios fire, were let go by RKO Pathé when their contracts expired. The Pathé Exchange (not RKO Pathé) continued to pay for the pair's legal defense when the criminal trial started in New York City.[9]

Even the venerable *Pathé News* became an additional burden to the nascent RKO Pathé. The advent of sound required newsreel trucks that were outfitted with recording equipment, something that the Pathé Exchange was unable to afford. The Pathé Exchange arranged to rent six trucks from Radio Corporation of America (RCA) Photophone, but it remained at a competitive disadvantage to its better-financed competition who had fleets of as many as forty sound trucks. On top of that, for much of the silent era *Pathé News* had been without competition that was backed by the major studios and their theater chains. Around the time that sound came in, both Paramount and Metro-Goldwyn-Mayer (MGM) started their own newsreels, and the addition of sound to the Fox newsreel in 1927 made it much more of a competitive threat than it had been as a silent reel. The theatrical bookings for *Pathé News* began to dry up.[10]

In late October 1931 rumors of what had likely been inevitable from the start began to swirl. By November it was confirmed: having been green-lighted by the Justice Department's antitrust enforcers, RKO Pathé was to be folded into RKO Radio.[11] The production executive who was brought in to facilitate the merger was David O. Selznick.[12] All feature-film production was moved to RKO's Hollywood studios, the former Film Booking Offices of America (FBO) lot, in December 1931, leaving the Comedy Village and independent producers renting space as the only occupants of the Culver City studio.[13] Since contracts with exhibitors for the 1931–32 movie season had already been completed by the time of the merger, RKO was obliged to release films under both the Radio and Pathé "brands" through the summer of 1932.

By February 1932 the trade advertising for the two product lines had been combined with one slogan: "A new day dawns! RKO Radio-Pathé leaps to attack."[14] One of the last RKO Pathé films from the summer of 1932 was *What Price Hollywood?* with Constance Bennett and Lowell Sherman. Based on an original story by Adela Rogers St. Johns, it served as the unofficial basis for David O. Selznick's *A Star Is Born* (1937) and its two remakes. One interesting project that was intended to mark the Pathé brand's return to the serial form wasn't quite completed in time to be an RKO Pathé release. *The Last Frontier*, starring Lon Chaney Jr., debuted in September 1932 as RKO Radio's one and only ever serial.

Once again Terry Ramsaye wrote an obituary for his old mascot: "By official announcement from Joseph I. Schnitzer the Pathé rooster trademark passes from the screen with the passing of the RKO Pathé trademark in the combination under the Radio banner for all dramatic product. However, the belligerent Gallic gamecock, selected as an emblem by Mr. Charles Pathé in Paris more than a quarter of a century ago and the oldest surviving trademark if the industry, will, on the word of Mr. Courtland Smith, continue on Pathé News, which has presented the doughty bird since 1910."[15]

Indeed, the rooster would live on as the herald of the newsreel, and for far longer than Ramsaye could have possibly imagined. The crowing cock would introduce the *RKO-Pathé News* until 1947, when the cash-strapped RKO sold the newsreel division to Warner Brothers.[16] Of the major studios Warner Brothers alone had never produced or distributed a newsreel. During the

Second World War, when newsreels peaked in popularity, Warner Brothers briefly considered launching one but then decided that the start-up costs and logistics were too great. Now, and probably at the worst possible time with television just around the corner, the *Warner Pathé News* made its debut. RKO retained the right to use the Pathé name for productions other than newsreels. It continued to make industrial and theatrical short films under the RKO Pathé banner, including *RKO Pathé Sportscopes*, *RKO Pathé Screenliners*, the *This Is America* documentary series, and even a 1953 Technicolor documentary feature-length picture, *Below the Sahara*. Director Stanley Kubrick made his first two films, *The Flying Padre* (*RKO Pathé Screenliner*, 1951) and *The Day of the Fight* (*This Is America*, 1951), for RKO Pathé. RKO used the Pathé brand name until its own demise as a film production company in 1957. As a result, for nearly a decade starting in 1947, no less than three separate entities used the Pathé name: Pathé Industries (the successor to the Pathé Exchange), *Warner Pathé News*, and RKO Pathé.

The economics of the motion-picture industry shifted radically from the late-1940s into the 1950s. The 1948 Consent Decree not only stripped the studios of their theater chains, it mandated that all films had to be sold to theaters individually and not in groups. This not only affected the way feature films were sold, it also meant that theaters could not be forced to accept short films as part of a package with features. At the same time, the rise of television and the shift of the middle-class population to the suburbs and away from the urban centers that housed most movie theaters caused a business downturn of epic proportions. Exhibitors began to reevaluate the need for an entire program that presented a prologue of short films before the featured attraction. Short films had already been squeezed off many screens due to the rise of double features and the resultant ballooning of program lengths. Now they faced complete extinction.

On top of these factors, the newsreel faced an additional problem with the advent of television. With few exceptions, some of which were mentioned earlier in this work, newsreels were not noteworthy for the timeliness of their news. Metropolitan newspapers issued multiple editions over the course of a normal day, updating the news with each printing. In the case of urgent news they would even print an "extra" edition. The beginning of commercial radio broadcasting in the United States in the 1920s meant that news could be delivered with the speed of light. But the one thing that newsreels could do that their two competitors could not was to present moving images, accompanied after 1927 by sound. Newsreels provided most Americans with their only opportunity to see *and* hear the president of the United States delivering a speech, or to witness a Second World War battle that may have involved their own sons. Television eliminated the newsreel's unique niche. It didn't matter that the presentation of news on television in the 1950s suffered mightily due to the limitations of the available technology, it was still more immediate than newsreels, it presented the same type of material, and it was free. Given these challenges, it is a wonder that the major newsreels held out as long as they did. Universal Pictures was the last to throw in the towel in 1967. The *Warner Pathé News*, on the other hand, was one of the first to go.

The death knell for the newsreel sounded in 1956. This time Terry Ramsaye wasn't available to write the obituary. He had passed away two years earlier. In his absence, an anonymous United Press reporter did the honors, reporting that "[t]he crowing rooster of Warner Pathé News will stop crowing Aug. 23, when the pioneer newsreel service will discontinue."[17] The story went on to say that approximately twenty-five million feet of Pathé newsreel footage dating to 1898 would be sold to an investor group headed by Serge Semenenko, senior vice president of the First National Bank of Boston.

The new ownership retained the name "Pathé News, Inc." but changed the focus. No longer a news-gathering organization, the company turned to the licensing of material from its library for use in documentaries. It also produced its own "new" films culled from its archive. Perhaps the best known was "Milestones of the Century," a series of three-minute made-for-television "filler" films narrated by Ed Herlihy, the announcing voice of newsreels, television programs, and Kraft cheese commercials. The new Pathé News also edited its old material into short educational historical films designed for classrooms.[18]

In 1971 the oldest newsreel company in existence embarked on an encounter with cutting-edge technology. It sold access to its entire archive, including "Milestones of the Century," to the Videorecord Corporation of America. Videorecord, in turn, was to distribute the Pathé material on the cartridge television home-video format. A *Billboard* article extolled Videorecord's altruistic project: "In transferring the Pathé programming to the cartridge TV format, the Videorecord Corp. feels it is performing a public service by preserving a documentary and nostalgic record of the 20th century in the new medium."[19] Cartridge television would make its commercial debut in 1972 and go bankrupt in 1973, doomed by expensive and unreliable machines and tapes. Undeterred, Pathé News stuck a deal later in the 1970s with Magnetic Video for distribution of "Milestones of the Century" on VHS (Video Home System) and Betamax videotape.[20] Pathé News, Inc., remained in business into the new millennium, finally closing up shop in June 2011. Its licensees still distribute material from the Pathé News archive.

THE OTHER PATHÉ

The Pathé Exchange, Inc., wobbled into 1931 largely as a holding company for the assets RKO did not want, facing a future that was uncertain at best. Its primary holdings were the 49 percent interest in the DuPont-Pathé Film Manufacturing Corporation (which would drop "Pathé" from its name in the summer of 1931),[21] the film processing and printing laboratory at Bound Brook, ownership of all but three of the Pathé Exchange–produced features (and box-office receipts from RKO for those that were still in theatrical distribution), ownership of the State Theatre in Denver, Colorado,[22] Pathé International Corporation (four foreign distribution branches that were not included in the sale), and stock and continuing payments from RKO for the purchase of the Pathé Exchange's production and distribution assets.[23] The Pathé Exchange also still owned its nontheatrical division, Pathé Films, Inc., but as part of its agreement with RKO not to use the name "Pathé" in the motion-picture field, that subsidiary was renamed "Pathegrams, Inc."[24] Pathé's ventures in the nontheatrical market will be discussed later.

It was Joseph Kennedy's intention to sell off the remaining assets and liquidate the company entirely.[25] However, at the end of April 1931 Kennedy resigned as Pathé Exchange chairman of the board and gave up his seat as a director of the company. Stuart Webb replaced Kennedy, and Webb apparently wanted to keep the company going.[26] In the short term, the fortunes of the Pathé Exchange improved through the mid-1930s.[27] In 1935 the company reorganized and rebranded itself from the Pathé Exchange, Inc., to the Pathé Film Corporation.[28] It sold a block of its DuPont stock, bringing its stake in the DuPont Film Manufacturing Company down to 35 percent.[29] It also sold practically all of the features and shorts that it had retained after the RKO deal. Columbia Pictures bought the library for $44,000, not with the intent of reissuing the old films but rather with the idea of remaking them.[30] *The Awful Truth* (1937) and *Holiday* (1938), both starring Cary Grant, were among the Columbia remakes that were far more memorable than the Pathé Exchange originals.

Undoubtedly the most significant event for the Pathé Film Corporation in the mid-1930s was the 1936 announcement that its five-year hiatus from filmmaking, required as a term of the RKO deal, was up and that it was interested in reentering the production field.[31] Then it bought an 8 percent interest in the newly formed Grand National Films.[32]

Grand National[33] had started life modestly enough in the spring of 1936 as a distributor of mostly low-budget independent films. It scored a major and unexpected coup just one month after Pathé Film Corporation's June stock purchase, when the popular but volatile star James Cagney walked off the Warner Brothers lot and signed a deal with Grand National. At around the same time, Grand National began the process of acquiring the Santa Monica Boulevard studio of the faltering Educational Pictures.[34]

However, Cagney proved to be more of a liability than an asset. His first Grand National film, *Great Guy* (1937), turned out well enough, but his second ruined the company. According to Ted Okuda, *Something to Sing About* (1937) went over budget, costing nearly $1 million before it was finished, and was a critical and commercial failure. Cagney, perhaps chastened by his experience working for a poverty-row studio, reached an accommodation with Warner Brothers and resumed his career there. Grand National was never able to dig its way back out of the money pit dug by *Something to Sing About*.[35] It managed to stagger on for two more years, releasing a diet mostly consisting of low-budget westerns and action films, supplemented by imports from Great Britain. When Grand National and its "movables" were auctioned off at the end of February 1940, the *Los Angeles Times* actually referred to the studio as having been founded four years earlier "as an outgrowth of Pathé."[36]

In the meantime there had been movement in the Pathé Film Corporation's film processing business. In early 1938 the Bound Brook facility suffered a massive fire in two of its film vaults, completely destroying one of the twenty buildings at the site and heavily damaging two others. Lost in the blaze was much of the collection of fiction features and shorts that had been purchased by Columbia in 1935. As one silver lining the Bound Brook processing laboratory itself escaped unscathed. In late 1939 the Pathé Film Corporation purchased a Los Angeles processing lab and set up a new subsidiary, Pathé Laboratories, Inc., of California to operate it.[37]

In 1939 and 1940 the Pathé Film Corporation once again acted primarily as a holding company, with majority ownership of the East Coast and West Coast processing labs, the nontheatrical division, and the State Theatre. During that period it attracted the attention of a financier and industrialist named Robert R. Young.

THE OTHER ROBERT YOUNG

Robert Ralph Young, no relation to the Robert Young of motion-picture and television acting fame, was the son of a cattleman, banker, and hotel proprietor in the Texas Panhandle. He amassed a fortune during the 1930s buying apparently worthless stock and turning it around. In 1937, after accumulating "another $4 million or $5 million," Young acquired control of the

Alleghany Corporation, a holding company that held controlling interests in the Chesapeake & Ohio, the Pere Marquette, and the Nickel Plate Railroads, and that had additional smaller interests in other railroads and industries.[38]

In 1940, and as an independent venture completely outside of the Alleghany Corporation, Robert Young bought a controlling interest in the Pathé Film Corporation. He installed his older brother, Kenneth, as president, and the two set about a reorganization of the company. To that end, the Young brothers sold the Pathé Film Corporation's remaining stake in the DuPont Film Manufacturing Company to DuPont.[39] They then dissolved the Pathé Film Corporation but retained the laboratory operations in both New Jersey and California as well as Pathé's nontheatrical division and the State Theatre.[40] Next on the agenda was to increase the revenues of those processing laboratories. And that led the Pathé Laboratories, Inc., of California directly to the Producers Releasing Corporation.

The Producers Releasing Corporation, commonly known as PRC, had begun life in early 1939 as Producers Distributing Corporation, an attempt to create a national distribution system for low-budget independent films. The company quickly got into financial difficulties and was reorganized as PRC in early 1940.[41] Money problems continued, though, until Pathé Laboratories of California, began advancing production funding to PRC's operation in late 1940. In exchange, PRC sent all of its processing and printing jobs to the Pathé lab.[42] The relationship between the two companies developed rapidly from that point. In January 1942 Pathé Laboratories of California bought a 68 percent controlling interest in PRC.[43] Only one month later Pathé Laboratories owned PRC outright.[44]

The Pathé Laboratories management was enthusiastic about PRC's potential. The major studios had recently signed a consent decree, a precursor to the draconian decree of 1948. The 1941 decree altered, but did not eliminate, block-booking practices in a way that promised to open up the marketing and distribution of motion pictures and put independents on more equal footing with the majors. It was a promise that went largely unfulfilled. The United States would soon be actively involved in the Second World War; enforcing antitrust laws against film studios would not be a top priority in the early 1940s.

In the short term, though, the business conditions for PRC seemed rosy. The company reported sales that were 100 percent better than the year before and that its films were being seen in 50 percent more theaters than previously. Because of this, PRC announced that it would increase its budgets on the remaining product of the 1941–42 season as well as for the entire product line for 1942–43.[45] For the 1942 season Pathé Laboratories even considered changing PRC's name to some iteration of "Pathé" but realized that would violate the terms of the RKO sale.[46] PRC remained PRC, although the copyright notices on some PRC releases from the late 1940s were taken out in the name of Pathé Industries.

Even after the takeover by Pathé Laboratories, PRC's product was being produced by independent producers, and it was being distributed by independent film exchanges that acted as PRC franchise holders in different regions of the United States. While they cheered the consent decree that promised to take power away from the vertically integrated studios, the Pathé Laboratories management very much wanted to make PRC itself into a vertically integrated studio. They decided first on making more of the PRC product in-house. In the summer of 1943 PRC borrowed $1 million to purchase some of the franchise exchanges and to increase film budgets on its 1943–44 features.[47]

To facilitate in-house feature production, PRC bought the Fine Arts Studio on Sunset Boulevard in Hollywood in August 1943, the same facility that had hosted some of the Pathé Exchange's serial production in the 1920s.[48] At the Fine Arts Studio PRC made its first "directly produced" feature, *Jive Junction* (1943), directed by PRC's resident auteur Edgar G. Ulmer and starring former child-star Dickie Moore.[49]

As part of its product announcement for the 1944–45 season, PRC was able to boast that one of its films of the current season, an independently produced musical drama titled *Men on Her Mind* (1944), had actually been played as the "B" picture in a double-feature bill at the Carthay Circle Theatre, the Grauman's Chinese Theatre, and both the Loews State and Loews Uptown theaters in Los Angeles. Normally having a film as the lesser half of a double feature was not cause for celebration, but in this case it represented one of the first times a PRC picture was played at all in some of the movie capital's most prestigious venues.[50] By the following year PRC was able to boast that a full 70 percent of its release schedule would be made up of in-house productions and that several of the films would be in color. Technicolor was out of PRC's price range, so it had to settle for the inferior Cinecolor process. The season also brought two of PRC's most memorable features: *The Mask of Diijon* (1946), starring the always interesting Erich von Stroheim, and Edgar Ulmer's film noir opus *Detour* (1945).[51]

Beyond the expansion in internal production during the mid-1940s, Pathé Industries also acquired no less than two companies that sold and rented films to the nontheatrical and home-movie markets: Pictorial Films and Official Films.[52] Earlier incarnations of Pathé had dipped a toe in that stream before.

MOVIES FOR THE HOME

Virtually from the beginning of the cinema, various inventors and entrepreneurs saw a market for films in educational institutions as well as for entertainment and preserving family history in home settings. There were at least three glaring problems with using standard 35-millimeter film in these venues. First and foremost, the nitrate film stock used by the professional industry until the early 1950s was as flammable as gasoline—not something that was safe in the hands of untrained projectionists. Nonflammable "safety film" was available early on, but it lacked the durability and optical quality of nitrate film, so it was not embraced by the professional motion-picture industry. While it would have been possible to sell 35-millimeter "safety" prints to the amateur market, there was a fear that if the public had easy access to 35-millimeter projectors, it would follow that nitrate prints would find their way into homes and schools. As it was, some 35-millimeter projectors were sold directly to the public. These were usually fully enclosed to limit, or at least delay, the effects of a fire. But there were fires. And there were fatalities. The most tragic of these occurred at children's parties where the films were shown for entertainment. In 1936 three children were killed and four others burned while a film was being shown at a party in Hattiesburg, Mississippi. The projectionist in this case apparently failed to notice that the take-up reel of the projector was not functioning properly, and the film was simply coiling up on the floor around the base of the projector where the children were sitting. An adult apparently sitting with the children inadvertently brushed the pile of film with a lit cigarette, sparking the blaze.[53]

Thus, the goal of most designers of home-cinema film and equipment was to produce a system that would run nonflammable safety film in a narrower width than 35 millimeters. These small-gauge systems made the purchase and production of films more affordable, since they consumed less bulk film stock than 35-millimeter gauge. In this, amateur-film gauges always had to balance two contradictory truths. The narrower the film, the less expensive it was, but also the lower in quality. As film stocks improved, with photographic quality becoming ever sharper, it became possible to develop narrower and cheaper film formats that still delivered acceptable quality for the amateur.

Many inventors, including Thomas Edison, worked on the problem of home cinema, and they came up with wildly divergent concepts. Pathé Frères introduced its first of several entrants in the home-movie race in 1912 in the form of the 28-millimeter Pathéscope Home Cinematograph, more commonly known as the Pathé KOK. An interesting feature of the early KOK machines was that the hand crank that advanced the film through the projector also turned a dynamo that powered the projection lamp, so the machine could be used in situations where no electric current was available. Since the 28-millimeter safety film was not much narrower than conventional 35-millimeter film, the image quality was quite good. By 1918 over ten thousand projectors had been sold worldwide, and an estimated twenty-five million feet of positive film had been printed, including the reedited European version of *The Perils of Pauline* from which all current copies derive.[54]

In the United States, most Pathéscope 28-millimeter films were available on a per-reel rental basis or through an annual subscription fee that gave the subscriber access to a certain number of reels per week.[55] The 1918 *Descriptive Catalogue of Pathéscope Films* available from Pathéscope of America contains a preponderance of films from Pathé Frères as might be expected, but it also includes American productions from Biograph, Vitagraph, Essanay, and Kalem. Two of Charlie Chaplin's three-year-old Essanay comedies, *A Jitney Elopement* and *In the Park*, are listed, along with a number of D. W. Griffith's Biograph productions including *The Battle at Elderbush Gulch* (1913). All fourteen chapters of the Pearl White Pathé serial *The Exploits of Elaine* (1914) are listed, but, curiously, the more famous *Perils of Pauline* is represented by only two chapters (*Thru Air and Fire* and *The Goddess of the Golden West*). One of the more intriguing titles is the 1914 Vitagraph short *Lincoln the Lover*, with Ralph Ince portraying Honest Abe.

The early success of 28-millimeter film dissipated fairly rapidly in the United States. In *Resurrecting the Lost History of 28mm Film in North America*, Anke Mebold and Charles Tepperman analyze the 28-millimeter format's decline in the 1920s. A major contributing factor was Kodak's introduction of the lower-cost 16-millimeter amateur format in 1923. The format was less expensive partially due to the smaller film size, and the cameras and projectors were certainly smaller than 28-millimeter equipment, but, additionally, Kodak dominated the amateur photographic marketplace in the United States. Willard Cook, a strong promoter of 28-millimeter format who had overseen the Pathéscope of America library, was employed to set up the new Kodascope 16-millimeter rental-library system.[56]

Following the failure of its 28-millimeter format, French Pathé's next attempt at creating a new nontheatrical film standard was as clever as it was unique, and it enjoyed a considerably longer life span than its predecessor. Introduced in 1922, the system used film that was 9.5 millimeters wide and sported sprocket holes that ran down the center of the film in the black line that separated one frame from the next.[57] This arrangement of perforations permitted the picture to take up the entire width of the film, rather than having the "waste" associated with 35 millimeters and 28 millimeters (and later 16 millimeters) that occurred when the perforations took up space on either side of the image. In this manner, 9.5 millimeters was able to enjoy the economy of a gauge that was narrower than 16 millimeters but that had a frame that was approximately the same size and quality as 16 millimeters.

Another innovation born out of a desire to make the projectors for Pathé's new system as foolproof as possible for the amateur projectionist would prove a hindrance. Pathé-Baby projectors took nonflammable films that were not on open reels, but rather encased in "bobbins," small metal canisters with a relatively small slot through which the film could be accessed. The bobbin was clamped firmly on the top of the projector, and the film was fed into an opening on the hand-cranked projector. The projector took it from there, threading itself and feeding the film onto a permanently mounted internal take-up reel.

The problems with this system began with the fact that each reel had to be rewound before the next could be shown, and if the end of the film became detached from the bobbin and was consumed by the projector, it could be quite difficult to extract. A far more significant limitation, though, was that having the films encased in bobbins meant that the running time of each reel was permanently fixed. Each bobbin could only hold a certain amount of film and no more. The initial bobbins held only thirty feet of film, although larger bobbins were soon introduced that doubled that amount. Even so, and acknowledging the fact that the hand-cranked projectors could be operated at an infinite variety of speeds, depending on the stamina of the projectionist, the average running time for a sixty-foot bobbin was three and a half minutes. While this may have been sufficient for a home movie of a family's seaside vacation, it was woefully short for the distribution of professionally made films. A one-reel (35 millimeter) short comedy was characteristically compressed into one or two three-and-half-minute bobbins. Two-reel comedies were often edited down to three bobbins, and feature-length films might be condensed into four or more bobbins. *Nanook of the North* was released as a series of eight single-bobbin films. Pathé would eventually create a "super arm" attachment for the Pathé-Baby that would permit the use of open reels containing up to three hundred feet of film.

In an effort to make the most out of the limited bobbin capacity, Pathé developed an "auto stop" feature on the Pathé-Baby projectors. Whenever the projector got to a title card or any other material that would play well as a freeze-frame (e.g., an insert shot of a hand holding a letter), a notch on the side of the film caused the projector to stop and hold the image on the screen for a few seconds before proceeding. Auto stop was only possible because the Pathé-Baby projectors came with low-wattage lamps that could only produce an acceptably bright image in a completely darkened room and a screen size that did not exceed three feet by four feet. While a higher-wattage lamp would have generated more light, permitting a brighter and larger image, it would also have produced enough heat to melt the film during a prolonged freeze-frame.[58]

Pathé-Baby made its American debut in 1925, two years after Kodak had introduced its 16-millimeter system. An outfit consisting of camera, projector, and accessories could be purchased for $100. A thirty-foot magazine of unexposed film for home-movie photography cost $2, processing and return postage included. On average, Pathé-Baby versions of commercially made films cost $1.75 per bobbin.[59] The U.S. incarnation was sold under the trade name "Pathex," an abbreviation of Pathé Exchange, and the manager of Pathex was none other than J. A. Berst.

Speaking about the genesis of Pathex many years after the fact, Elmer Pearson claimed that the 9.5-millimeter system was forced upon the Pathé Exchange by Charles Pathé in a last-minute stipulation to the agreement that permitted the Pathé Exchange to use Pathé Frères' film-manufacturing patents. Pearson further related that the Pathé Exchange was coerced into taking thirty thousand Pathé-Baby projectors, which proved very difficult to sell.[60] As with some of his other recollections about the Pathé Exchange, Pearson's account doesn't entirely line up either chronologically or logically with the manner in which events unfolded.

The Pathé Exchange may well have been less than enthusiastic about the Pathé-Baby, for 16 millimeter and its potential for longer film lengths had been introduced in the United States two years before the arrival of 9.5 millimeter. Still, the Pathé Exchange appears to have made an honest effort to promote 9.5 millimeter, making a large cross section of their films, from Hal Roach comedies to Leo Maloney westerns, available in miniaturized form. The Pathex catalog even included one film each featuring Douglas Fairbanks, William S. Hart, and Lillian Gish.

Pathé's "super arm" attachment as well as an electric motor attachment that replaced the hand crank arrived in the United States too late to help Pathé-Baby sales. Pathex released only a handful of films in three-hundred-foot form, mostly complete versions of one- and two-reel comedies, before pulling the plug on the operation completely. In Europe and elsewhere, 9.5-millimeter film flourished as a viable home-movie format for decades.

At some point in the late 1920s, the Pathé Exchange began selling single-reel subjects in 16 millimeters under the trade name "Pathegrams."[61] The initial offering of Pathegrams appears to have mostly been educational (*Our Four-Footed Helpers [Ruminants]*), cultural (*The Little Indian Weaver*), and comedy (*Where's the Fire?*, a Hal Roach comedy starring Snub Pollard). They were not inexpensive. A four-hundred-foot 16-millimeter print of *The Little Indian Weaver* on amber-tinted DuPont-Pathé film stock retailed for $35.

As the Great Depression set in, Pathegrams' business fell off. Its output consisted largely of highly abridged versions of the Pathé Exchange's shorts and features of the 1920s, printed and distributed by the Allied Manufacturing Company of Chicago. Some of these Pathegrams ran as short as twenty-five feet in 16 millimeter, running approximately one minute at the "silent" projection speed of sixteen frames per second. Pathé Exchange's 1927 one-hour feature *Combat* was cut to the bone, issued to the home-movie market as a one-minute short titled *Fighting Men*. Some of the miniature Pathegrams were advertised as "colored films," using DuPont and Agfa tinted film stock in which the entire image was shaded in a single color like amber, sepia, and fuchsia.

In 1937 the Pathé Film Corporation sought to revive its flagging home-movie division. Gene Castle, a newsreel cameraman and editor as well as a producer and distributor of institutional films, had decided to try his hand at the growing 8-millimeter[62] and 16-millimeter home-movie market. Using his newsreel connections for source material, he edited three single-reel news films for exclusive sale to home-projector owners: *Hindenburg Explodes!*, *The Coronation of Their Majesties King George VI and Queen Elizabeth*, and *The Life of Edward—Britain's Ex-King*. He contracted with Pathé to use the "Pathegrams" name in connection with sales and promotion of the films, then used his existing institutional distribution channels to market them.[63] The films were released in both sound and silent versions in 16 millimeters, since 16-millimeter silent projectors vastly outnumbered sound projectors in 1937, a year in which 8 millimeters was a silent-only format.

The films were wildly successful, but Gene Castle took the proceeds and split with Pathegrams. He founded Castle Films, a highly successful home-movie company that survived well into the age of home video. For its part Pathegrams contracted with a retail distributor and issued a fourth release, a 1934 theatrical short titled *A Day with the Dionne Quintuplets*. Pathegrams then used its ongoing relationship with the RKO Pathé newsreel[64] to release monthly news-highlights reels in 8 millimeters.[65]

The 8-millimeter newsreel was not successful enough to be sustained, and the Pathegrams brand was allowed to die. However, in the early 1940s, no doubt spurred on by the success of Castle Films, Pathé Industries purchased control of both Official Films and Pictorial Films, the number two and number three home-movie distributors behind Castle Films. Official Films had begun distributing public-domain silent comedies with music and sound effects added; then it obtained the home-movie rights to many of Amadee J. Van Beuren's early 1930s cartoons. Additionally it produced and distributed a color travelogue of the 1939 New York World's Fair. Photographed and printed using Kodak's amateur color film stock, Kodachrome, a ten-minute 16-millimeter sound copy cost a whopping $100.[66] As was the case with Castle Films, Official offered most of its films in a one-hundred-foot version (approximately two and a half minutes at sound projection speed) and a four-hundred-foot version (approximately ten minutes at sound speed) in 16 millimeters; in 8 millimeters, there were corresponding fifty-foot and two-hundred-foot versions. Pictorial Films ran a 16-millimeter rental library under its own name and sold 8-millimeter and 16-millimeter one-reel subjects under the trade name "Pictoreels." The Pictoreels catalog was somewhat smaller than that of Official. The catalog listed black and white editions of several of Hugh Harman and Rudolf Ising's Technicolor Metro-Goldwyn-Mayer cartoons of the mid-to-late 1930s, a handful of George Pal "Puppetoons," a number of RKO musical shorts, and a healthy lineup of sports reels and nature studies, mostly from independent producers.[67]

Pathé Industries' home-movie empire of the mid-1940s was divided along the following lines. Official Films seems to have largely continued operating as it did before its acquisition by Pathé. It continued to offer the Van Beuren cartoons, several of Charlie Chaplin's Keystone comedies from 1914,[68] and the World's Fair film, augmented by news and sports films (some with sound, some silent) compiled in the manner of Gene Castle for exclusive sale to the home-movie market. Official Films also released a handful of two-reel films, mostly theatrical comedies that had been produced by Educational Pictures in the 1930s and musical shorts, as well as a large library of three-minute miniature musicals called "soundies" that had been produced for coin-operated movie "jukeboxes" found in bars, lounges, and amusement parks during the Second World War. Among Official Films' more offbeat releases were its "De Luxe Musical Classics" series, which featured the likes of Ignacy Paderwaski (culled from the 1937 British feature *Moonlight Sonata*) and Jose Iturbi, and the "Broadway Handicap Home Movie Racing Game," which supplied six three-minute race films, betting tickets, and play money. To play the game, a reel was drawn at random, the bets were placed with a player acting as "cashier," the projector was started, and, as described in the Official Films catalog, "you're off to the races. Results flash on screen at end of race—and the lucky winner collects the 'pay-off.'"[69] During Pathé Industries' ownership, Official began selling one-reel abridgments of entertainment feature-length pictures.

Pathé Industries' impact on Pictorial Films was much greater. As it had done with Official, Pathé Industries pushed Pictoreels to begin releasing abridgements of dramatic features. The only problem was that the pool of entertainment films available to Official, Pictorial, and Pictoreels was drawn almost exclusively from PRC, and, despite the occasional *Bluebeard* or *Detour* (both of which could be rented from Pictorial), PRC's films were among the least desirable in all of Hollywood.[70]

Ignoring the poor quality of the product, some in Pathé Industries' management expressed dismay at the lackluster performance of the home-movie divisions. Robert Benjamin, Pathé Industries' general counsel and the man who would soon purchase and revitalize United Artists with his business partner Arthur Krim, reported to top management that he had received calls expressing a need for an investigation of Pictorial Films. He noted that Castle Films demonstrated that there was a potentially lucrative market but that Pictorial was underperforming.[71]

Part of Pictoreels' problems in the late 1940s may have been the result of marketing budgets that were too thin. Both 16-millimeter and 8-millimeter home-movie prints were characteristically displayed in department stores and camera stores on showcase racks. Since the product itself, the film, could not be seen without a projector, the home-movie companies put their films in elaborate and colorful boxes to promote sales in much the way movie posters enticed patrons into theaters. Castle Films always had the most elaborate box art. In fact some film collectors today prize their Castle Films as much for the artwork as for the films themselves. Official and Pictoreel boxes were never as elaborate as Castle boxes, but they did the job. However, if one 1947 Pictoreel box is typical of most from the Pathé Industries period, Pictoreel's films were going to have to be purchased on the merits of the contents alone. The box in question goes with a 1947 one-reel, silent 8-millimeter abridgement of a 1945 Buster Crabbe PRC western titled *Fighting Bill Carson*. The film is in a blank white box, which has the legend "it's a Pictoreel" written in fairly small letters on one side only. The film's title is stamped on one end of the box, but there is no mention of the star. It would have taken someone with foreknowledge of the film to want to buy it, something of a long shot considering this was a "B" western geared primarily to children's Saturday matinees. In short, the packaging is cheap and shabby, and it has every appearance of being an economy measure imposed by someone with no idea of how to market the product.

Pathé Industries apparently spun Official Films off around 1950. Official Films then became a major early syndicator of filmed television programming, offering local U.S. stations a wide array of subjects ranging from 1920s-era silent Felix the Cat cartoons (with music and sound effects added) to the British-produced Richard Greene television series *The Adventures of Robin Hood*. Pictorial Films and Pictoreels remained with Pathé Industries, dying a quiet death in the 1950s.

EAGLE-LION

Nineteen forty-five was a banner year for Pathé Industries. Its headquarters office in New York City relocated to 105 East 106th Street, along with the main offices of Pathé Labs, Pictorial Films, and Pathé's sibling, *RKO Pathé News*. Additionally, an adjacent building was converted for use as Pathé's New York City film processing lab, a move that would soon render the Bound Brook plant obsolete.[72]

Also in 1945 Robert R. Young merged two more nonfilmmaking subsidiaries into Pathé Industries: Commonwealth Securities and V. D. Anderson, the latter being a manufacturer of presses to extract oil from seeds and meat by-products.[73] Pathé Industries' holdings were becoming so diversified that one 1949 board of directors meeting followed a discussion of film studio management with an examination of a new type of air brake for possible use on Young's railroads.[74] The *Wall Street Journal* praised the "spectacular performance of Pathé Industries," noting that its August 1945 stock value was $70 per share, up from $6 per share a year earlier.[75]

Perhaps the most significant development of 1945, though, was Pathé Industries' involvement with British producer J. Arthur Rank and the creation of Eagle-Lion. Tired of his films receiving what he considered second-rate distribution in the United States, Rank's idea was to set up a company to handle his British-made films as well as some from American independents who would be financed by Rank. As part of the deal, Rank would distribute the American productions in the United Kingdom through his existing channels there.[76]

Eagle-Lion Films, it was announced, would release a total of twenty features for the 1946–47 movie season, ten from Rank and ten from Pathé Industries, to be distributed throughout the United States and Central and South America by PRC and throughout the rest of the world by Rank.[77] Kenneth Young took pains to emphasize to the press that PRC was not being replaced by Eagle-Lion, but, rather, that each entity would have its own slate of films.[78]

Eagle-Lion's releases were a wildly divergent lot, with British imports such as the Ealing Studios comedy *Passport to Pimlico* (1949) and Michael Powell and Emeric Pressburger's *The Red Shoes* (1948) mixing it up with the likes of Anthony Mann's gritty American films noir *T-Men* (1947) and *Raw Deal* (1948). However, even with an intriguing lineup that included a few genuinely prestigious productions, Eagle-Lion was to have a fairly short life. On the production side, already thin budgets were further stretched by the skyrocketing labor costs in Hollywood following the Second World War. A series of strikes beginning in 1945 had resulted in a 25 percent wage increase for most union employees.[79]

Beyond that, even as it was in the process of being stripped of its theater chains because of its oligopolistic tendencies, the Hollywood studio system was as difficult and unrepentant as ever when it came to market access for independent producers. Writing in 1948, Robert Benjamin lamented that no studio since Columbia in the late 1920s and early 1930s had gone from start-up to major studio.[80]

He noted that PRC, along with Monogram and Republic, had met with little real success because of their inability to attract top producing, directing, and acting talent.[81] In this he believed Eagle-Lion had finally turned the corner, with independent producer Walter Wanger signed to do two films and single-picture contracts with Hedy Lamar and Robert Cummings (*Let's Live a Little*, 1948), Paul Henreid and Joan Bennett (*Hollow Triumph*, 1948), and Bud Abbott and Lou Costello (*The Noose Hangs High*, 1948). However, none of these films did enough business to save Eagle-Lion.[82]

As quickly as it had arisen, Pathé Industries' film empire began to contract. The 1947–48 movie season was the last for PRC. It released nine films, mostly Lash LaRue and Eddie Dean westerns, and closed up shop. Eagle-Lion split out its product lines in 1950 by shifting its British films to a new subsidiary, Eagle-Lion Classics. In 1950 Pathé Industries closed Eagle-Lion Films, quit distributing British films, and began handling its U.S. releases through Eagle-Lion Classics. In April of the following year Pathé sold Eagle-Lion Classics to United Artists, which was in the process of being taken over by Robert Benjamin and Benjamin's law partner and former Eagle-Lion president Arthur Krim. As part of the Eagle-Lion Classics sale, United Artists signed a ten-year processing deal with Pathé Industries' laboratories.[83] Even though Eagle-Lion had not been successful, its passing was mourned in the film industry, especially among independent producers who would now have nowhere to go but United Artists for distribution.[84]

SIGNIFICANT PASSINGS

Of course there was still film to be processed, and Pathé Industries still operated laboratories on both coasts. In 1946 Pathé Industries had signed a contract to be the exclusive processing and printing labs for Universal Pictures.[85] Pathé would get another large exclusive processing deal with a major studio in 1958, signing with Columbia Pictures and its television subsidiary, Screen Gems, to do all of their processing and printing.[86] Very likely the last time that the Pathé name received wide U.S. circulation was when the title "Color by Pathé" appeared on the closing credits of countless Screen Gems television programs during the 1960s. By that time Pathé's corporate landscape had changed dramatically.

In 1953 Robert Young, perhaps discouraged by the failure of PRC and Eagle-Lion, changed the name of Pathé Industries to Chesapeake Industries.[87] Young had refocused on his railroads, and in 1954 he won a proxy battle to become chairman of the New York Central.[88]

The day after Christmas 1957 Charles Pathé, the man who had started it all, died at the age of ninety-four. He had enjoyed a very long and wealthy retirement overlooking the Mediterranean Sea in Monaco. The *Los Angeles Times*, the primary newspaper in a city that owed much of its success to the industry that Pathé and a few other visionaries had pioneered, buried the three-paragraph obituary on page six, next to a story about a rabid dog in Lakeland, Florida.[89]

One month later the newspapers had another death to report. This one commanded space on the front page of the *New York Times*. On January 25, 1958, in the billiard parlor of his twenty-five-room mansion in Palm Beach, Florida, Robert R. Young put the twin barrels of a twenty-gauge shotgun to his head and simultaneously pulled both triggers. He was sixty years old.[90] Although no reason for the suicide was ever made public, it was known that Young had struggled with depression since the death of his only child, Eleanor, in a plane crash in 1940. To make matters worse, the New York Central Railroad, along with many other railroads in the northeast United States, was beginning to feel the financial pinch that would lead to bankruptcy in the early 1970s.[91]

NEW BEGINNINGS . . . AND ENDINGS

It only took three months for Robert Young's estate to liquidate his estimated 15 percent to 20 percent interest in Chesapeake Industries. In April William Zeckendorf, chairman of Webb & Knapp, Inc., a real estate holding company, acquired Young's ownership stake for a reported $750,000.[92] By 1960 Chesapeake Industries had been rechristened the America Corporation, and it was becoming even more diversified.[93]

Incredibly enough, the newly enlarged America Corporation decided that its next venture would return the Pathé name to the big screen, once again as the distributor of independently produced features. Possibly because those in charge were unaware of the clause in the Pathé Exchange deal that gave RKO the exclusive rights to the name "Pathé" in connection with filmmaking endeavors or possibly because RKO itself had exited film production in 1957, the new enterprise was called Pathé-America. One of its first films was also Sam Peckinpah's feature-film debut, following his three-year career as a director of television westerns. Starring Maureen O'Hara and Brian Keith, *The Deadly Companions* was the only Pathé-America release shot in Pathé Color, this time simply Kodak's Eastman Color film stock processed at Pathé's labs.[94]

Pathé-America would only release seven films during its 1961–62 life span. Most notable, in addition to *The Deadly Companions*, was a pair of British films (*Victim*, starring Dirk Bogarde, and *Whistle Down the Wind*, produced by Richard Attenborough and featuring Allen Bates and Hayley Mills) and Roger Corman's striking race-relation drama *The Intruder*, starring William Shatner and written by frequent *Twilight Zone* contributor Charles Beaumont.

After the failure of Pathé-America, the America Corporation spun off Pathé Labs as an independent company, which reverted to the old name of Pathé Industries.[95] It continued to operate processing labs on both coasts until 1967, when it announced that it was going to close its New York City lab and focus solely on the lab in Los Angeles.[96] At the same time, Pathé razed its venerable Bound Brook plant. Despite the serious fire in 1938, the facility had remained actively engaged in film processing until 1946, when it was replaced by the New York City lab. At that time, Pathé management had described the Bound Brook plant as "outmoded and impossible to modernize." The film storage vaults continued to be used for a time after that, but by 1957 the site was deserted to the point that it was used for a practice fire drill by the Middlesex County disaster forces.[97]

It appears that Pathé Industries did not close the New York lab as planned, but it did enlarge its Hollywood facility with the idea of that becoming its primary lab. If the hope was that the expanded Los Angeles lab would retain all of Pathé's previous business and pick up even more, reality set in very quickly. As Pathé management should have already known, Technicolor was already the laboratory of choice for practically every studio in Hollywood. Pathé threatened to sue Technicolor for $30 million in damages for "attempting to monopolize the color film processing business of major motion picture distributors,"[98] but the case apparently never went to trial.[99]

In October 1967 Pathé Industries sold its laboratory subsidiary to Perfect Film, a New York company that "operates a national photo finishing chain, imports novelties and sells mail-order prescriptions."[100] Martin Ackerman, president of Perfect Film, became chairman and president of Pathé Industries. Only in his mid-thirties at the time, Ackerman had already established himself as a specialist in turning around troubled companies, although he is possibly best remembered today as the man who bought and then closed the 148-year-old *Saturday Evening Post* magazine, the publication that during much of the twentieth century was home to the nostalgic Americana illustrations of Norman Rockwell.

By early 1969, at about the same time as he closed the *Post*, Ackerman was facing a stockholders' rebellion. Kent MacDougall, a reporter for the *Wall Street Journal*, detailed Ackerman's woes in an article titled "The Trials of Marty." Not the least of these trials was Pathé. MacDougall wrote, "Pathé Laboratories, Inc., which he acquired for Perfect [Film] in 1967, suffered from overexpansion in the professional-movie-processing industry and lost $1.2 million last year before Mr. Ackerman unloaded it (Pathé Labs is not to be confused with Pathé Industries, a company Mr. Ackerman still heads. Pathé Industries is basically a holding company whose main holding is Perfect Film stock. Perfect Film, in turn, holds about 10% of Pathé Industries stock.). He now concedes that buying Pathé Laboratories was a mistake."[101]

In October 1970 Ackerman announced his resignation as president of Pathé Industries. William J. Mockridge was elected chairman, president, and chief executive officer of Pathé Industries. Pathé Industries' offices, it was announced, would be relocated to Mockridge's home base of Beverly Hills.[102]

The company to which Martin Ackerman "unloaded" Pathé Labs in 1968 was Berkey Photo, Inc. Founded by Benjamin Berkey in 1932, the company was second only to Eastman Kodak in the photofinishing industry by the mid-1960s, with sales of over $60 million. Purchasing Pathé Labs would allow Berkey to expand beyond the realm of amateur photography and into the related world of professional motion-picture processing and printing.[103]

Benjamin Berkey must have realized his mistake almost immediately, because in June 1969 he sold Pathé's Hollywood lab to Movielab, a company that was already well established in motion-picture processing in New York City and that wanted to establish a beachhead in Hollywood. Berkey Photo continued to own and operate the New York lab until around 1978, at which time it converted the space into a rental film-production stage. By 1988 the film stage was no longer in operation, and the space was repurposed for new, nonfilm tenants.[104]

In 1970 Berkey and Movielab became embroiled in a legal dispute. Berkey sued Movielab, charging that the latter was in arrears in its payments for the purchase of Pathé Labs.[105] In its suit against Berkey, Movielab claimed that Berkey had used fraudulent means to sell Pathé Labs, using "various false representations and concealment of certain material facts (e.g., the price Berkey had paid for the assets being sold to Movielab; the extent of losses that had been suffered; the status of the assets and equipment; and Berkey's relationships with customers), with the result that Movielab was unable efficiently to use the assets acquired from Berkey and suffered heavy losses."[106]

Late in 1972 Movielab and Berkey settled their dispute, with Movielab agreeing to pay Berkey the money it still owed on the purchase of Pathé Labs.[107] Movielab never really recovered from its legal losses. In 1985 it closed the Hollywood lab, and the following year its remaining assets were purchased by Viacom International.[108]

The history of the Hollywood studio system is often cast as a story of those who had a place at the table (after having first *built* the table) and those who stood around hungrily trying to get in and diving for any crumbs that dropped to the floor. In the first camp were the eight major studios, who got into the game early enough and with enough foresight and business acumen to control 95 percent of the industry's revenues. The others were the niche players, forced into the margins of the industry either because they arrived too late or lacked the vision or financial resources necessary to expand into areas like exhibition. Belonging to the latter group didn't automatically guarantee a short corporate life. What it did mean, though, was that the studios outside of the oligopoly were typically obliged to make films for market segments ignored by the majors, usually because of low profit margins. Thus, the Hal Roach Studios enjoyed its most successful years as a producer of short comedies and half-hour episodic television series, and Republic Pictures thrived as a purveyor of Saturday matinee fodder to rural theaters.

The Pathé Exchange really doesn't fit into either category, suggesting that perhaps it is time for a third classification: the "self-marginalized." In that regard the Pathé Exchange really had less in common with Roach and Republic and far more in common with one of the least powerful of the oligopolists, Universal Pictures. Founded the same year as Paramount, Universal under Carl Laemmle followed a very comfortable policy through the silent era of supplying the small independent and rural market and largely remaining out of theater ownership.[109] In fact, it would likely have survived the 1930s with its original management structure intact had it not been for a tragically ill-advised production loan mid-decade.[110] Universal controlled its own production in a way that the Pathé Exchange did not, but Pathé's "subcontractor" system was entirely of its own choosing, not something that was imposed on it from outside. While both Universal and Pathé distributed thousands of reels of undistinguished program fare annually, Universal was capable of pulling off truly memorable if infrequent "A" pictures like von Stroheim's *Blind Husbands* (1919) and *Foolish Wives* (1922), the Lon Chaney classics *The Hunchback of Notre Dame* (1923) and *The Phantom of the Opera* (1925), and Lewis Milestone's *All Quiet on the Western Front* (1930). The closest Pathé was able to come to that level of success was with the Harold Lloyd and Rex, King of Wild Horses, pictures.

Pathé Frères certainly commenced film production in the United States early enough to become an industry powerhouse; after all, the Pathé Exchange was founded a mere three years after Paramount and Universal. As part of an international media empire, the Pathé Exchange should have been able to tap into the resources needed to expand the business had that been the will of the management. And Charles Pathé was every bit as much an industry visionary as Adolph Zukor. What defined the Pathé Exchange's operations, from its management strategies to its production slates during its formative years, was the niche it filled as part of Pathé Frères' international organization, not the niche it filled as part of the Hollywood studio system. Had Charles Pathé been more concerned about positioning his American branch to best compete in the U.S. film industry, the story may have played out differently.

Even as late as 1921 when Merrill Lynch acquired the Pathé Exchange, it may have been possible to propel the company into the ranks of the major studios with an influx of money and strong studio management attuned to the industry. Warner Brothers was still a minor studio at that point, and Columbia Pictures had not even been founded yet. Merrill and Lynch, though, were more interested in operating the Pathé Exchange as an investment. Every profitable year seemed to be confirmation of a winning strategy. They celebrated weathering a 1921–22 business recession in better shape than their competitors while totally missing the import of the sea change around them. Charles Pathé may have ignored the changes in the American market, but at least his Pathé Exchange was a logical piece to a much bigger puzzle. Now it just operated as if in a vacuum, continuing to follow its own path, although that path no longer served a "greater good," and led only to an ever-diminishing status.

When Merrill and Lynch finally awoke to how badly their strategy of the 1920s had positioned the Pathé Exchange to enter the era of the talking picture, it was probably too late to do anything other than what any good investor would do: sell. The new owners had even less passion for filmmaking and absolutely no sentimental attachment to the legacy of the company. They threw the Pathé Exchange into the Mixmaster of an ill-conceived merger and began speaking about liquidation almost immediately.

By every expectation the Pathé Exchange should have ceased to exist after 1931. That was certainly Kennedy's intent. But a strange sort of institutional self-preservation kicked in at that point, and the company refused to die. It actually demonstrated a resilience and adaptability that had largely been absent in the 1920s, continuing on with film processing as its core business but expanding into the ownership of multiple film production studios and home-movie distributors. Taken as a whole, the Pathé Exchange and its corporate successors remained active in some aspect of the film business from 1915 until it sold its last laboratory in 1968, a total of fifty-three years, most of which was *after* its studio operation was folded into RKO. Its newsreel division, included in the 1931 sale to RKO and subsequently sold to Warner Brothers, emerged as an independent company in 1956 and continued to be active as a repackager and licensor of archival footage until 2011, one hundred years after the inauguration of the *Pathé Weekly*.

So, is it finally time to write the rooster's obituary? Probably not. At the time of this writing, Pathé subsidiaries and spin-offs continue to operate in Europe and in other parts of the world. In the United States, multiple corporations carrying some variant of the Pathé name are still listed in government records as alive but inactive.[111]

Corporate remnants aside, the Pathé Exchange and its successors left a large imprint on American culture that will not disappear for a very long time. Its pioneering newsreel left us with an invaluable record of the first half of the twentieth century and paved the way for a new type of journalism using moving images to tell a story that carries on in the television journalism of today. The short comedies Pathé distributed are among the very finest ever made. Laurel and Hardy, Harold Lloyd, Harry Langdon, and Our Gang all had their earliest efforts released under the Pathécomedy banner. And Pathé's late-life, and largely failed, experience with the PRC created *Detour*, one of the seminal films noir. Even now it is hard to imagine that a single day goes by without a Pathé Exchange film being shown somewhere in the world. To paraphrase Terry Ramsaye, we have come to the end of the lovely story of how the little red rooster cast a very long shadow. Vive le coq!

SELECT FILMOGRAPHY

NOTES

BIBLIOGRAPHY

INDEX

SELECT FILMOGRAPHY

The Pathé Exchange and its predecessors and successors released well over 5,000 films, most of them short subjects, during their collective history. The filmography for the Pathé Exchange alone runs some 141 pages, far too long to be included here. It may be found online and is accessible through http://siupress.siu.edu/books/978-0-8093-3496-4.

What follows is a select group of Pathé Exchange releases, plus a few films of Pathé Frères, Pathé Industries, *Pathé News* and Pathé-America. For the most part, these titles represent films that were either mentioned in the text by name or are part of a film series that was discussed.

Disclaimer: Films appear and disappear on Internet sites with amazing rapidity (as do the sites themselves). This list was accurate as this book went to press, and hopefully the titles will remain available in some form on the Internet for years to come.

1910–19

PRE–PATHÉ EXCHANGE

White Fawn's Devotion (1910). Pathé Frères American production. https://www.youtube.com/watch?v=7mlazzAsUTw

Max and the Fair M.D. (1914). Max Linder comedy. https://archive.org/details/MaxLinderInMaxAndTheLadyDoctormaxEtLaDoctoresse1914

The Perils of Pauline, chapter 2 (1914). https://archive.org/details/THEPERILSOFPAULINE1914Ch.2PearlWhite

ANIMATION

Colonel Heeza Liar at the Bat (1915).
http://www.youtube.com/watch?v=D3mJBLVzEpw

"Jerry on the Job" cartoon fragment (ca. 1918).
https://www.youtube.com/watch?v=hHj50VoylTo

SERIAL

The Iron Claw, chapter 7 (1916). Feature Film Corporation serial starring Pearl White. https://www.youtube.com/watch?v=ZNBD5kva60E

COMEDIES

Heinie & Louie (ca. 1916). European release copy of a Mittenthal comedy.
https://www.youtube.com/watch?v=4AJxCXRoibk

Are Crooks Dishonest? (1918). Harold Lloyd, Bebe Daniels, and Snub Pollard in a Rolin comedy. https://archive.org/details/Are_Crooks_Dishonest

FEATURES

The Queen of Spades (1916). "Russian Art Film."
https://www.youtube.com/watch?v=60GFl-WvdXI

The World and the Woman (1916). Thanhouser.
http://thanhouser.org/films/world.htm

The Vicar of Wakefield (1917). Thanhouser.
http://thanhouser.org/films/Vicar-1917.htm

The Woman in White (1917). Thanhouser.
http://www.thanhouser.org/films/woman_white.htm

1920–29

Pathé News

1923. https://archive.org/details/4076_1923_Pathe_Newsreel

Pathé Review

ca. 1928–30, includes Pathéchrome segments.
https://www.youtube.com/watch?v=YZN2cVFzwyo

Pathé Review PATHÉCOLOR SEGMENTS

1922. https://www.youtube.com/watch?v=ecpyxNtDIvY
1927. https://www.youtube.com/watch?v=LuIjKA_MwX8
1928. https://www.youtube.com/watch?v=AhGPnisQL40

SPORTLIGHTS

Alien Antics (1927). https://www.youtube.com/watch?v=t1RpWu8yK88

The Sport Almanac (1929). This sound Sportlights "special" highlights the different sports played each month of the year. https://www.youtube.com/watch?v=OqmSmpwbghc

Aesop's Fables

The Bear and the Bees (1921). https://www.youtube.com/watch?v=xpYl8Jnn2YM

The Cat and the Magnet (1924). https://www.youtube.com/watch?v=yXHjB_XOwM8

The Faithful Pup (1929). Excerpts. https://www.youtube.com/watch?v=S266R32nD9Q

Custard Pies (1929). Excerpts. https://www.youtube.com/watch?v=BwWq5wmVlCc

DOCUMENTARIES

Trailing the Coyote (1921). Excerpt of "An Adventure of Bill and Bob." https://www.youtube.com/watch?v=YvK7217wH3Y

Mysterious Tracks (1922). Excerpt of "An Adventure of Bill and Bob." https://www.youtube.com/watch?v=GncBHgOI1QM

Whiskey Rebellion (1924). A condensed version of one of the Pathé-Yale Chronicles of America. https://archive.org/details/whiskey_rebellion

Our Four-Footed Helpers (Ruminants) (ca. 1925). https://www.youtube.com/watch?v=zoDuYy15SzI

Hiking through Holland with Will Rogers (1927). Condensed version of Rogers' second "Unofficial Ambassador" short. https://www.youtube.com/watch?v=xZicrhWmD4Q

SHORT DRAMAS

The Ballad of Fultah Fisher's Boarding House (1922). https://www.youtube.com/watch?v=BqZy2VR9YH0

The Timber Queen (1922). Excerpt. https://www.youtube.com/watch?v=k_EYF9–3Hqc

Little Indian Weaver (1928). https://www.youtube.com/watch?v=ZJcXSCaU90Q

COMEDIES

Fresh Paint (1920). Rolin comedy with Snub Pollard. https://www.youtube.com/watch?v=tcT22a40kFc

Harvest Hands (1922). Hal Roach comedy starring James "Paul" Parrott. https://www.youtube.com/watch?v=44cULEqDgQg

Too Many Mamas (1924). Hal Roach comedy starring Charley Chase. https://archive.org/details/ManyMammas

The Buccaneers (1924). Hal Roach Our Gang comedy. https://archive.org/details/TheBuccaneers

The Hansom Cabman (1924). Mack Sennett comedy starring Harry Langdon. https://archive.org/details/TheHansomCabman

WESTERNS

100% Nerve (1923). Retitled, one-reel abridgment of a Leo Maloney two-reeler. https://www.youtube.com/watch?v=KZ4-s-im27U

The Ridin' Rowdy (1927). Excerpt. https://www.youtube.com/watch?v=HOFB7yCqMqk

FEATURES

Combat (1927). Pathegrams excerpt. https://www.youtube.com/watch?v=kkVaAALquVc

Blonde for a Night (1928). Silent comedy with Marie Prevost, Harrison Ford, and Franklin Pangborn. https://archive.org/details/BlondeForANight1928

High Voltage (1929). William Boyd and Carol Lombard in an early Pathé talkie. https://archive.org/details/High_Voltage_

The Flying Fool (1929). William Boyd in an early Pathé talkie. https://archive.org/details/TheFlyingFool1929

The Racketeer (1929). Robert Armstrong and Carol Lombard in an early Pathé talkie. https://archive.org/details/The.Racketeer

Big News (1929). Robert Armstrong and Carol Lombard in an early Pathé talkie. https://archive.org/details/BigNews

PATHEX 9.5-MILLIMETER FILMS

Hints (ca. 1925). Tips and pointers on how to project and photograph movies with Pathex 9.5-millimeter equipment. https://www.youtube.com/watch?v=CHfjZo6T3Vw

Travel, Laugh, Thrill and Learn with Pathex (ca. 1925). A film promoting the Pathex entertainment films available to the home-movie market. https://www.youtube.com/watch?v=1YpGEUW6LIk

Flashes of the Past (1925). Highlights of Pathé's newsreel coverage of events from 1910 to 1925. https://www.youtube.com/watch?v=zo3pamXhyu8

Man from Mars (1925). A *Pathé Review* "scientific" speculation on what a Martian might look like. https://www.youtube.com/watch?v=CJQkvWI6e5E

Juggling Balls (1921). Novagraph motion study. https://www.youtube.com/watch?v=O_V1AD13Vy8

Thumbelina (from a 1924 *Pathé Review*). A silhouette animation by Herbert M. Dawley. https://www.youtube.com/watch?v=-E2vFfi7iDQ

Lindbergh's Paris Flight and *Welcome Home* (1927). https://www.youtube.com/watch?v=3fxve9CKD_o

1930–39

Pathé Audio Review (ca. 1930). https://www.youtube.com/watch?v=xT_Hy4-ehi8

FEATURES

Sin Takes a Holiday (1930). Constance Bennett and Basil Rathbone. https://archive.org/details/SinTakesAHoliday

Pardon My Gun (1930). https://archive.org/details/PardonMyGun

Lonely Wives (1931). Edward Everett Horton. https://archive.org/details/Lonely_Wives_1931

The Painted Desert (1931). https://archive.org/details/ThePaintedDesert1931ClarkGable

PATHEGRAMS

Allied Manufacturing Pathegrams

Hardy Heroes. Home-movie version of a mid-1920s film about college football. https://www.youtube.com/watch?v=npmXB8aiUvE

Four Pathegrams: Milton Caniff, Monty Banks, Bill and Bob, and Charlie Chaplin. https://www.youtube.com/watch?v=sAYqZ92EDlc

Gene Castle Pathegrams

Hindenburg Explodes! (1937). https://www.youtube.com/watch?v=TnmOe_obghU

The Coronation of Their Majesties King George VI and Queen Elizabeth (1937). https://www.youtube.com/watch?v=FXG8y99lB9c

1940–49

OFFICIAL FILMS

News Thrills of 1946. https://www.youtube.com/watch?v=tkSjnqlgQvo
Touchdown Thrills of 1948. https://www.youtube.com/watch?v=8t6lPltGVcs

PICTOREEL

Snow Fun (early 1940s). Number 101 in the Pictoreel Catalog. https://www.youtube.com/watch?v=GSFmeGYTlDM

PRC (PRODUCERS RELEASING CORPORATION)

Detour (1945). https://archive.org/details/Detour_movie

EAGLE-LION

He Walked by Night (1948). https://archive.org/details/He_Walked_by_Night_1948

1950–59

The Erie Canal (1957). Pathé Educational film, number 702, culled from the *Pathé News Magazine of the Screen*. https://www.youtube.com/watch?v=Drardk31stM

1960–69

PATHÉ-AMERICA

The Intruder (1962). Roger Corman production starring William Shatner. http://www.youtube.com/watch?v=DGkLnjn8E3k

NOTES

INTRODUCTION

1. Stephanie Salmon, *Pathé: À la conquête du cinéma 1896–1929* (Paris: Tallandier, 2014), 353, 356; "France Increases Film Imports," *Moving Picture World* (hereinafter *MPW*), November 18, 1916, 995.

2. A very strong link between the two words indeed, since the firm referred to its serials as "Pathéserials."

3. Salmon, *Pathé*, 354.

4. Gilles Willems, "The Origins of Pathé-Natan," in *Une histoire économique du cinéma français (1895–1995), Regards croisés franco-américains*, ed. Pierre-Jean Benghozi and Christian Delage, trans. Annabelle de Cröy (Paris: Harmattan, Collection Champs Visuels, 1997); Salmon, *Pathé*, 395.

CHAPTER ONE
CHARLES PATHÉ, FILM PUBLISHER: 1908–14

1. One of the quickest ways to start an argument between two silent-film aficionados is to ask them the running time of a thousand-foot reel of film during the silent era. The fact is there was no absolute standard until the arrival of sound. Around 1915 most films were shot and projected at around fifteen minutes per reel. The speed gradually increased after 1915 and into the early 1920s. By the end of the silent era in the late 1920s, most films were projected at an average of ten minutes per reel. But throughout the silent era, these running speeds were only an approximation. Theater managers sometimes deliberately ran films too fast to squeeze in an extra showing per day. Some projectionists saw themselves as being part of the artistic process and would speed films up or slow them down, depending on whether the audience seemed to be bored or seemed to want more. Another complication was the fact that most makers

of silent films agreed that their films played better if they were sped up a little. Thus, films were often shot at one speed but edited with the assumption that they would be played faster. If a contemporary projectionist or video-transfer house attempts to show a silent film at the "correct" speed based on the speed of the onscreen action, the scenes often seem to drag on forever.

2. Jacques and Théophile had dropped out of Pathé Frères by this time.

3. "Romance Hovers Around House of Pathé in Its Rise," *Motion Picture News* (hereinafter *MPN*), January 8, 1916, 52; Richard Abel, *The Cine Goes to Town: French Cinema 1896–1914* (Berkeley: University of California Press, 1994), 9–22; Ephraim Katz, "Charles Pathé," in *Film Encyclopedia*, 3rd ed. (New York: Harper Perennial, 1998), 1069–70.

4. "Berst Returns to Pathé," *MPW*, February 5, 1916, 751.

5. Abel, *The Cine Goes to Town*, 23–24.

6. Today this part of "East Bound Brook" is located within the town of Middlesex, New Jersey.

7. "Pathé Ends an Era in Middlesex," *Courier-News* (New Jersey), January 6, 1967.

8. "Berst Returns to Pathé," *MPW*, February 5, 1916, 751.

9. Ed Hulse, *Distressed Damsels and Masked Marauders* (Morris Plains, NJ: Murania Press, 2014), 75.

10. Abel, *The Cine Goes to Town*, 52.

11. "Fined for Inhumane Realism," *MPW*, April 26, 1913, 367.

12. George Blaisdell, "At the Sign of the Flaming Arcs," *MPW*, May 24, 1913, 820.

13. "Comments on the Films," *MPW*, January 31, 1914, 543.

14. "Pauline Ends with 20th Episode," *MPW*, November 14, 1914, 941; "Expediting Service," *MPW*, July 11, 1914, 284.

15. Eclectic ads for *The Perils of Pauline*, *MPN*, July 18, 1914, 4.

16. Review of episode 13 of *The Perils of Pauline*, *MPN*, September 19, 1914, 49.

17. Sadly, and with no small irony considering the number of prints made for *The Perils of Pauline*'s theatrical run, the series no longer exists in its original twenty-episode form. A 1935 inventory of Pathé's vault does not contain an entry for *The Perils of Pauline*; Pathé had sold the remake rights to Universal Pictures two years earlier. However, all negatives and prints of two other Pearl White serials from after 1910, *The Exploits of Elaine* (1914) and *The Iron Claw* (1916), are listed in the inventory as having been scrapped sometime prior to 1935. In all likelihood the same fate befell *The Perils of Pauline*. If some film element of *Perils* did manage to survive into the 1930s, it probably would have been lost in

the massive vault fire suffered by Pathé in 1938 or else (if it was included with the sale of the remake rights) willfully destroyed by Universal Pictures when it discarded the bulk of its silent films in the late 1940s.

All of today's copies of *The Perils of Pauline* descend from a badly worn 28-millimeter home-movie print of a reedited nine-episode French release. The subtitles were poorly translated back into English from a French text and include such gems as Pauline being given a challenge to determine her "immoral strength," rather than "immortal strength" as intended.

18. Edward J. Perkins, *Wall Street to Main Street: Charles Merrill and Middle-Class Investors* (Cambridge: Cambridge University Press, 1999), 95.

19. "Pathé News Has Had Long History," *MPW*, January 11, 1919, 190.

20. "Romance Hovers around House of Pathé in Its Rise," *MPN*, January 8, 1916, 52.

21. Ad for the *Pathé Daily News*, *MPW*, July 4, 1914, 30.

22. "Pathé's Weekly Twice a Week," *MPW*, June 21, 1913, 1261.

23. "Brunet Answers International," *MPN*, November 23, 1918, 3053.

24. Ad for the *Pathé Daily News*, *MPW*, June 20, 1914, 1630–31.

25. "Newspaper Man to Pathé Weekly," *MPW*, January 10, 1914, 182.

26. "Pathé's Weekly Gets Newspaper Service," *MPW*, January 24, 1914, 393.

27. "Boosting Pathé Pictures," *MPW*, March 14, 1914, 1392–93.

28. "Pathé Shows Subway Accident within Five Hours," *MPN*, October 9, 1915, 60.

29. In mid-May 1914 the pattern of Pathé Frères' releases through General Film was a one-reel short per day Monday–Wednesday, a two- or three-reeler on Thursday and Saturday, and no release on Friday. General Film had no releases on Sunday.

By comparison, in the spring of 1914 Biograph had four reels per week, Edison six (four one-reelers and one two-reeler), Kalem six (two one-reelers and two two-reelers), Selig eleven (five one-reelers, including *Hearst-Selig News*, and two two-reelers), Vitagraph eight (four one-reelers and two two-reelers), Essanay six (four one-reelers and one two-reeler), and Lubin seven (three one-reelers and two two-reelers). On Tuesdays, General Film would distribute a film from a European studio like Cines, Ambrosio, and Celio. These special Tuesday releases were two- and three-reel films. See "Calendar of Licensed Releases," *MPW*, May 16, 1914, 990.

30. Ibid.

31. Ad for CGPC, *MPW*, August 10, 1912, 563.

32. Ad for CGPC, *MPW*, August 17, 1912, 613.

33. Ad for Eclectic Films, *MPW*, January 11, 1913, 181.

34. "Malitz Succeeds Roussel as Pathé President," *MPN*, January 16, 1915, page number missing.

35. Ad for Eclectic Films, *MPW*, January 18, 1913, 225; Abel, *The Cine Goes to Town*, 40.

36. Pathé ad for *A Leech of Industry*, *MPW*, March 7, 1914, 1206.

37. Ad for Pathé, *MPW*, May 9, 1914, 835.

38. Ad for Pathé, *MPW*, May 16, 1914, 1000.

39. Ad for Eclectic Films, *MPW*, August 8, 1914, 4–5.

40. Abel, *The Cine Goes to Town*, 41.

41. W. Stephen Bush, "Charles Pathé's Views," *MPW*, January 24, 1914, 390–91.

42. Ibid.

43. *The Exploits of Elaine* appears to have been primarily shot in and around the Pathé studio in Jersey City, but by the time *The New Exploits of Elaine* was in production, Theodore and Leopold Wharton had leased a forty-five-acre lakeside resort and amusement park near Ithaca, New York, for their studio. In the April 17, 1915, *MPN* story announcing the lease, the Whartons noted that the park already had "frontier settlement streets and log cabins" that could be used for the production of westerns.

44. "Pathé Dinner a Love Feast," *MPW*, January 22, 1916, 570.

45. Bonvillain had already earned a spot in history by taking the first-ever photograph from a Wright brothers airplane when the plane was brought to France in 1908.

46. "Deceased Pathé Vice-President a Film Expert," *MPN*, January 2, 1915, 29.

47. "Felix Malitz—Pathé Guiding Spirit," *MPW*, March 13, 1915, 1583.

48. "Malitz Succeeds Roussel as Pathé President," *MPN*, January 16, 1915, page number missing.

CHAPTER TWO
"A PROGRAM WHICH WILL GO INTO EVERY PART OF THE WORLD": 1915–18

1. "Pathé Sails for Europe," *MPW*, January 16, 1915, 342.

2. Perkins, *Wall Street to Main Street*, 95.

3. "Felix Malitz—Pathé Guiding Spirit," *MPW*, March 13, 1915, 1583.

4. "Charles Pathé the Guiding Spirit," *MPW*, March 27, 1915, 1914H.

5. "Pathé's New Home a Fine Establishment," *MPN*, April 10, 1915, 37.

6. Salmon, *Pathé*, 249.

7. "Pathé Dinner a Love Feast," *MPW*, January 22, 1916, 570.

8. "Pathé Announces New Program," *MPN*, January 16, 1915, 27.

9. "Fitzmaurice, Formerly of Pathé, with Old Company," *MPN*, July 19, 1915, 42; "Pathé Will Release One Gold Rooster a Week," *MPN*, October 7, 1916, 2175; "Edward José, Producer of 'The Iron Claw,'" *MPW*, April 8, 1916, 270; "Pathé Plans Greater Program," *MPW*, July 15, 1916, 459.

10. "Pathé Will Release One Gold Rooster a Week," *MPN*, October 7, 1916, 2175.

11. "Fitzmaurice, Formerly of Pathé, with Old Company," *MPN*, June 19, 1915, 42.

12. "Producer Settles Here," *Los Angeles Times* (hereinafter *LAT*), August 4, 1919, sec. 2, p. 8.

13. "Kismet," *MPW*, December 4, 1920, 636.

14. Katz, "Louis J. Gasnier," *Film Encyclopedia*, 515–16.

15. "Wharton Doing General Producing," *MPW*, January 22, 1916, 570.

16. "All International Films to Be Released Through Pathé," *MPN*, January 13, 1917, 227.

17. "Reviewers High in Praise of 'Patria' Serial," *MPN*, February 17, 1917, 1061.

18. "Mrs. Castle Signs Long Contract with Pathé," *MPN*, April 28, 1917, 2666.

19. "Arrow to Produce for Pathé," *MPW*, October 23, 1915, 634.

20. *Who Is Guilty?* (location report), *MPW*, November 20, 1915, 1460.

21. "'The Red Circle' Pathé's Next Special," *MPW*, November 27, 1915, 1643.

22. "Anna Nilsson in Pathé's 'Who's Guilty?,'" *MPW*, April 29, 1916, 805.

23. "'Who's Guilty?' Series Popular," *MPW*, June 10, 1916, 1869.

24. "Seven and Eight Reel Productions Planned by Arrow," *MPN*, September 30, 1916, 2012.

25. "Arrow Shows Objector Why He Should Buy Film," *MPN*, August 25, 1917, 1302.

26. "Pathé Will Release One Gold Rooster a Week," *MPN*, October 7, 1916, 2175.

27. "Edwin Thanhouser Retires," *MPW*, March 2, 1918, 1230; "Thanhouser Back as Head of New Rochelle Concern," *MPN*, March 6, 1915, 33; Victor Graf, liner notes to the Thanhouser Collection DVD volumes 7, 8, and 9, Thanhouser Film Preservation Company, 2007.

28. "Thanhouser in New Studio," *MPW*, January 17, 1914, 268–69.

29. Ad for Thanhouser, *MPW*, July 29, 1916, 732; "Pathé Exchange Gets the Thanhouser Product," *MPW*, July 29, 1916, 765; "Edwin Thanhouser Now Has Four Companies at Work," *MPN*, September 9, 1916, 1527.

30. "Thanhouser Will Continue Trade Showing," *MPW*, July 21, 1917, 441.

31. "Thanhouser to Go In for 'Americanism and Sunshine,'" *MPN*, July 28, 1917, 601.

32. "Miss Young Leases Thanhouser Studio," *MPW*, August 4, 1917, 804.

33. "Fun-Art Film Begins Work in New Rochelle," *MPN*, October 6, 1917, 2393.

34. "Edwin Thanhouser Retires," *MPW*, March 2, 1918, 1230.

35. Edwin Thanhouser biography, http://www.thanhouser.org/people/thanhousere.htm.

36. Ad for Balboa, *MPN*, December 12, 1914, 61.

37. "Ruth Roland Goes to Balboa for Three Years," *MPN*, December 19, 1914, 57.

38. "'Neal of Navy' Gets Big Ovation at First New York Showing; Triumph for Pathé and Balboa," *MPN*, September 18, 1915, 79.

39. Review of *The Shrine of Happiness*, *MPW*, November 13, 1915, 1326; Review of *Adventures of a Madcap*, *MPN*, November 13, 1915, 86.

40. E. D. Horkheimer, "Studio Management," *MPW*, October 30, 1915, 982.

41. "Veterans of Balboa," *MPW*, October 9, 1915, 267.

42. "Balboa's Plant Growing Steadily," *MPW*, September 23, 1916, 1977.

43. Peter Milne, review of *Sold at Auction*, *MPN*, February 10, 1917, 921.

44. "Pathé Activity at Coast Studio," *MPW*, February 16, 1918, 986; "Pathé Uses Paralta Studios," *MPN*, February 2, 1918, 686.

45. "Balboa Plant May Be Sold," *MPW*, October 12, 1918, 203.

46. "At the Diando Studios," *MPW*, December 15, 1917, 1638.

47. While Marie Osborne's starring film career ended in early childhood, she lived to be ninety-nine years old, dying in 2010.

48. For information on the Mittenthal brothers, see http://www.kpl.gov/local-history/biographies/mittenthal-brothers.aspx.

49. When Kendig died in 1915, the series continued with another actor as Louie.

50. Richard Ward, *A History of the Hal Roach Studios* (Carbondale: Southern Illinois University Press, 2005), 8–14.

51. Dwight Whiting, in New York City, telegrams to Rolin Film Company, March 25 and 26, 1915, Hal Roach Collection, University of Southern California (hereinafter USC) Cinematic Arts Library, 1914–15 business correspondence file.

52. Roach to Whiting, October 27, 1917, Hal Roach Collection, USC Cinematic Arts Library, 1917 business correspondence file.

53. Whiting to Roach, October 28, 1917, Hal Roach Collection, USC Cinematic Arts Library, 1917 business correspondence file.

54. Roach to Whiting, October 29, 1917, Hal Roach Collection, USC Cinematic Arts Library, 1917 business correspondence file.

55. Whiting to Roach, October 28, 1917, Hal Roach Collection, USC Cinematic Arts Library, 1917 business correspondence file.

56. "The Motion Picture News Chart of National Film Trade Conditions," *MPN*, October 31, 1914, 20–21.

57. "Pathé Acquires Savage's Plays," *MPW*, December 18, 1913, 2187.

58. "Pathé Gets A. H. Woods Play," *MPW*, November 20, 1915, 1467.

59. "Pathé Gets Rights to Screen First Kipling Novel," *MPN*, December 11, 1915, 53.

60. "Pathé Will Issue 'Gold Rooster' Features," *MPN*, July 17, 1915, 68.

61. Ibid.

62. Ad for *The Spender*, *MPW*, October 9, 1915, 219.

63. Joshua Yumibe, *Moving Color: Early Film, Mass Culture, Modernism* (New Brunswick, NJ: Rutgers University Press, 2012), 79.

64. A good example of this process may be seen in most video copies of *The Great Train Robbery* (1903). Color is reserved for orange puffs of smoke from a dynamited safe and gunfire, for the purple riding hood of a little girl, and for the dresses in a brief square-dance sequence.

65. In a five-color example given by Coe, the colors are red, blue, brown, green, and yellow.

66. Brian Coe, *The History of Movie Photography* (London: Ash & Grant, 1981), 115.

67. Supplement to *Kinematograph Weekly*, dated December 11, 1924, at http://www.cinerdistan.co.uk/pathécolor.htm.

68. Paul Read, "Unnatural Colours: An Introduction to Colouring Techniques in Silent Era Movies," *Film History* 21, no. 1 (2009): 16. At the time of this writing, an excellent example of an entire silent feature done in Pathécolor can be seen in the DVD release of *Cyrano de Bergerac* (1925).

69. Yumibe, *Moving Color*, 79.

70. "Does Color Enhance Dramatic Realism?," *MPW*, July 1, 1916, 84.

71. Review of *The Galloper*, *MPW*, August 28, 1915, 1496.

72. Review of *Comrade John*, *MPN*, November 6, 1915, 85.

73. "The Shrine of Happiness Beautifully Colored by Pathé," *MPW*, February 19, 1916, 1153.

74. Review of *Here and There in Spain*, *MPW*, November 25, 1916, 1189.

75. "Pathé's *Sultana*, a Gold Rooster in Natural Colors, Ready on October 29," *MPN*, October 28, 1916, 2668.

76. Review of *Adventures of a Madcap*, *MPN*, November 13, 1915, 86.

77. Review of *The Beloved Vagabond*, *MPW*, December 18, 1915, 2196.

78. Review of *The Beloved Vagabond*, *MPN*, December 11, 1915, 94.

79. Ad for Pathé, *MPW*, April 8, 1916, 329.

80. Ad for Pathé, *MPW*, July 8, 1916, 194.

81. "Serial Program to Cost $5,000,000," *MPW*, May 27, 1916, 1519.

82. "Pathé Serials for 1917 Are Based on Three Widely Read Novels," *MPN*, September 16, 1916, 1682.

83. "What the Public Wants in 'Shielding Shadow'—Gasnier," *MPN*, September 9, 1916, 1557.

84. "Pathé Plans Greater Program," *MPW*, July 15, 1916, 459.

85. "Pathé Will Release One Gold Rooster a Week," *MPN*, October 7, 1916, 2175.

86. "Pathé Plans Five Reelers to Equal Serials," *MPN*, December 30, 1916, 4187.

87. Peter Milne, review of *The Empress*, *MPN*, March 10, 1917, 1570.

88. *MPN*'s Peter Milne didn't care for this one either, saying, "It is something of a pity that Bessie Love makes her debut on the Pathé program under such adverse conditions." *MPN*, March 9, 1918, 1467.

89. "Pathé Announces New Policy of Expansion," *MPW*, October 13, 1917, 216.

90. Peter Milne, review of *Crime and Punishment*, *MPN*, February 24, 1917, 1255.

91. Peter Milne, review *The Vicar of Wakefield*, *MPN*, March 17, 1917, 1717.

92. Frederick Warde, "A Legitimate Player in the Films," *MPW*, July 21, 1917, 400.

93. Ibid.

94. "Seven Year Chart of Film Production," *MPN*, July 28, 1917, 658.

95. "The Beggars" (editorial cartoon), *MPN*, March 3, 1917, 1370.

96. "Pathé Announces New Policy of Expansion," *MPW*, October 13, 1917, 216.

97. "Pathé Acquires 'Runaway Romany,'" *MPW*, December 8, 1917, 1519.

98. Peter Milne, review of *Runaway Romany*, *MPN*, December 29, 1917, 4585.

99. "Pathé Policy for 1918," *MPW*, November 10, 1917, 893.

100. "Pathé Will Also Release; Pathé Studio Facilities Greatly Enlarged," *MPN*, October 20, 1917, 2723.

101. After the First World War, American producers returned the favor by selling *their* films for low prices on the world market, a practice that continues to this very day.

102. Review of *The Shadow of Her Past*, *MPN*, September 5, 1916, 785.

103. W. Stephen Bush, review of *Germinal*, *MPW*, January 24, 1914, 416.

104. "A Chapter of the Foreign Film," *MPW*, November 4, 1916, 671.

105. "Pathé's Les Misérables Is Capacity Play," *MPN*, August 11, 1917, 990.

106. "In a Box Office Report," *MPN*, November 17, 1917, 3432.

107. "Pathé Policy for 1918," *MPW*, November 10, 1917, 893.

108. "Russian Art Films Artistic and True to Life," *MPN*, August 25, 1917, 1276.

109. "Kaplan Returning to Moscow," *MPW*, October 20, 1917, 369.

110. Peter Milne, review of *The Queen of Spades*, *MPN*, November 3, 1917, 3133.

111. Peter Milne, review of *Her Sister's Rival*, *MPN*, December 15, 1917, 4222.

112. "All International Films to Be Released Through Pathé," *MPN*, January 13, 1917, 227.

113. Another dramatic effort by International, *When My Ship Comes In*, was announced as an upcoming Gold Rooster Play early in 1917 but was never released as part of that series. It was ultimately released to poor reviews in 1919 through the Independent Sales Corporation.

114. "The Weekly News Reel," *MPW*, July 21, 1917, 419–20.

115. "Pathé and International Weeklies Combine," *MPN*, January 20, 1917, 386.

116. "All International Films to Be Released Through Pathé," *MPN*, January 13, 1917, 227.

117. Hulse, *Distressed Damsels*, 77–79.

118. "Hearst-Pathé News Consolidation Profitable," *MPN*, April 28, 1917, 2663.

119. Hulse, *Distressed Damsels*, 129.

120. Ibid., 130.

121. "Pathé Bars Hearst Name on Pictorial," *LAT*, October 10, 1918, sec. 1, p. 3; "Brunet Answers International," *MPN*, November 23, 1918, 3053.

122. Pathé had discontinued distribution of Hearst's cartoons the previous March.

123. Tino Balio, *Grand Design: Hollywood as a Modern Business Enterprise, 1930–1939* (New York: Charles Scribner's Sons, 1993), 365.

124. "Pathé Claims Costly Program Film," *MPN*, February 16, 1918, 1013.

125. Exhibitors have traditionally disliked long films. The longer a film, the fewer showings an exhibitor can fit into a day; hence fewer people will be able to pay to see it.

126. Goldfish would soon adopt the name of his company and become Samuel Goldwyn.

127. "Goldfish Denounces Extravagance in Industry," *MPW*, December 15, 1917, 1613–14.

128. "The Public Must Pay the Tax," *MPN*, December 1, 1917, 3776–77.

129. "Amalgamation Would Throttle Exhibitors, says Berst," *MPN*, December 15, 1917, 4143.

130. "Goldfish Denounces Extravagance in Industry," *MPW*, December 15, 1917, 1613–14.

131. Two-page ad for Pathé, *MPW*, December 22, 1917, 1732–33.

132. Ad for Pathé, *MPW*, January 12, 1918, 174.

133. "Box Office Report," *MPN*, December 15, 1917, 4157; "Box Office Report," *MPN*, December 22, 1917, 4331.

134. "Box Office Report," *MPN*, January 5, 1918.

135. "Pathé Plays Every Two Weeks," *MPN*, January 26, 1918, 574.

136. "'Hysteria Worst,' Says Pathé," *MPN*, February 16, 1918, 998.

137. "Pathé Uses Paralta Studios," *MPN*, February 2, 1918, 686.

138. "Paralta to Build Elaborate Studio," *MPW*, March 30, 1918, 1833.

139. "Berst Withdraws from Pathé Organization," *MPN*, March 23, 1918, 1707.

CHAPTER THREE
"IN CLOSER TOUCH WITH THE WORLD ORGANIZATION OF PATHÉ": 1918–21

1. Ad for Paramount, *MPN*, January 9, 1915.

2. "Famous Players and Lasky in $12,500,000 Combine," *MPN*, July 15, 1916, 223.

3. "Samuel Goldfish Resigns as Chairman of Lasky Directors," *MPN*, September 30, 1916.

4. "Another Big Merger of Producing Interests," *MPN*, October 21, 1916, 2513.

5. "Famous Players-Lasky Takes Over Paramount," *MPW*, December 23, 1916, 1778.

6. The "Famous" name would continue to surface throughout the years. Paramount's music publishing business was known as Famous Music, and its animation division was known for most of the 1940s and 1950s as Famous Studios.

7. "Paul Brunet Takes Pathé Management," *MPN*, March 23, 1918, 1707.

8. Ibid.

9. Salmon, *Pathé*, 355.

10. Ibid.

11. "Brunet Talks of Pathé Policies under His Administration," *MPW*, March 30, 1918, 1842; "Ferdinand Zecca an Old-Timer," *MPW*, April 6, 1918, 99.

12. "Pathé to Cancel Paralta Contract," *MPW*, April 13, 1918, 253.

13. "Pathé Active East and West," *MPW*, March 30, 1918, 1851.

14. The Paralta and Anderson-Brunton facility would be purchased by Famous Players–Lasky in 1926 and would become the permanent home of Paramount Pictures.

15. "Brunet Plans Four Serials," *MPN*, March 30, 1918, 1858.

16. Ad for Pathé, *MPW*, April 13, 1918, 194.

17. "Pathé to Combine Open Booking and Program Methods," *MPW*, April 20, 1918, 415.

18. "Brunet Favors Sane Limit on Films," *MPN*, August 10, 1918, 869.

19. "Fear" (editorial), *MPW*, December 4, 1920.

20. "Brunet Favors Sane Limit on Films," *MPN*, August 10, 1918, 869.

21. Ibid.

22. "Pathé Plans in Two Broadway Houses," *MPW*, June 8, 1918, 1420.

23. Theaters did employ very large fans to circulate the air. One of the most heavily promoted was branded the Typhoon.

24. "'One Hour Before Dawn' to Be Warner's First Production under the Pathé Banner," *MPW*, June 26, 1920, 1782.

25. "Pathé Has Two on Broadway," *MPN*, July 17, 1920, 625.

26. "Fourth Blanche Sweet Film in Year Shown at Broadway," *MPW*, September 4, 1920, 105.

27. "Pathé Wins Place on Broadway," *MPN*, July 31, 1920, 961.

28. "Big Features Will Soon Run Full Year on Broadway, Predicts Adolph Zukor," *MPW*, December 4, 1920, 574.

29. "Charles Pathé Expected in New York April 15," *MPN*, April 5, 1919, 2150.

30. "American Organization Dines Charles Pathé," *MPN*, June 21, 1919, 4121.

31. "Pathé's New Year Force Is Strong," *MPN*, November 15, 1919, 3647.

32. "Blackton Releases through Pathé," *MPN*, August 30, 1919, 1824.

33. "Blackton Producing Pathé Pictures in His New Plant," *MPW*, September 20, 1919, 1806.

34. Tom Hamlin, review of *The Moonshine Trail*, *MPN*, November 1, 1919, 3346.

35. Laurence Reid, review of *Man and His Woman*, *MPN*, July 24, 1920, 865.

36. "Blackton Films in Demand," *MPN*, April 24, 1920, 3677.

37. Review of *Forbidden Valley*, *MPW*, October 16, 1920, 996.

38. Katz, "Stuart Blackton," *Film Encyclopedia*, 133–34.

39. Review of *The Little Café*, *MPW*, June 12, 1920, 1504.

40. Katz, "Max Linder," *Film Encyclopedia*, 830–31.

41. "Pathé Reports a Big Increase," *MPN*, March 20, 1920, 2729.

42. "Pathé Erecting Twelve Story Building to Accommodate Business Increase," *MPW*, February 14, 1920, 1094.

43. "Art in Motion Picture Advertising," *MPW*, October 2, 1915, 63; "Pathé Puts Out Beautiful Posters," *MPW*, December 25, 1915, 2397; "Fine Posters Hallmark of Good Films, Says Pathé," *MPN*, January 1, 1916, 46.

44. "Pathé Erecting Twelve Story Building to Accommodate Business Increase," *MPW*, February 14, 1920, 1094.

45. "Pathé Sales Force Wide Awake," *MPW,* July 12, 1919, 227.

46. "Pathé Celebrates the 10th Anniversary of Its Newsreel in November 1920," *MPW,* November 20, 1920, 312.

47. "Pathé News to Record Large Local Happenings," *MPW,* December 28, 1918, 1543.

48. "Programs of the First Runs," *MPN,* March 20, 1920, 2706.

49. "Pathé's Short-Subject Schedule," *MPN,* July 24, 1920, 785.

50. "Zoology and Science in Current Pathé Review," *MPW,* February 7, 1920, 909.

51. Review of *Pathé Review No. 79*, *MPW,* November 27, 1920, 508.

52. "Pathé's Short-Subject Schedule," *MPN,* July 24, 1920, 785.

53. "To Release 'Topics' Each Week," *MPN,* April 19, 1919, 2478.

54. "Drive for Pathé 'Topics,'" *MPN,* January 3, 1920, 423.

55. Ad for Pathé's *Topics of the Day*, *MPN,* January 3, 1920, unnumbered page.

56. White's feature-film career would be short lived. In 1922 she was back at George B. Seitz Productions to make one final Pathé serial, *Plunder* (1923), before retiring to France. She came out of retirement long enough to star in a single French feature, *Terror* (1925).

57. "Serial Program for Coming Year," *MPN,* July 24, 1920, 781, 783.

58. "Pathé Reports Many Contracts for Serials Offered as Special Attraction for Summer," *MPW,* July 10, 1920, 228.

59. First-run theaters played films when they were new, and these theaters were more prestigious than "subsequent-run" houses that reran films that had already been out for a while and had already played in the town in which the theater was located.

60. "Record Number of First-Run Bookings Announced for 'Ruth of the Rockies,'" *MPN,* September 4, 1920, 88.

61. "Says That Serials Interest Picture Patrons of All Ages," *MPW,* September 10, 1921, 198.

62. "Ruth Roland in Atlanta Kept the Coppers Busy," *MPW,* April 2, 1921, 487.

63. "With First Run Theaters," *MPN,* January 31, 1920, 1253.

64. "'Box Office Stars' Only New Pathé Program Rule," *MPN,* March 17, 1917, 1702.

65. "Lloyd-Pathé Bookings Climb Steadily," *MPN,* January 25, 1919, 553.

66. Taking such care with a short series was unusual, but not unheard of. In 1920 Roscoe "Fatty" Arbuckle had just completed a series of elaborate and highly valued two-reelers, and Buster Keaton, who had been a member of Arbuckle's supporting cast, was just embarking on his own series. Then there

was Charlie Chaplin, who, as his own producer, spent all of 1918 making two three-reel comedies and making a half-reel plug for the sale of bonds to finance the United States' effort in the First World War. The next year he produced two two-reelers.

67. "Sidney Drew Dies," *MPN*, April 19, 1919, 2445.

68. "Pathé Signs Hobart Henley and Mrs. Sidney Drew," *MPW*, September 27, 1919, 1962.

69. Pathé ad for *The Gay Old Dog*, *MPN*, October 18, 1919.

70. "Two Notable Acquisitions by Pathé," *MPN*, September 27, 1919, 2602.

71. "Mrs. Sidney Drew Returns to Films in Third of Her Pathé Comedies," *MPW*, February 28, 1920, 1503.

72. "Pathé Says Short Features Are Coming Again into Public Favor," *MPW*, January 29, 1921, 588.

73. "Short Subjects in Demand," *MPN*, July 17, 1920, 627; "Pathé Contracts to Release Fifteen Two Reel Westerns with Tom Santschi," *MPW*, September 4, 1920, 64.

74. "Pathé 'Bob and Bill' Series to Show Thrilling Hunting Scenes," *MPW*, February, 12, 1921, 846.

75. "'Pathé Playlets' to Be Re-issued in Three Reels of Big Pathé Features," *MPW*, December 31, 1921, 1081.

76. Ad for Pathé, *MPN*, January 28, 1922, unnumbered page.

77. "Three Reel Harold Lloyd Comedy to Be Featured by S. L. Rothafel," *MPW*, July 2, 1921, 107; "Popularization of Short Subject Programs Foreseen by Pathé Man," *MPW*, July 23, 1921, 424.

78. "Under American Control Pathé Will Enlarge Its Activities, Brunet Says," *MPW*, August 27, 1921, 924; "Pathé Classifies 450 Pictures under Title of Short Subjects for Next Year," *MPW*, August 6, 1921, 628.

79. "Charles Pathé Sees No Film Monopoly," *MPN*, May 24, 1919, 829.

80. "Pathé's New Year Force Is Strong," *MPN*, November 15, 1919, 3647.

81. "Resolutions Adopted at Cleveland by Exhibitors' Convention," *MPN*, June 26, 1920, 57.

82. Ibid.

83. "King Vidor Contracts to Release a Series of Special Productions through Associated Producers," *MPW*, February 26, 1921, 1083.

84. "1918–1919—Thumbnails of Men Making Film History," *MPN*, December 28, 1918.

85. "United Theaters Takes 'T' Exchanges," *MPN*, January 24, 1920, 1033.

86. Ad for First National, *MPW*, July 28, 1917, 601.

87. Ad for First National, *MPW*, December 20, 1919, unnumbered page.

88. "First National's Defense Expansion," *MPN*, December 6, 1919, 4063.

89. "'Community of Interest' Will Be Fostered by Pathé in Special Exhibitor Partnership," *MPW*, December 27, 1919, 1118.

90. "Pearson Succeeds Quimby as Pathé's Exchange Head," *MPW*, February 7, 1920, 927.

91. "Fred C. Quimby Leaves Associated Exhibitors to Become a Producer; Will Star Jack Dempsey in Serial," *MPW*, October 30, 1920, 1273.

92. "Harold Lloyd Signs Contract with Associated Exhibitors," *MPN*, July 3, 1920, 223.

93. "Associated Exhibitors Is Reorganized to Greatly Extend Present Activities," *MPW*, March 5, 1921, 33.

94. "Arthur Kane," *MPW*, February 7, 1920, 926; "Eclectic Shows 'Em," *MPW*, October 31, 1914, 644; "Arthur S. Kane Elected President of Associated Exhibitors," *MPN*, March 18, 1922, 1603.

95. "Associated Exhibitors, Inc., Starts with New York Capitol Chief Unit," *MPW*, 861.

96. "Associated Exhibitors' Power Is Shown in Analysis by General Manager Quimby," *MPW*, March 13, 1920, 1769.

97. "Four Weeks Before Its Release Date 'Riddle: Woman' Promises New Records," *MPW*, October 16, 1920, 991.

98. "Associated Exhibitors Secure Rights to 'The Devil,' Starring George Arliss," *MPW*, October 30, 1920, 1230.

99. "Release Date Set for Third Associated Exhibitors' Feature," *MPW*, February 12, 1921, 838.

100. Ad for Associated Exhibitors, *MPW*, February 5, 1921, unnumbered page.

101. *The Extra Girl* was to have been the first of a series of three or four feature pictures per year produced by Sennett, starring Normand and released through Associated Exhibitors. However, due largely to her implication in no less than two of the scandals that rocked Hollywood in the early 1920s, Normand withdrew from films for three years following the production of *The Extra Girl*.

102. Ad for Pathé, *MPN*, September 22, 1923, unnumbered page; Ad for Associated Exhibitors, *MPN*, November 10, 1923, unnumbered page.

103. "To the Exhibitors of America," *MPW*, June 11, 1921, 568.

104. "Marcus Loew Buys Interest in Metro," *MPN*, January 17, 1920, 815.

105. "Brunet Forecasts Pathé's Season," *MPW*, July 12, 1919, 231.

106. "Pathé Assumes Protector's Role: Styles Itself as Friend of the Small-Town Exhibitor," *MPN*, January 17, 1920, 865; "Small Theatres Continue to

Place Heavy Bookings for Pathé," *MPW*, February 7, 1920, 921; "Pathé Assumes Protector's Role," *MPN*, January 17, 1920, 865.

107. "Small Houses Fly Pathé Banner," *MPN*, February 7, 1920, 1487.

108. "Pathé Issues Statement Showing Business Done by Its Short Subjects," *MPW*, February 21, 1920, 1242.

109. Douglas Gomery, *The Hollywood Studio System* (New York: St. Martin's Press, 1986), 2.

110. Editorial cartoon, *MPW*, January 22, 1921, 382.

111. "Industry Is Seriously Threatened as 'Reformers' Besiege Congress," *MPW*, December 11, 1920, 696.

112. Paul Brunet, "Sunday Shows and Bolshevism," *MPN*, April 19, 1919, 2444.

113. "Knights of Columbus to Fight Blue Laws," *MPW*, February 26, 1921, 1017.

114. "Ministers Deal Blow to Blue Laws, Declaring Christianity Stands for Freedom as Well as Righteousness," *MPW*, April 30, 1921, 944.

115. "Fox and Pathé Win Victory Over Keystone Censors," *MPN*, April 1, 1916, 1904.

116. "Berst Asks Exhibitor Aid to Push Federal Censorship," *MPN*, July 29, 1916, 623.

117. "Pathé Giving Direct Support to Local Bodies Opposing Censorship and Blue Laws," *MPW*, February 19, 1921, 913.

118. "New York State passes a censorship law," *MPW*, April 30, 1921, 948.

119. "Pathé Starts a War on Censors," *MPW*, August 20, 1921, 782.

120. "Censors Again Cut Pathé News," *MPW*, August 27, 1921, 883.

121. "News Reels Liable to Censor Dictum," *MPW*, May 19, 1923, 214.

122. "Newsreel Non-Censor Bill Is Passed," *MPN*, April 16, 1926, 1581.

123. "Pathé Re-Affirms Its Intention to Only Distribute Pictures That Are Wholesome," *MPW*, March 26, 1921, 364.

124. Ad for Pathé, *MPN*, March 18, 1922, 1637.

125. "Nationwide Censorship Agitation," *MPW*, March 26, 1921, 356.

126. "Pathé Gets Kipling's First Scenario," *MPW*, February 19, 1921, 943; "Pathé Releases Big Kipling Film to Aid Theatres' Summer Business," *MPW*, June 18, 1921, 727.

127. "'Without Benefit of Clergy' Is Praised by New York Critics," *MPW*, July 9, 1921, 217.

128. "Boston, Atlanta and Cincinnati Critics Praise Highly Kipling's 'Without Benefit of Clergy,'" *MPW*, July 30, 1921, 524.

129. "Present American Stockholders Acquire Control of Pathé; Brunet Retains Office," *MPW*, July 2, 1921, 39.

CHAPTER FOUR
BANKING INTERESTS: 1921–26

1. "Brunet Succeeds Charles Pathé as President," *MPN*, September 25, 1920, 2496; "President Brunet Names Elmer Pearson General Manager of the Pathé Exchange," *MPW*, October 15, 1921, 749.

2. Willems, "The Origins of Pathé-Natan," 395.

3. Perkins, *Wall Street to Main Street*, 96.

4. Robert Lewis, "Edmund Lynch Biography" (unpublished manuscript, 1949), Merrill Lynch Corporate Archives, World Financial Center, New York, 92.

5. Willems, "The Origins of Pathé-Natan," 395.

6. Lewis, "Edmund Lynch Biography," 94.

7. Ibid.

8. Ibid., 95.

9. Perkins, *Wall Street to Main Street*, 97.

10. "New Pathé President Not to Be Elected Now," *MPN*, October 7, 1922, 1735.

11. "All Branches of Pathé Exchange Unite to Honor Paul Brunet," *MPN*, April 15, 1922, 2171.

12. Ibid.

13. "New Pathé President Not to Be Elected Now," *MPN*, October 7, 1922, 1735.

14. Perkins, *Wall Street to Main Street*, 97.

15. "Pearson Studies Growing Market, Pathé Executive Believes Short Subjects of Great Importance," *MPN*, November 25, 1922, 2675.

16. "Roach Congratulations to Pathé Officials," *MPN*, May 19, 1923, 2410.

17. Richard W. Bann, *Max Davidson—Blow by Blow* (2011). Retrieved from www.dick-und-doof.com/archive/articles/2011–01-davidson/davidson-2.html.

18. Perkins, *Wall Street to Main Street*, 97.

19. Lewis, "Edmund Lynch Biography," 96.

20. Ibid.; "Pathé Sales Show Increase," *MPN*, May 13, 1922, 2694; "Pathé Product Determined by Exhibitor Demand by Elmer Pearson," *MPN*, August 26, 1922, 1041.

21. "Brunet Says Depression Has Hit Bottom; Exhibitors Must Reduce Admission Fee," *MPW*, December 3, 1921, 525; "Pathé Bond Issue Rapidly Bought Up by Investing Public," *MPN*, December 3, 1921, 2929.

22. Raw stock is unexposed or blank film that can be used to photograph a movie or to make the copies that are shown in theaters.

23. U.S. Congress, House Committee on Ways and Means, *Photographic Film and Motion Pictures: Hearings on General Tariff Revision before the House*

of Representatives, Part 5, Schedule N—Sundries. 66th Cong., 3rd sess., 1921. Washington, DC: Government Printing Office, 1921, 3472–73.

24. Ansco, the only other manufacturer of raw film in the United States, provided rather feeble competition for Kodak, but its existence did preserve the illusion of free-market competition.

25. Perkins, *Wall Street to Main Street*, 98.

26. The Pathé Cinema Société Anonyme of Paris also held a minority stake in the new firm, a stipulation laid down when Charles Pathé granted the film patent rights with the sale of Pathé to Merrill Lynch.

27. "Du Pont Holds Control in New Organization," *MPN*, December 27, 1924, 3299.

28. Perkins, *Wall Street to Main Street*, 98.

29. "Government Charges Eastman with Conspiracy," *MPW*, May 12, 1923, 115; "Dissolution Demanded," *MPW*, May 3, 1924, 44.

30. "Pathé Classifies 450 Pictures under Title of Short Subjects for Next Year," *MPW*, August 6, 1921, 628; "Under American Control Pathé Will Enlarge Its Activities, Brunet Says," *MPW*, August 27, 1921, 924.

31. "Present American Stockholders Acquire Control of Pathé; Brunet Retains Office," *MPW*, July 2, 1921, 39.

32. Ad for Pathé, *MPN*, August 26, 1922, 1025.

33. "Pearson Talks of New Pathé Films; Sees Good Fall Business," *MPW*, July 28, 1923, 290.

34. Laurence Reid, review of *The Ballad of Fisher's Boarding House*, *MPN*, April 15, 1922, 2216.

35. "'The Price of Progress,' a Kiser Artfilm, 2 Reels, Dist. by Pathé," *MPN*, November 18, 1922, 2562; Ad for Pathé, *MPN*, January 20, 1923, 328.

36. "High Class Patronage Won by Pathé Pictures," *MPW*, December 22, 1923, 715.

37. Richard Koszarski, *Hollywood on the Hudson: Film and Television in New York from Griffith to Sarnoff* (New Brunswick, NJ: Rutgers University Press, 2008), 112. Koszarski goes on to report that the American Museum of Natural History circulated three sets of *Chronicles of America* in 35-millimeter film and another nine sets in 16-millimeter until 1941, and that *Chronicles* "became the first documentary film series ever shown on American television, when New York station WNBT aired nine of the episodes between July 3 and October 16, 1941."

38. "Pathé Acquires 'Famous Melody Series,'" *MPN*, January 2, 1926, unnumbered page; Ad for *Famous Melody Series*, *MPN*, February 6, 1926, 690; Review of *Famous Melody Series*, *MPN*, February 6, 1926, 699.

39. First National's contract with Chaplin actually paid him $1 million to produce eight films. Although that sum was renegotiated upward when Chaplin made the fifth film, *The Kid* (1921), as a feature, for publicity purposes Pathé simply halved the original purchase price for half as many films: $500,000 for four films.

40. *Exhibitors' Trade Review* (hereinafter *ETW*), January 21, 1922, 514.

41. Hoping for audience amnesia was probably overly optimistic; all four films had already been reissued by First National in 1922.

42. "Pathé Buys Chaplin Re-Issue Rights," *MPN*, October 3, 1925, 1581, 1583.

43. "Each Pathé Release Stands on Own Merit, Says Pearson," *MPW*, January 6, 1923, 31.

44. As late as the mid-1920s, there were only three major newsreels competing with Pathé's: International News, which was produced by Hearst and distributed by Universal; Kinograms, which was distributed by short-subject specialist Educational Pictures; and Fox News.

45. William Sheafe Chase, *Catechism on Motion Pictures in Inter-state Commerce*, 3rd ed. (New York: New York Civic League, 1922), 40–41; "Pathé Starts a War on Censors," *MPW*, August 20, 1921, 782; "Censors Again Cut Pathé News," *MPW*, August 27, 1921, 883.

46. Sumner Smith, "Pathé Strategy Deposes Ohio Censor; A Victory Not without Comic Touches," *MPW*, June 24, 1922, 695.

47. Chase, *Catechism on Motion Pictures*, 40–41.

48. Sumner Smith, "Pathé Strategy Deposes Ohio Censor; A Victory Not without Comic Touches," *MPW*, June 24, 1922, 695.

49. Ibid.

50. Among the other cities that received the *Pathé Newsletter* were New Orleans, Cleveland, Philadelphia, and Dallas.

51. "Pathé News in Radio Tie-Up, Ten Broadcasting Stations to Handle Matter Publicising [*sic*] Topical Subject," *MPN*, January 17, 1925, 242-D; "Add New Stations to Pathé News Broadcast System," *MPN*, January 31, 1925, 455; "Pathé News-Radio Tie-Up," *MPW*, April 11, 1925, 588.

52. "Studios Broadcast Laugh Month Program," *MPN*, January 30, 1926, 593.

53. "Cross-Country Radio Boosts 'Laugh Month'; Screens and Press Continue Fine Support," *MPW*, January 23, 1926, 325.

54. "'The Best Picture I Have Seen in Five Years'—Roxy," *MPW*, May 30, 1925, 567.

55. Review of *Pathé Review*, *MPW*, July 30, 1927.

56. "Use of Pathécolor in Review Now Increased," *MPN*, April 7, 1923, 1699.

57. Ad for Pathé, *MPW*, April 5, 1924, unnumbered page.

58. "Pathé Celebrates Anniversary of Its Better Serial Movement," *MPW*, February 7, 1925, 596.

59. "'The Way of a Man' Made by Pathé as Feature and Serial," *MPW*, November 3, 1923, 155; Pathéserial and Pathépicture ad for *The Way of a Man*, *MPW*, December 1, 1923.

60. Phil M. Roe, "At the World's Crossroads," *MPW*, August 13, 1927, 462.

61. "Pathé," *MPW*, March 26, 1927, 398.

62. "Fine Arts Soon to Close Doors," *MPW*, October 22, 1927, 497.

63. "Pathé Serials Reach Forty Per Cent of American Theatres," *MPW*, February 5, 1927, 417, 421.

64. Leonard Maltin, *Of Mice and Magic* (New York: Plume, 1987), 128–29.

65. Ibid, 130.

66. Michael Barrier, *The Animated Man: A Life of Walt Disney* (Berkeley: University of California Press, 2007) 33.

67. Ibid., 67.

68. Ibid.

69. Maltin, *Of Mice and Magic*, 130.

70. "Animated Cartoon Suit Over Patents Settled," *MPW*, September 11, 1926, 3.

71. Maltin, *Of Mice and Magic*, 131.

72. Ibid., 207–8.

73. Ad for Pathé, *MPN*, August 26, 1922, 1025, 1045.

74. "Pathé Announces Acquisition of Noted European Production," *MPW*, January 28, 1922, 394.

75. Laurence Reid, review of *Isle of Zorda*, *MPN*, March 25, 1922, 1756; "*Isle of Zorda* Scores Big Bookings, Some for Long Runs," *MPW*, May 27, 1922, 388.

76. Among Pathé's other feature documentaries were *Black Shadows* (1923), which was set in the Solomon Islands, produced by World Tours, Inc., and edited and subtitled at the Hal Roach Studios; and 1925's *Kivalina of the Ice Lands*, which promised scenes of the aurora borealis in "natural colors." But the studio that experienced the greatest success with feature documentaries after *Nanook* was Paramount, which released *Grass* (Merian C. Cooper and Ernest B. Schoedsack, 1925), *Moana* (Flaherty, 1926), *Chang* (Cooper and Schoedsack, 1927), and *Tabu* (Flaherty and F. W. Murnau, 1931).

77. Ad for Pathé–Associated Exhibitors, March 18, 1922, unnumbered page.

78. A similar report in *MPN* on August 12, 1922, demonstrates how much higher the 87 percent ratings for *A Sailor-Made Man* were than the ratings for the other releases from Associated Exhibitors and Pathé. Associated Exhibitors' *Handle with Care* averaged 63 percent, *Hills of Missing Men* averaged 54

percent, and *Woman Wake Up* earned 59 percent. Pathé's *Isle of Zorda* earned 72 percent, *Nanook of the North* received 70 percent, and *The Power Within* averaged 66 percent.

79. "Exhibitor Reports in Percentages," *MPN*, May 4, 1922, 2548.

80. And it should be remembered that this record would have surpassed the Los Angeles run of Charlie Chaplin's wildly successful comedy-drama *The Kid* (1921).

81. "Records for Grandma's Boy," *MPN*, September 9, 1922, 1282; Ad for Associated Exhibitors, *MPN*, October 7, 1922; "Lloyd's Latest Is Popular," *MPN*, June 3, 1922, 3054.

82. Associated Exhibitors ad reprints an editorial from *The Portland Telegram*, Portland, Oregon, September 2, 1922.

83. "Straight from the Shoulder Reports," *MPW*, March 10, 1923, 221.

84. "Dr. Jack Breaking Records," *MPW*, January 27, 1923, 376.

85. "'Dr. Jack' to Soon Attain 100 Per Cent Distribution," *MPW*, February 23, 1924, 637.

86. "Straight from the Shoulder Reports," *MPW*, March 10, 1923, 226–27.

87. "Straight from the Shoulder Reports," *MPW*, February 3, 1923, 470.

88. "Lloyd's Seven Reel Comedy Full of Thrills," *MPW*, March 10, 1923, 236.

89. "Novelties Supplied for 'Safety Last,'" *MPW*, March 24, 1923, 456.

90. "Straight from the Shoulder," *MPW*, May 12, 1923, 153; "Exhibitors Say Harold Lloyd's 'Safety Last' Is in Class by Itself," *MPW*, March 17, 1923, 359; "'Safety Last' Is Breaking Records," *MPW*, May 5, 1923, 80.

91. "Pathé Films Lead List in Sherwood Selection," *MPW*, December 15, 1923, 638.

92. Tom Dardis, *Harold Lloyd: The Man on the Clock* (New York: Viking Press, 1983), 88.

93. "Lloyd and Roach Terminate Relations in Friendly Way," *MPW*, July 7, 1923, 52; "Lloyd, Roach Terminate Business Relations," *MPN*, July 7, 1923, 51.

94. "Lloyd and Valentino to Distribute Their Pictures through Paramount," *MPW*, October 11, 1924, 472.

95. Ad for Pathé, *MPW*, August 1, 1925, unnumbered page.

96. W. B. Frank to Warren Doane, October 3, 1924, Hal Roach Collection, USC Cinematic Arts Library, box 5, 1924 file.

97. Frank to Doane, November 14, 1924, Hal Roach Collection, USC Cinematic Arts Library, box 5, 1924 file.

98. "Pathé to Distribute Series of Charles Ray Productions," *MPW*, May 24, 1924, 362.

99. "Pathé's 1924–25 Program," *MPW*, July 26, 1924, 279.

100. "The Check Up," *MPN*, May 9, 1925, 2151; "The Check-Up," *MPN*, September 12, 1925, 1258–59.

101. "Semon Dons Straight Make-up For Role in 'Stop, Look, Listen,'" *MPW*, January 2, 1926, 69.

102. George T. Pardy, review of *Stop, Look, and Listen*, *MPN*, January 30, 1926, 600.

103. Ward, *A History of the Hal Roach* Studios, 55; "The Check-Up," *MPN*, November 8, 1924, 2365; C. S. Sewell, review of *Black Cyclone*, *MPW*, May 30, 1925, 537; "The Check Up," *MPN*, May 9, 1925, 2151.

104. Compare this to Charles Ray's first film for Pathé, *Dynamite Smith* (1924), which averaged only 50 percent.

105. "'Atta Boy' Unit Only One at Hal Roach Studio," MPN, August 7, 1926, 498. In fact, the only production companies shooting when the regular Roach producing units took their summer break in July 1926 were for Banks' *Atta Boy* and Rudolph Valentino's swan song, *Son of the Sheik*.

106. "That Pathé Rooster," *MPN*, October 10, 1925, 1674.

107. "Edna Murphy to Star in Pathé's Novel Serial 'Dangerous Paths,'" *MPW*, May 26, 1923, 337.

108. "'Way of Man' Marks Decided Pathé Serial Policy Change," *MPW*, February 2, 1924, 416.

109. "Pathé to Handle Ben Turpin and Mack Sennett Comedies," *MPW*, March 24, 1923, 407; "Pathé Has Huge 2-Reel Comedy Program; Sennett and Roach Signed Up to Supply 104," *MPW*, June 6, 1925, 662.

110. "Paramount in Short-Subject Field; Re-enters Market with Series of 25 Mack Sennett Re-Issues; Due Aug. 5," *MPN*, July 7, 1923, 75.

111. Our Gang received universally positive reviews as a crowd pleaser from theater managers. A specific example is quoted in a Pathé ad, *MPW*, March 10, 1923, unnumbered page.

112. Chase spelled his first name "Charley," not "Charlie." Unfortunately, even studio documents and reissue film credits occasionally got it wrong.

113. T. C. Kennedy, "Opinions on Current Short Subjects," *MPN*, November 29, 1924, 2857.

114. W. B. Frank letter to Warren Doane, December 4, 1926, Hal Roach Collection, USC Cinematic Arts Library, box 5, file within 1924 file: Warren Doane Dec. 1924; Frank to Doane October 9, 1924, Hal Roach Collection, USC Cinematic Arts Library, box 5, file within 1924 file: Warren Doane Dec. 1924.

115. Frank to Doane, December 4, 1926, Hal Roach Collection, USC Cinematic Arts Library, box 5, file within 1924 file: Warren Doane Dec. 1924; Frank

to Doane, November 26, 1924, Hal Roach Collection, USC Cinematic Arts Library, box 5, file within 1924 file: Warren Doane Dec. 1924.

116. Frank to Doane, December 4, 1926, Hal Roach Collection, USC Cinematic Arts Library, box 5, file within 1924 file: Warren Doane Dec. 1924; Doane to Frank, October 7, 1924, Hal Roach Collection, USC Cinematic Arts Library, box 5, file within 1924 file: Warren Doane Dec. 1924.

117. Frank to Doane, December 4, 1926, Hal Roach Collection, USC Cinematic Arts Library, box 5, file within 1924 file: Warren Doane Dec. 1924; Doane to Frank January 26, 1926, Hal Roach Collection, USC Cinematic Arts Library, box 5, file within 1924 file: Warren Doane Jan. 1926.

118. Frank to Doane, December 4, 1926, USC, Hal Roach Collection, USC Cinematic Arts Library, box 5, file within 1924 file: Warren Doane Dec. 1924; Doane to Frank, January 26, 1926, Hal Roach Collection, USC Cinematic Arts Library, box 5, file within 1924 file: Warren Doane Jan. 1926.

119. "Keith-Albee Theatres Exploit 'Our Gang;' Hippodrome Prologue for 'Your Own Back Yard,'" *MPW*, October 17, 1925, 573.

120. Frank to Doane, December 4, 1926, Hal Roach Collection, USC Cinematic Arts Library, box 5, file within 1924 file: Warren Doane Dec. 1924; Frank to Doane, October 30, 1925, Hal Roach Collection, USC Cinematic Arts Library, box 5, 1925 file.

121. Frank to Doane, December 4, 1926, Hal Roach Collection, USC Cinematic Arts Library, box 5, file within 1924 file: Warren Doane Dec. 1924; Frank telegram to Doane, March 23, 1926, Hal Roach Collection, USC Cinematic Arts Library, box 5, file within 1924 file: Warren Doane March 1926.

122. Hal Roach Studios, telegram to Red Kahn of the *Film Daily*, May 26, 1926, in answer to inquiries from Kahn, Hal Roach Collection, USC Cinematic Arts Library, box 6, 1926 file.

123. Warren Doane to Fred Quimby, June 10, 1927, Hal Roach Collection, USC Cinematic Arts Library, box 6, Fred Quimby 1926–27 file; Doane to H. M. Walker, April 19, 1927, and Walker to Doane, April 25, 1927, Hal Roach Collection, USC Cinematic Arts Library, H. M. Walker New York April 1927 file.

124. Roach could produce feature-length films for MGM while still under contract to Pathé. To this end the studio made two westerns: *The Desert's Toll* (1926) and *The Valley of Hell* (1927).

125. Frank to Doane, December 4, 1926, Hal Roach Collection, USC Cinematic Arts Library, box 5, file within 1924 file: Warren Doane Dec. 1924; Frank to Doane, April 2, 1926, Hal Roach Collection, USC Cinematic Arts Library, box 5, file within 1924 file: Warren Doane April 1926.

126. "Educational Planning Sound Newsreel; 114 Short Subjects on '30-'31 Schedule," *MPN*, May 24, 1930, 98; Ad for Educational Film Exchanges, *MPH*, August 29, 1931, 31; "Christie, Al(bert)," Katz, *Film Encyclopedia*, 236–37.

127. "Arthur S. Kane Elected President of Associated Exhibitors," *MPN*, March 18, 1922, 1603.

128. Ad for Associated Exhibitors, *MPN*, November 10, 1923, unnumbered page.

129. "Associated Exhibitors' Plan Reduces Distribution Costs," *MPW*, August 23, 1924, 530.

130. "Selznick Liquidates; Associated Gets Features and F. B. O. Shorts," *MPW*, November 29, 1924, 406.

131. "Arthur S. Kane with Universal; Resigned Associated Presidency," *MPW*, March 28, 1925, 343.

132. "Associated Exhibitors Elects Woody; Radical Policy Changes Are Planned," *MPW*, April 4, 1925, 445.

133. "Associated Exhibitors Will Release Guaranteed Pictures, Announces Woody," *MPW*, June 6, 1925, 675.

134. "P. A. Powers Heads Board of Directors of Reorganized Associated Exhibitors," *MPN*, October 3, 1925, 591.

135. Clive Hirschhorn, *The Universal Story* (New York: Crown Publishers, 1983), 8–11.

136. Richard B. Jewell and Vernon Harbin, *The RKO Story* (London: Octopus Books, 1982), 8.

137. "Associated's New Directorate Named, with Powers Chairman," *MPW*, October 3, 1925, 384.

138. "Associated Establishes Own Booking Service; Install New Branch Managers," *MPW*, November 21, 1925, 235; "States Associated Exhibitors Policy," *MPN*, December 19, 1925, 2998.

139. "Associated Busy on New Product," *MPN*, January 9, 1926, 169.

140. "Selznick Heads Assoc. Exhibs.: Company Reorganized, Plan Being to Release One a Week in Addition to Twelve Specials," *MPN*, July 3, 1926, 34.

141. "Pathé Assumes Distribution of All Associated Product," *MPW*, October 30, 1926, 1; "Eschmann Heads Pathé Feature Sales," *MPN*, November 6, 1926, 1758A.

142. William A. Johnston, "An Editor on Broadway," *MPN*, November 20, 1926, 1925.

143. To make matters confusing, Associated Exhibitors and Pathé released another series of westerns with an actor whose actual name was Bill Cody. He was no relation to either the famous Buffalo Bill Cody or to "Buffalo Bill Jr."

144. Quick Reference Picture Chart, *MPW*, September 24, 1927, 266.

145. "Covarrubias Presents Distinguished Picture People," *MPW*, April 17, 1926, unnumbered page.

146. "Pathé Profits Show an Increase," *MPN*, April 17, 1926, 1794.

147. "Warner Bros. Buy Vitagraph; Acquire 50 Branches throughout the World," *MPW*, May 2, 1925, 25; Thomas Schatz, *The Genius of the System* (New York: Pantheon Books, 1988), 60–61; Tony Thomas and Aubrey Solomon, *The Films of 20th Century Fox: A Pictorial History* Secaucus, NJ: Citadel Press, 1979), 13.

148. Perkins, *Wall Street to Main Street*, 98.

149. Ibid., 99.

150. "Blair & Company in Film Field," *New York Times* (hereinafter *NYT*), October 9, 1926, p. 25, col. 4.

CHAPTER FIVE
"TRYING TO FIGURE WHETHER PRODUCERS BOUGHT PATHÉ OR PATHÉ, PRODUCERS": 1926–28

1. While his last name is also variously spelled de Mille and De Mille, even in studio correspondence, DeMille is the spelling of choice.

2. "Hodkinson Changes Corporate Name to Producers Distributing Corporation," *MPW*, June 28, 1924, 780; "Hodkinson Changes Corporate Name," *MPN*, June 28, 1924, 3062; "De Mille and F. P. Sever; Future Berth Unannounced," *MPW*, January 24, 1925, 323; "De Mille Affiliation Pending, Purchase of Interest in Producers Distributing Corporation Rumored," *MPN*, January 31, 1925, 426; "Cecil B. De Mille and Prod. Dist. Corp. Affiliate in New $10,000,000 Company, New Company Takes Over De Mille Unit, with Stars, and Control of Distributing Organization—Ince Studio in Deal," *MPW*, February 21, 1925, 770–72. Robert S. Birchard, *Cecil B. DeMille's Hollywood* (Lexington: University Press of Kentucky, 2004), 200–1.

3. Birchard, *Cecil B. DeMille's Hollywood*, 205.

4. Ibid., 201.

5. Ibid., 211.

6. Pathé Exchange records, Margaret Herrick Library, Academy of Motion Picture Arts and Sciences, folder 7, Financial Matters 1925–28; Birchard, *Cecil B. DeMille's Hollywood*, 211.

7. "Keith and Orpheum Buy a Half Interest in Pro. Dis. Co.," *MPW*, May 15, 1926, 1; William Reilly, editorial, *MPW*, May 22, 1926, 1.

8. In 1916 Paramount had distributed the *Paramount Pictograph*, a newsmagazine reel similar to the *Pathé Review*.

9. "Paramount Short Subjects to Be Widely Advertised by Emmanuel Cohen," *MPN*, April 15, 1927, 1343.

10. "'Our Gang' Comedy on Pathé Program for July 31," *MPW*, July 23, 1927, 260.

11. Ad for Pathé, *MPW*, April 9, 1927, 530–31.

12. Ray Hall, Emanuel Cohen's replacement as editor, was assisted by Louis de Rochemont, a future documentarian who was one of the founding filmmakers behind the *March of Time* newsreel series of the 1930s and 1940s.

13. Two-page ad for *Pathé News*, *MPW*, April 29, 1927, unnumbered page.

14. Ad for Paramount News, *MPW*, August 6, 1927, unnumbered page.

15. Ad for Pathé, *MPW*, November 12, 1927, unnumbered page.

16. "Blair & Company in Film Field," *NYT*, October 9, 1926, 25:4.

17. "Merger Is Only Planned," *NYT*, March 13, 1927, 22:2; "Keith-Pathé Merger Nearing Completion," *NYT*, April 1, 1927, 26:2.

18. The film's premiere was pushed back two months while construction of the theater was being completed. *King of Kings* would run constantly at the Chinese Theatre for over six months.

19. "King of Kings to Charge Only $11 Per Person," *MPW*, March 5, 1927, 31; "'King of Kings' to Rate N.Y. Premiere?," *MPW*, March 19, 1927, unnumbered page; Birchard, *Cecil B. DeMille's Hollywood*, 232.

20. T. C. Streibert memo to Joseph Kennedy, February 23, 1928, regarding Pathé-DeMille contract dated April 11, 1927, John F. Kennedy Presidential Library, Joseph P. Kennedy Personal Papers.

21. Tom Waller, "New Combine Will Banner 486 Pictures as 1927–28 Schedule," *MPW*, June 11, 1927, unnumbered page.

22. "James Cruze Joins P.D.C.—Pathé Unit," *MPW*, June 4, 1927, 325.

23. Letter from Cecil B. DeMille Pictures to Price Waterhouse, December 7, 1927, Pathé Exchange records, Margaret Herrick Library, Academy of Motion Picture Arts and Sciences, folder 1, Auditing Matters; W. G. Hutchinson, comptroller for Cecil B. DeMille Pictures, to Price Waterhouse, January 16, 1928, Pathé Exchange records, Margaret Herrick Library, Academy of Motion Picture Arts and Sciences, folder 1, Auditing Matters; W. G. Hutchinson to William Sistrom, April 3, 1928, Pathé Exchange records, Margaret Herrick Library, Academy of Motion Picture Arts and Sciences, folder 3, James Cruze Production Costs.

24. Thomas C. Kennedy, review of *The Country Doctor*, *MPN*, September 9, 1927, 786.

25. Facts Which Made It Desirable for Pathé to Accept the RKO Deal, undated, unsigned, Joseph P. Kennedy Personal Papers, John F. Kennedy Presidential Library, Joseph P. Kennedy Personal Papers.

26. "Buyers Index," *Exhibitors Herald and Moving Picture World* (hereinafter *EH & MPW*), April 28, 1928, 64–66, 73, 76.

27. Herbert Knicht Cruikshank, "They Don't Like 'Em—Not Much," *MPW*, October 22, 1927, 501.

28. "More Than Million to Glimpse Pathé Films on Broadway in Week," *MPW*, October 29, 1927, 553.

29. Cari Beauchamp, *Joseph P. Kennedy Presents His Hollywood Years* (New York: Vintage Books, 2009), 143.

30. "F.B.O. Changes Hands," *Film Daily* (hereinafter *FD*), February 8, 1926, 1, 3.

31. Donald Crafton, *The Talkies: American Cinema's Transition to Sound, 1926–1931* (New York: Charles Scribner's Sons, 1997), 136; Beauchamp, *Joseph P. Kennedy*, 11, 13.

32. Beauchamp, *Joseph P. Kennedy*, 17, 19.

33. Ibid., 35–36.

34. Jewell and Harbin, *The RKO Story*, 8–10.

35. "P. A. Powers Joins Robertson-Cole," *Exhibitors Trade Review* (hereinafter *ETR*), February 18, 1922, 800.

36. Jewell and Harbin, *The RKO Story*, 8; "F.B.O. Changes Hands," *FD*, February 8, 1926, 1, 3.

37. "Kennedy Elected F. B. O. Chairman; Derr Treasurer," *MPW*, March 20, 1926, 1, 2.

38. Crafton, *The Talkies*, 136.

39. "Kennedy Elected F. B. O. Chairman; Derr Treasurer," *MPW*, March 20, 1926, 1, 2; "Derr Starts Movie Career from Top," *Sunday News*, March 16, 1930, John F. Kennedy Presidential Library, Joseph P. Kennedy Personal Papers.

40. Joseph P. Kennedy letter to Guy W. Currier, April 7, 1928, John F. Kennedy Presidential Library, Joseph P. Kennedy Personal Papers.

41. "Mr. Joseph P. Kennedy," *EH & MPW*, March 3, 1928, 14.

42. Beauchamp, *Joseph P. Kennedy*, 145.

43. Crafton, *The Talkies*, 138.

44. Beauchamp, *Joseph P. Kennedy*, 148.

45. Ibid., 144.

46. Ibid., 151.

47. Cecil B. DeMille letter to Joseph P. Kennedy at FBO, March 14, 1928, John F. Kennedy Presidential Library, Joseph P. Kennedy Personal Papers.

48. George Armsby telegram to Elisha Walker, March 16, 1928, John F. Kennedy Presidential Library, Joseph P. Kennedy Personal Papers.

49. "De Mille-Kennedy Confer on Future Plans," *MPN*, March 24, 1928, 949.

50. Joseph P. Kennedy to Elisha Walker, April 4, 1928, John F. Kennedy Presidential Library, Joseph P. Kennedy Personal Papers.

51. Brent E. Walker, *Mack Sennett's Fun Factory* (Jefferson, NC: McFarland, 2010), 179.

52. Ibid., 218.

53. Despite their exotic stage names, both actresses were American.

54. Urson had worked as DeMille's assistant director on *The King of Kings* and *The Godless Girl*, but he was also a director in his own right. The most common explanation for why DeMille did not take credit for *Chicago* is that he thought his association with a film about the amoral Roxie Hart might blunt the box-office potential of *The King of Kings*, which would not go into general release until September 1928. Robert Birchard, who has written the definitive book on DeMille, says that both DeMille and Urson alternated directing during the principal photography of *Chicago*, with DeMille doing the retakes and supervising the editing. Tragically, Urson would drown while on vacation in the summer of 1928.

55. Birchard, *Cecil B. DeMille's Hollywood*, 232.

56. Crafton, *The Talkies*, 25, 52.

57. Ibid., 134.

58. Ibid., 131.

59. Ibid., 136–37.

60. Richard B. Jewell, *The Golden Age of Cinema: Hollywood, 1929–1945* (Malden, MA: Blackwell Publishing, 2007), 94.

61. The general release version ran 112 minutes, as compared to the 155-minute version that ran at Grauman's Chinese Theatre.

62. "Straight from the Shoulder," *MPW*, November 5, 1927, 45.

63. Beauchamp, *Joseph P. Kennedy*, 193.

64. Memo on RCA Photophone stationery concerning a conference held in Elisha Walker's Office on July 24, 1928, John F. Kennedy Presidential Library, Joseph P. Kennedy Personal Papers.

65. Ibid.

66. There was at least one other operational difference between Photophone and Movietone. In the early days of sound, before the art and technology of audio mixing was perfected, films were actually released with cue sheets that instructed projectionists on where the sound would need to be turned up or down in a film and by how much. GE's engineers discovered that RCA and Western Electric sound readers behaved differently in this regard, with RCA fader settings operating at approximately twice the value of Western Electric settings. For example, if the proper fader setting was "4 above normal" on an RCA system playing a Photophone sound track, it would only be "2 above normal" for a Western Electric system playing the same sound track.

67. Memo on RCA Photophone stationery concerning a conference held in Elisha Walker's Office on July 24, 1928, John F. Kennedy Presidential Library, Joseph P. Kennedy Personal Papers; Crafton, *The Talkies*, 139–40.

68. During this period, the *Exhibitors Herald World* (hereinafter *EHW*) launched a campaign to find a replacement for the word "talkie" in connection with sound films. The magazine's own choice was "audien," and for a time it routinely published stories using the word. As an example, the title of one article published on January 26, 1929, was "George LeMaire, Comedy Maker, Signed to Make 12 Pathé Audiens." Pathé's Colvin Brown suggested "electrical entertainment," adding that "any effort to kill the word 'talkie' is commendable, and if the word is killed, the industry will have been rendered a great favor." See *EH & MPW*, December 22, 1928, 16. William LeBaron banned the word "talkie" at his studio, preferring "dialogue film." See *EHW*, January 12, 1929, 29. In the end, of course, all of the efforts to dislodge "talkie" from the lexicon failed.

69. Memo on RCA Photophone stationery concerning a conference held in Elisha Walker's Office on July 24, 1928, John F. Kennedy Presidential Library, Joseph P. Kennedy Personal Papers.

70. Birchard, *Joseph P. Kennedy*, 232.

71. Memo on RCA Photophone stationery concerning a conference held in Elisha Walker's Office on July 24, 1928, John F. Kennedy Presidential Library, Joseph P. Kennedy Personal Papers.

72. "New Amusement Combination," Boston News Bureau, Friday, June 15, 1928, John F. Kennedy Presidential Library, Joseph P. Kennedy Personal Papers.

73. Crafton, *The Talkies*, 141–42.

CHAPTER SIX
"I HAVEN'T ANY HI-FALUTING THEORIES ABOUT PRODUCTION": 1928–31

1. Ad for FBO, *EH & MPW*, June 9, 1928, unnumbered page.

2. Crafton, *The Talkies*, 139–40.

3. Byron Haskin, *Hollywood: A Celebration of the American Silent Film—The Autocrats*, VHS, directed by Kevin Brownlow and David Gill (HBO Home Video, 1998).

4. William LeBaron, Los Angeles, letter to Joseph Kennedy, New York, September 25, 1928, John F. Kennedy Presidential Library, Joseph P. Kennedy Personal Papers.

5. Crafton, *The Talkies*, 139–40.

6. Ibid.

7. Ibid., 141.

8. Ibid.

9. Price Waterhouse report dated February 4, 1931, on Gloria Productions accounts, December 1, 1928, to December 31, 1930, John F. Kennedy Presidential Library, Joseph P. Kennedy Personal Papers.

10. Pathé Studios, Inc., interoffice communication from E. A. Tambert to Charles Sullivan, June 21, 1930, John F. Kennedy Presidential Library, Joseph P. Kennedy Personal Papers; Walter Brooks letter to H. S. Brown, September 26, 1930. Brown sent copies to Elisha Walker at the Transamerica Corporation and to J. P. Kennedy, John F. Kennedy Presidential Library, Joseph P. Kennedy Personal Papers.

11. Pathé interoffice communication to Mr. Tambert, cc: Mr. Sullivan, from William Sistrom, March 8, 1929, John F. Kennedy Presidential Library, Joseph P. Kennedy Personal Papers; Pathé Studios interoffice communication from E. A. Tambert to William Sistrom, with answers from Sistrom, June 12, 1929, John F. Kennedy Presidential Library, Joseph P. Kennedy Personal Papers; C. J. Dunphy, president of Gloria Productions, to Pathé board of directors, April 23, 1931, John F. Kennedy Presidential Library, Joseph P. Kennedy Personal Papers.

12. E. A. Tambert to Charles Sullivan, Pathé Studios interoffice communication, June 21, 1930, John F. Kennedy Presidential Library, Joseph P. Kennedy Personal Papers.

13. C. J. Dunphy, president of Gloria Productions, to Pathé board of directors, April 23, 1931, John F. Kennedy Presidential Library, Joseph P. Kennedy Personal Papers.

14. Ibid.; "Pathé Units Twiddle Thumbs as Gloria Uses 11 Stages—All for One Production," *MPN*, April 12, 1930, 19.

15. Postal telegram from Pat Scollard in New York to C. E. Sullivan of Pathé Studios, Inc., Culver City, California, July 18, 1930, Pathé Exchange records, Margaret Herrick Library, Academy of Motion Picture Arts and Sciences, folder 1, Auditing Matters.

16. Letter on Pathé Exchange letterhead, New York, from A. B. Poole, treasurer, to Joseph P. Kennedy in Palm Beach, Florida, March 18, 1931, John F. Kennedy Presidential Library, Joseph P. Kennedy Personal Papers.

17. Letter to Pathé from president of Gloria Productions, C. J. Dunphy, April 23, 1931, John F. Kennedy Presidential Library, Joseph P. Kennedy Personal Papers.

18. Ad for Pathé product, *EH & MPW*, June 16, 1928, 27.

19. Ibid., 28.

20. "Fifteen Elected to Pathé Board; Officers Chosen," *EH & MPW*, June 2, 1928, 75.

21. "Ramsaye Editor Pathé Eastern Productions," *EH & MPW*, August 4, 1928, 396.

22. Ad for Pathé product, *EH & MPW*, June 16, 1928, 29.

23. "Pathé Concentrating at Culver City," *MPN*, August 25, 1928, 607.

24. "Derr Starts Movie Career from Top" *Sunday News*, March 1?, 1930, John F. Kennedy Presidential Library, Joseph P. Kennedy Personal Papers.

25. Ibid.

26. E. B. Derr letter to William Sistrom, June 7, 1928, John F. Kennedy Presidential Library, Joseph P. Kennedy Personal Papers.

27. Document titled "Financing," April 29, 1928, John F. Kennedy Presidential Library, Joseph P. Kennedy Personal Papers.

28. Ibid.

29. Ibid.

30. Ibid.

31. Fourth Year Productions (1928–29), Pathé Exchange records, Margaret Herrick Library, Academy of Motion Picture Arts and Sciences, folder 5, De Mille Metropolitan Pictures.

32. Facts Which Made It Desirable for Pathé to Accept the RKO Deal, undated, unsigned, John F. Kennedy Presidential Library, Joseph P. Kennedy Personal Papers.

33. Colvin W. Brown memo to J. P. Kennedy, October 23, 1928, John F. Kennedy Presidential Library, Joseph P. Kennedy Personal Papers.

34. "Old Pathé Plant in N.Y. Remodeled as Manhattan Studio," *EH & MPW*, July 7, 1928, 42.

35. "Sound Studios, Inc., Now in Work," *EH & MPW*, September 29, 1928, 33.

36. Father of the infamous 1980s talk-show host, Morton Downey Jr.

37. Ad for Pathé, *EH & MPW*, June 30, 1928, 12.

38. Giovanna Fossati, "When the Cinema Was Colored," in *All the Colors of the World: Colors in Early Mass Media 1900–1930*, ed. Luciano Berriatúa (Reggio Emilia: Diabasis, 1998), 124.

39. "Pathéchrome, New Color Process, to Make Bow in Pathé Review," *EH & MPW*, November 24, 1928, 34.

40. "First Pathéchrome Sound Pictures on Way to America," *EHW*, May 11, 1929, 26. Experiments are completed, and the first shipment is on its way to America. The first color image will be of Mr. Pathé, the rooster, crowing.

41. "Pathé Rooster to Crow as Picture Starts," *EH & MPW*, July 7, 1928, 21.

42. Anthony L'Abbate, film preservation officer at the George Eastman House, email to the author, March 11, 2015.

43. British Pathé. *Pathecolor Sic Nature's Teacup—Crater Lake In Oregon (1927)*, 3 min., 50 sec., YouTube, https://www.youtube.com/watch?v=Lu1jKA_MwX8.

44. British Pathé. *Pathe Review—Colour Clips (1928)*, 12 min., 20 sec., YouTube, https://www.youtube.com/watch?v=AhGPnisQL4o.

45. Review of *Pathé Audio Review #13*, *MPN*, March 29, 1930, 56.

46. Review of *Pathé Audio Review #23*, *MPN*, June 7, 1930, 138; Review of *Pathé Audio Review #30*, *MPN*, July 26, 1930, 63; Review of *Pathé Audio Review #36*, *MPN*, September 13, 1930, 59; Review of *Pathé Audio Review #39*, *MPN*, September 27, 1930, 44.

47. Salmon, *Pathé*, 516.

48. Paul Read, "Unnatural Colours: An Introduction to Colouring Techniques in Silent Era Movies," *Film History* 21, no. 1 (2009): 16.

49. "Pathé Sound News Issues Color Film as Fast as Black and White," *EHW*, March 22, 1930, 49.

50. *New York Sun*, March 25, 1930.

51. As an interesting side note, former Pathé producer Mack Sennett made some of his comedies in the very early 1930s in his own version of Prizma under the name Sennett-Color.

52. M. Robach, "Color in Motion Pictures," *International Projectionist*, November 1931, 11–12.

53. Terry Ramsaye to E. B. Derr, March 31, 1930, Pathé Exchange records, Margaret Herrick Library, Academy of Motion Picture Arts and Sciences.

54. Review of *Pathé Audio Review #23*, *MPN*, June 7, 1930, 138; Review of *Pathé Audio Review #30*, *MPN*, July 26, 1930, 63; Review of *Pathé Audio Review #36*, *MPN*, September 13, 1930, 59; Review of *Pathé Audio Review #39*, *MPN*, September 27, 1930, 44.

55. "Pathé Sound News Issues Color Film as Fast as Black and White," *EHW*, March 22, 1930, 49.

56. "Pathé Audio Review Makes Its Bow with Terry Ramsaye Editor," *EHW*, March 30, 1929, 32.

57. J. J. Murdock cover letter to Pathé stockholders, dated May 19, 1928, accompanying the balance sheet as of December 31, 1927, John F. Kennedy Presidential Library, Joseph P. Kennedy Personal Papers.

58. Rob King, "The Spice of the Program: Educational Pictures, Early Sound Slapstick, and the Small-Town Audience," *Film History* 23, no. 3 (2011): 322.

59. Review of *Syncopated Trial* (Morgan Morley and Lew Seymour, 2 reels, Melody all-talking comedy), *MPN*, September 14, 1929, 989. "[T]he less said about it the better"; Review of *All Stuck Up* (Harry McNaughton, 2 reels, Checker all-talking comedy), *MPN*, February 1, 1930, 81. "Inexcusable"; Review

of *Pick 'Em Young* (Robert Agnew, 2 reels, Melody comedy), *MPN*, May 10, 1930, 56. "Weak in every department."

60. Associated Press report printed in the *Freeport Journal-Standard* (Freeport, Illinois), December 10, 1929, 1, 4.

61. Richard Koszarski, "Laughter, Music and Tragedy at the New York Pathé Studio," *Film History* 14, no. 1 (2002): 36.

62. Terry Ramsaye, Western Union telegram to E. B. Derr, December 10, 1929, Pathé Exchange records, Margaret Herrick Library, Academy of Motion Picture Arts and Sciences, Folder 10, General Matters.

63. Terry Ramsaye letter to E. B. Derr, December 14, 1929, Pathé Exchange records, Margaret Herrick Library, Academy of Motion Picture Arts and Sciences, folder 10, General Matters.

64. "Pathé Studio Heads Fined in Fire Case," *NYT*, March 18, 1930, 29:1.

65. "Inspector Testifies on Pathé Plant Visit," *NYT*, January 18, 1930, 9:2.

66. "Refuses to Indict Pathé Studio Heads," *NYT*, March 25, 1930, 31:1.

67. "Says Pathé Studio Ignored Fire Rule," *NYT*, March 6, 1930, 25:8; "Says Pathé Studio Lacked Fire Hose," *NYT*, March 11, 1930, 56:2.

68. "Refuses to Indict Pathé Studio Heads," *NYT*, March 25, 1930, 31:1.

69. "Pathé Studio Heads Blamed by M'Adoo" *NYT*, March 27, 1930, 1:5.

70. "Crain Will Reopen Pathé Fire Inquiry," *NYT*, March 28, 1930, 27:6; "Indicts Pathé Heads in Fatal Studio Fire," *NYT*, April 4, 1930, 27:1

71. "Indictments Delayed in Pathé Fire Case," *NYT*, April 5, 1930, 4:5.

72. Stephen G. Christianson, "Triangle Shirtwaist Factory Fire," in *Great American Trials*, ed. Edward W. Knappman (Detroit: Visible Ink, 1994), 257.

73. "Scandals of New York," *Time*, April 20, 1931; "Study Crain Action in Pathé Film Fire," *NYT*, March 22, 1931, 25:1; "Crain Faces Charges on Pathé Fire Next," *NYT*, April 12, 1931, 1:7.

74. "Clears Pair in Studio Fire," *NYT*, April 27, 1932, 13:5; Koszarski, "Laughter, Music and Tragedy at the New York Pathé Studio," 39, note 28.

75. "Producers Seek New Studios as Remodeling Starts at Gramercy," *EHW*, January 18, 1930, 46.

76. Dancers Catherine Porter, 16; Norine Byrd, 23; and Jola Sparks, age unreported, died at the scene. Edna Burford, 23, died later in the hospital. The four dancers were the victims named in the second-degree manslaughter charges against Flinn and Lalley. Incidentally, Eddie Elkins, the orchestra leader who was readying his musicians on the stage when the fire erupted, survived the inferno but never appeared in another film. Thelma White, the star of *The Black and White Revue/Sixteen Sweeties* and a supporting player in the Ginger Rogers vehicle *A Night in a Dormitory*, also survived and went on to find screen

immortality as the pot-pushing Mae in Pathé veteran Louis Gasnier's 1936 opus *Tell Your Children/Reefer Madness.*

77. "George LeMaire, Pathé Producer, Dies in N.Y.," *FD*, January 21, 1930, 1–2.

78. C. J. Scollard, Western Union telegram to [unknown recipient], February 4, 1930, John F. Kennedy Presidential Library, Joseph P. Kennedy Personal Papers.

79. E. B. Derr, Western Union telegram to Phil Reisman, February 7, 1930, Pathé Exchange records, Margaret Herrick Library, Academy of Motion Picture Arts and Sciences.

80. "Full Speed on Pathé's Comedies," *EHW*, March 22, 1930, 24; "Pathé Is in the Race for Strong Shorts in '30–'31," *MPN*, March 22, 1930, 49.

81. C. J. Scollard, Western Union telegram to E. B. Derr, April 9, 1930, Pathé Exchange records, Margaret Herrick Library, Academy of Motion Picture Arts and Sciences; E. B. Derr, Western Union telegram to C. J. Scollard, April 5, 1930, Pathé Exchange records, Margaret Herrick Library, Academy of Motion Picture Arts and Sciences.

82. "Pathé Completes Fourth of 52 Short Comedies in Eight Series," *EHW*, June 7, 1930, 96.

83. Review of *Two Plus Fours*, *MPN*, July 26, 1930, 63.

84. Review of *One Nutty Night*, *MPN*, November 22, 1930, 46.

85. C. J. Scollard to E. B. Derr, August 5, 1930, Pathé Exchange records, Margaret Herrick Library, Academy of Motion Picture Arts and Sciences.

86. Don Ashbaugh, review of *Pardon My Gun*, *MPN*, July 5, 1930, 42.

87. Pathé ad for new serial series, *EHW*, September 13, 1930, unnumbered page.

88. "Pathé Halts Plan to Remake Serials," *MPN*, November 8, 1930, 54.

89. "Canned by Pathé, Armstrong Back and Nicks Roll," *MPN*, April 12, 1930, unnumbered page.

90. "Axe to Swing at Pathé L.A. Studio," *MPN*, November 23, 1929, 23; "Sistrom out of Pathé; Glazer In," *MPN*, November 30, 1929, 27; "Derr Takes Charge of Pathé Culver Studios," *EHW*, February 15, 1930, 32.

91. "Constance Bennett to Make Sound Films under Pathé Banner," *EHW*, April 13, 1929, 40; "Pathé Assumes Strong Position; Is Assembling Array of Screen Talent," *EHW*, April 27, 1929, 44.

92. "Louise Brooks Refuses to Sign Pathé Contract," *MPN*, February 23, 1929, 545.

93. Ad for Pathé season lineup, *EHW*, July 6, 1929, unnumbered page.

94. Ibid.

95. Since Pathéchrome was applied to prints after the film was shot on a regular black and white negative, it is technically possible that the process could have been used for some prints of *The Painted Desert*. This seems unlikely, though, given the state of Pathé's finances in 1930–31.

96. Ad for Pathé season lineup, *EHW*, July 6, 1929, unnumbered page.

97. Admittedly this is pure speculation, but it might be noted that *The Great Gabbo*, a 1929 film from another studio whose Multicolor sequence is also unfortunately lost, does give Multicolor a credit in the opening titles.

98. "Joseph P. Kennedy Elected to Head Pathé Exchange Board of Directors," *EHW*, May 11, 1929, 23.

99. "Kennedy to Model Pathé after U.A.," *MPN*, December 7, 1929.

100. E. B. Derr letter to Terry Ramsaye, January 4, 1930, Pathé Exchange records, Margaret Herrick Library, Academy of Motion Picture Arts and Sciences, folder 10, General Matters.

101. E. B. Derr, Western Union telegram to C. J. Scollard, February 25, 1930, Pathé Exchange records, Margaret Herrick Library, Academy of Motion Picture Arts and Sciences, folder 11, General Matters no. 2.

102. "Completion of First Special Launches Pathé's Aggressive Campaign," *EHW*, March 29, 1930, 20.

103. Review of *Swing High*, *MPN*, May 3, 1930, 95.

104. "'Swing High' Flops in L.A. Taking $7500," *MPN*, June 28, 1930, 72.

105. "Derr Denies Pathé, RKO to Merge; Tells Plans," *EHW*, February 22, 1930, 33.

106. E. E. Moore, Western Union telegram to E. B. Derr, April 17, 1930, Pathé Exchange records, Margaret Herrick Library, Academy of Motion Picture Arts and Sciences, folder 11, General Matters no. 2.

107. "3 Stockholders Sue to Halt Pathé Sale," *NYT*, December 30, 1930, 30:2.

108. "Pathé Limiting Output; Loans Stars to Others," *MPN*, October 18, 1930, 22.

109. "Pathé Bettering Status; Receiver Suit Dismissed," *MPN*, August 9, 1930, 32.

110. "'Why' of Rumored RKO-Pathé Deal Is Hinted as Out on Booking Contract," *MPN*, February 22, 1930, 16.

111. "Kennedy Retirement from Pathé Seen as Speeding Reported RKO Merger," *MPN*, May 10, 1930, 19.

112. "RKO-Pathé Terms," *MPN*, October 11, 1930, unnumbered page.

113. Letter to stockholders dated New York, December 8, 1930, over the signature of Joseph P. Kennedy, chairman of the board, John F. Kennedy Presidential Library, Joseph P. Kennedy Personal Papers.

114. J. P. Kennedy memo to "All Home Office Employees," December 9, 1930, John F. Kennedy Presidential Library, Joseph P. Kennedy Personal Papers.

115. "3 Stockholders Sue to Halt Pathé Sale," *NYT*, December 30, 1930, 30:2.

116. "Pathé Sale Voted at Stormy Meeting," *NYT*, January 6, 1931, 29:7.

117. "Assert Pathé Sale Violates Sherman Act," *NYT*, January 7, 1931, 14:4; "Writ Asked to Stop Pathé Sale to RKO," *NYT*, January 25, 1931, 23:2; "R.-K.-O. Consummates Pathé Acquisition," *NYT*, January 31, 1931, 29:2.

118. "Lee Marcus Operating Chief of Pathé; Likely to Replace Derr at Coast Studios," *MPH*, January 24, 1931, 34.

119. "Derr Looks Back, and Ahead," *MPH*, January 3, 1931, 107.

120. "Derr and Sullivan Quit Caddo Nov. 20," *MPH*, October 31, 1931, 10.

121. "Terry Ramsaye Records!," *MPH*, February 7, 1931, 18.

122. Ibid., 54.

123. Ibid.

CHAPTER SEVEN
THE BELLIGERENT GALLIC GAMECOCK: 1931–PRESENT

1. Since multiple "Pathés" have once again entered the narrative, the full name of the Pathé Exchange will be used to specify that entity.

2. Full-page ad for RKO Pathé, *MPH*, March 21, 1931, unnumbered page.

3. "Brown Borrows Six Million for RKO Pathé," *MPH*, June 20, 1931, 11.

4. Crafton, *The Talkies*, 187, 210.

5. Ibid., 210; Tino Balio, *Grand Design: Hollywood as a Modern Business Enterprise* (New York: Charles Scribner's Sons, 1993), *1930–1939*, 15.

6. Beauchamp, *Joseph P. Kennedy*, 311.

7. John T. Flynn, "Other People's Money," *New Republic*, 264–65, retrieved from the Securities and Exchange Commission Historical Society website, http://www.sechistorical.org/.

8. Betty Lasky, *RKO: The Biggest Little Major of Them All* (Englewood Cliffs, NJ: Prentice-Hall, Inc., 1984), 58.

9. "Kennedy Still in Pathé Picture as Deal Closes," *MPH*, March 7, 1931, 50.

10. Facts Which Made It Desirable for Pathé to Accept the RKO Deal, undated, unsigned, John F. Kennedy Presidential Library, Joseph P. Kennedy Personal Papers; Letter to Pathé Exchange stockholders, dated New York, December 8, 1930, over the signature of Joseph P. Kennedy, chairman of the board, John F. Kennedy Presidential Library, Joseph P. Kennedy Personal Papers.

11. "Unified Distribution for Radio and Pathé Believed Probable; Combined Production Held Less Likely," *MPH*, October 31, 1931, 10; "Radio and Pathé Sales Forces Consolidate under Lee Marcus," *MPH*, November 7, 1931, 9, 30.

12. At about the same time, E. B. Derr and Charles Sullivan resigned from Howard Hughes' Caddo Company after less than a year on the job. Hughes diplomatically stated that the duo was departing because "the program outlined for them has been completed." See *MPH*, October 31, 1931, 10.

13. The Thomas Ince Studio in Culver City, which subsequently became the DeMille Studio, then Pathé Exchange, then RKO Pathé, still stands today at 9336 West Washington Boulevard. Operating as a rental facility for independent producers, it is now known simply as "The Culver Studios." One of the highlights of its long career came when David O. Selznick returned as an independent producer in the 1930s and 1940s. The studio's colonial-style administration building was featured in the opening logo for *Gone with the Wind* (1939) and other Selznick International Pictures.

14. *MPH*, February 20, 1932, advertising pages between 18, 19.

15. "The Old Red Rooster," *MPH*, February 13, 1932, 7.

16. Associated Press, "Warner Brothers Buys Pathé News," *St. Petersburg Times* (St. Petersburg, Florida), July 28, 1947, 12.

17. United Press, "Warner Pathé News to Discontinue Aug. 23," *The Milwaukee Journal*, July 25, 1956, 23.

18. *Pathé Educational Films*, (New York: Pathé News, Inc., 1959), collection of the author.

19. "Videorecord Corp. Obtains Pathé Film Archives for CTV," *Billboard*, June 24, 1971, 22.

20. If Magnetic Video's *Milestones of the Century, Volume I*, is any indication, very little effort was put into presentation of the material for home-video release. The tape, presented "by special arrangement with Pathé News," consists of two solid hours of three-minute milestones of the century back to back, chronologically covering the period from the First World War through the beginning of U.S. involvement in the Second World War, then, curiously, backing up and covering such preludes to the First World War as Japan's invasion of China, the Spanish Civil War, and the Munich peace agreement before returning to the First World War and concluding with the Korean conflict.

21. "DuPont Changes Name," *MPH*, July 11, 1931, 10.

22. The State Theatre is a mystery. There is no mention in the company records or the trade journals of when or how the theater was acquired, and it is not listed as being among the assets to be retained by the Pathé Exchange. It suddenly appears in documents generated immediately following the sale.

23. Draft of letter to stockholders from the board, February 24, 1931, John F. Kennedy Presidential Library, Joseph P. Kennedy Personal Papers.

24. Unsigned, undated draft report, early 1931, John F. Kennedy Presidential Library, Joseph P. Kennedy Personal Papers.

25. Draft of letter to stockholders from the board, February 24, 1931, John F. Kennedy Presidential Library, Joseph P. Kennedy Personal Papers.

26. "Kennedy Ends Last Film Connection," *MPH*, May 2, 1931, 10, 30.

27. "Pathé Exchange Plans Return to Film Activities," *LAT*, July 21, 1933, 12; "Pathé Film Out of Red in Quarter," *LAT*, May 15, 1934, 14.

28. "Court Hears Pathé Fight," *LAT*, July 10, 1935, 18.

29. "Pathé Exchange Sells Block of Dupont Shares," *LAT*, August 1, 1935, 16.

30. David Pierce, "Forgotten Faces: Why Some of Our Cinema Heritage Is Part of the Public Domain," *Film History* 19 (2007): 133.

31. "New Pathé Unit Formed," *LAT*, April 3, 1936, 15.

32. "Pathé Acquires Stock," *LAT*, June 28, 1936, 18.

33. There is some question about whether the company name was Grand National Pictures, Grand National Films, or Grand National Studios. The studio's logo simply read, "Grand National." The copyright notices of both *Great Guy* and *Something to Sing About* give the corporate name as "Grand National Films, Inc."

34. Ted Okuda, *Grand National, Producers Releasing Corporation, and Screen Guild/Lippert* (Jefferson, NC: McFarland, 1989), 2.

35. Ibid.

36. "Bankrupt Film Studio Goes on Auctioneer's Block Today," *LAT*, February 28, 1940, A3.

37. "Pathé Acquires Local Plant," *LAT*, December 20, 1939, A13.

38. "Railroads: Galahad on Wheels," *Time*, February 3, 1947.

39. "Transfer of Stock to Dissolve Pathé," *MPH*, September 13, 1941, 34.

40. "Pathé Film Corp. Plans Dissolution," *LAT*, September 11, 1941, 21; "Pathé Film Holders Approve Stock Sale," *LAT*, October 4, 1941, 12; "Pathé Film to Dissolve," *NYT*, September 24, 1941, 35; "Du Pont Seeks Pathé Stock," *MPH*, August 2, 1941, 23; "Transfer of Stock to Dissolve Pathé," *MPH*, September 13, 1941, 34; "SEC Studies Pathé Deal," *MPH*, September 20, 1941, 40; "Pathé Stock Plan Finally Approved," *MPH*, October 14, 1941, 53; "Pathé Tax Free in Stock Shift," *MPH*, November 22, 1941, 62–64.

41. Okuda, *Grand National*, 32.

42. Robert Benjamin of Phillips, Nizer, Benjamin, and Krim, New York, draft of letter to Donald Sherwood of Constock and Co., Chicago, January 29, 1948, Wisconsin Center for Film and Theatre Research, United Artists Collection.

43. "Pathé Lab Buys PRC," *MPH*, January 10, 1942, 8; "Pathé-PRC Deal before Regionals," *MPH*, January 17, 1942, 37.

44. "Pathé Now Owns 100 Per Cent of PRC Stock," *MPH*, February 28, 1942, 46.

45. "Increased Film Budget Planned for PRC Product," *MPH*, January 31, 1942, 59; "Pathé Now Owns 100 Per Cent of PRC Stock," *MPH*, February 28, 1942, 46; "PRC to Have 18 Westerns and 24 Features," *MPH*, May 9, 1942, 21.

46. "PRC May Change Name to Pathé," *MPH*, August 1, 1942, 15; Summary of the December 2, 1930, agreement between Pathé and RKO, John F. Kennedy Presidential Library, Joseph P. Kennedy Personal Papers.

47. "Million Dollar Loan for PRC Expansion," *MPH*, June 12, 1943, 29.

48. "Pathé," *MPW*, March 26, 1927, 398.

49. "PRC Starts First," *MPH*, October 2, 1943, 45.

50. "PRC to Release 40 Films Next Year: Fromkess," *MPH*, February 26, 1944, 42.

51. "PRC Will Produce 70 Per Cent of Own Pictures," *MPH*, December 23, 1944, 24; "PRC Will Deliver 50 in 1945–46; Eight in Color," *MPH*, July 7, 1945, 40; "More Color Films in PRC's New Expansion Plan," *MPH*, September 29, 1945, 33.

52. "Pathé Industries Net Is $489,352," *MPH*, July 7, 1945, 40.

53. Associated Press, "Three Dead in Home Film Fire," *Denton Record-Chronicle* (Denton, Texas), July 10, 1936; Associated Press, "Children Die in Film Fire," *Amarillo Globe-Times* (Amarillo, Texas), July 10, 1936.

54. Coe, *The History of Movie Photography*, 164.

55. *1918 Descriptive Catalogue of Pathéscope Films* (New York: Pathé, 1918), 130–31.

56. Ibid.

57. Coe, *The History of Movie Photography*, 162–63.

58. "Pathex Provides Camera and Projector for Non-Theatricals," *MPW*, August 29, 1925, 896.

59. Ibid.

60. Lewis, "Edmund Lynch Biography," 97.

61. Alas, some subsequent distributors replaced the *replacement* titles with much simpler titles of their own, leaving out important information like actor and crew credits and copyright information. As they exist today, some of these films just begin with a single card containing only the title of the film before launching directly into the movie.

62. Kodak had introduced 8-millimeter film in 1932. It was much cheaper than 16-millimeter but also decidedly inferior.

63. Scott MacGillivray, *Castle Films, A Hobbyist's Guide* (New York: iUverse, 2004), 2–3.

64. Despite their separation in 1931, *Pathé News* had continued to be processed and printed at Pathé Laboratories. This relationship continued even after Warner Brothers acquired *Pathé News*. Additionally, *Pathé News* and Pathé Laboratories had adjacent headquarters offices in New York City into the 1950s.

65. MacGillivray, *Castle Films*, 3.

66. *Official Films* catalog, 1947, 13.

67. *Pictoreels* catalog, undated but from the era of Pathé Industries.

68. Official Films did a fair amount of damage to at least two of Chaplin's 1914 Keystone comedies. *The Face on the Barroom Floor* was completely mutilated. The film was a comic take on Hugh Antoine d'Arcy's tragic poem of the same name, and the plot is played against subtitles drawn from the poem. Inexplicably, Official removed all of the subtitles except for the very first *and* rearranged the sequence of the film, rendering it incomprehensible. The other casualty was *Caught in the Rain*. Relatively little damage was done to the content, but, again for reasons unknown, Official changed the title to *In the Park*. The problem is that in 1915 Chaplin actually made a single-reeler titled *In the Park*. Official's version has created a fair amount of confusion through the decades.

69. *Official Films* catalog, 1947, 7.

70. Okuda, *Grand National*, 31.

71. Robert Benjamin letter to Purcell, Pathé, Chrysler Building, November 1, 1947, Wisconsin Center for Film and Theatre Research, United Artists Collection.

72. "A New Home for Pathé," *MPH*, October 6, 1945, 39; STV Inc., preparer, "Phase I Environmental Site Assessment of M895, 105 East 106th Street, New York, New York, 10029," prepared January 19, 2012, 15–16, 18.

73. "Pathé Industries Merges Units," *MPH*, December 22, 1945, 13.

74. Board of directors meeting of Pathé Industries, at Chrysler Building, August 15, 1949, Wisconsin Center for Film and Theatre Research, United Artists Collection.

75. "Fromkess Leaves PRC Presidency over Differences," *MPH*, September 1, 1945, 42.

76. "Rank Starts Triple Play for American Market," *MPH*, February 19, 1944, 33.

77. "Rank Signs Another 2-Way Deal, This Time with Young," *MPH*, December 22, 1945, 13.

78. "Young Scotches PRC Reports," *MPH*, May 18, 1946, 29.

79. "Eagle-Lion Increases Its Budget by $5,000,000," *MPH*, July 27, 1946, 36.

80. Robert Benjamin of Phillips, Nizer, Benjamin and Krim, New York, draft of a letter to Donald Sherwood of Constock and Co., Chicago, January 29, 1948, Wisconsin Center for Film and Theatre Research, United Artists Collection.

81. Robert Benjamin letter to Wayne Estes, Topeka, Kansas, October 24, 1947, Wisconsin Center for Film and Theatre Research, United Artists Collection.

82. Robert Benjamin of Phillips, Nizer, Benjamin and Krim, New York, draft of a letter to Donald Sherwood of Constock and Co., Chicago, January 29, 1948, Wisconsin Center for Film and Theatre Research, United Artists Collection.

83. "Eagle Lion Is Sold to U.A. Film Firm," *NYT*, April 12, 1951, 40.

84. "United Artists Buys Eagle-Lion Classics," *LAT*, April 12, 1951, 16; Pathé Industries, Inc., salaries of over $10,000 per annum, June 5, 1947, Wisconsin Center for Film and Theatre Research, United Artists Collection.

85. "Pathé Sets Deal to Process All Universal Films," *MPH*, October 19, 1946, 25.

86. "Columbia, Pathé in Film Deal," *LAT*, September 23, 1958, C7.

87. Letterhead from November 27, 1953, is Chesapeake Industries, Inc., formerly Pathé Industries, Inc., Wisconsin Center for Film and Theatre Research, United Artists Collection; Seymour Peyser to Bernard Reich, Esq., March 18, 1954, Wisconsin Center for Film and Theatre Research, United Artists Collection; Seymour M. Peyser letter to Bernard Reich, Esq., October 10, 1958, Wisconsin Center for Film and Theatre Research, United Artists Collection.

88. "Robert Young, Financier, Ends Life in Palm Beach," *NYT*, January 26, 1958, 1, 78.

89. "Charles Pathé, French Film Pioneer, Dies," *LAT*, December 27, 1957, 6.

90. "Robert Young, Financier, Ends Life in Palm Beach," *NYT*, January 26, 1958, 1, 78.

91. H. Allen Anderson, "Young, Robert Ralph," Handbook of Texas Online (http://www.tshaonline.org/handbook/online/articles/fy012), accessed June 18, 2013. Published by the Texas State Historical Association.

92. John S. Tompkins, "Zeckendorf Buys Young Holding in Chesapeake Industries, Inc.," *NYT*, May 1, 1958, 45, 52.

93. "America Corporation," *NYT*, September 2, 1960, 33, 39.

94. "Chill Wills Assists at Pathé's Revival," *LAT*, January 10, 1961, C9.

95. Andrew Leckey, "Successful Investing," *Observer-Reporter* (Washington, Pennsylvania), February 15, 1987, B8.

96. "Pathé to Expand L.A. Film Facility," *LAT*, March 7, 1967, C7.

97. "Pathé Ends an Era in Middlesex," *Courier-News*, January 6, 1967, newspaper clip collection of the Bound Brook Memorial Library of the Somerset, New Jersey, county library system.

98. "Pathé Labs Sues Technicolor; Claims Monopolizing Attempt," *LAT*, June 1, 1967, B14.

99. Pathé had brought suit against Technicolor once before. By 1954 Technicolor had largely abandoned the "glorious Technicolor" process of *Gone with the Wind* (filmed by David Selznick on the old Pathé Culver City lot), *The Wizard of Oz*, and *Singin' in the Rain* and had become just one more developing lab for Eastman Kodak's "Eastman Color" process. Pathé claimed, rightly in the opinion of this author, that Technicolor should not be allowed to use the name "Technicolor" in connection with any process other than "classic" Technicolor three-color system. For reasons unknown, just before the trial date set for *Pathé v. Technicolor Motion Picture Corporation, Technicolor, Inc., and De Luxe Laboratories, Inc.*, Pathé filed a motion. The court ruled as follows:

> [The plaintiff] now, at this late date, comes in and asks that the action be discontinued without prejudice, claiming that certain changes have been made in the advertising program of the defendants which make the present continuing of this action unnecessary. It is hard to see where a mere change in the advertising program, if it took place (which is denied), would have been sufficient ground for discontinuing the action and relinquishing all of the relief asserted in the complaint if, in fact, plaintiff, in good faith, had believed that it was entitled to the relief claimed in the complaint.
>
> By bringing this action, plaintiff has caused the defendants the expense of retaining lawyers to defend the action. It would be the height of injustice to allow a party to commence an action, putting the defendant to the expense of defending it, and then shortly before the case was to be reached for trial, cause the action to be discontinued without reimbursement of the expenses to which the defendant has been put. Defendants' counsel have submitted an affidavit showing the services performed by them and their estimate of the reasonable value of those services.
>
> The motion for the voluntary dismissal of this action without prejudice is granted, conditioned upon payment to the attorneys for the defendants of the sum of $1,000 which the Court finds constitutes reasonable attorneys' fees for the services of such attorneys in this action to date.

100. "Perfect Film Acquires Pathé Industries Unit for Total of $9,751,420," *Wall Street Journal*, October 30, 1967, 15.

101. Kenneth MacDougall, "The Trials of Marty," *Wall Street Journal*, February 26, 1969, 1, 25.

102. "President of Pathé Relinquishes Post," *NYT*, October 7, 1970, 78.

103. Thomas W. Ennis, "Benjamin Berkey Dies at 73; Founder of Photo Company," Associated Press report printed in the *Telegraph* (Nashua, New Hampshire), December 19, 1984, 27.

104. STV, Inc., preparer, "Phase I Environmental Site Assessment of M895, 105 East 106th Street, New York, New York, 10029," prepared January 19, 2012, 16.

105. "Berkey Officials Quit Movielab Jobs in Row," *LAT*, August 24, 1970, D11.

106. *Movielab, Inc., v. Berkey Photo, Inc.*, 321 F.Supp. 806, No. 70 Civ. 3800 (S.D. New York 1970).

107. "Movielab Accord on Berkey Deal," *NYT*, November 24, 1972.

108. "Briefly," *LAT*, May 1, 1986.

109. Universal did own a chain of mostly small rural and neighborhood theaters briefly in the late 1920s and early 1930s.

110. Schatz, *The Genius of the System*, 235.

111. Pennsylvania's Department of State lists Pathé, Inc.; Pathé Industries, Inc.; and Pathé-America Distributing Co., Inc., as technically alive, if inactive. Similarly, Pathé Communications Corporation; Pathé Films, Inc.; Pathé Productions Corporation; and Pathé Releasing Corporation are still carried on the books of the New York Department of State, Division of Corporations. Pathé Films, Inc., is listed in California as well, with an address in Beverly Hills. The Delaware Department of State, Division of Corporations, still shows Pathé Exchange, Inc., and Pathé Frères Phonograph Company as inactive, but not dead, and Pathé Industries, Inc., as active, with a trust company listed as its agent.

BIBLIOGRAPHY

ARCHIVES

Hal Roach Studios Collection, USC Cinematic Arts Library, University of Southern California, Los Angeles, California.

Joseph P. Kennedy Personal Papers, John F. Kennedy Presidential Library, Boston, Massachusetts.

Pathé Exchange records, Margaret Herrick Library, Academy of Motion Picture Arts and Sciences, Beverly Hills, California.

United Artists Collection, Wisconsin Center for Film and Theatre Research, State Historical Society, Madison, Wisconsin.

JOURNALS AND NEWSPAPERS

Amarillo Globe-Times, Amarillo, Texas

Denton Record-Chronicle, Denton, Texas

Exhibitors Herald and Moving Picture World

Exhibitors Herald World

Exhibitors' Trade Review

Film Daily

Freeport Journal-Standard, Freeport, Illinois

Milwaukee Journal

Motion Picture Herald

Motion Picture News

Moving Picture World

New York Sun

New York Times

Observer-Reporter, Washington, Pennsylvania

Plainfield Courier-News (later *Courier-News*), New Jersey

St. Petersburg Times, St. Petersburg, Florida
Time
Wall Street Journal
Wid's

VIDEO

British Pathé. *Pathe Review—Colour Clips (1928)*. 12 min., 20 sec. YouTube, https://www.youtube.com/watch?v=AhGPnisQL40 (accessed April 13, 2014).

———. *Pathecolor Sic Nature's Teacup—Crater Lake In Oregon (1927)*. 3 min., 50 sec. YouTube, https://www.youtube.com/watch?v=LurjKA_MwX83:50 (accessed April 13, 2014).

Haskin, Byron. *Hollywood: A Celebration of the American Silent Film—The Autocrats*. VHS. Directed by Kevin Brownlow and David Gill. HBO Home Video, 1998.

WEBSITES

1918 Descriptive Catalogue of Pathéscope Films. New York: Pathé, 1918. http://www.archive.org/stream/descriptivecataloopath#page/n7/mode/2up.

About Pathécolor Films. (article taken from a supplement to *Kinematograph Weekly*, December 11, 1924). http://www.cinerdistan.co.uk/pathécolor.htm.

Anderson, H. Allen. "Young, Robert Ralph," Handbook of Texas Online www.tshaonline.org/handbook/online/articles/fyo12. Published by the Texas State Historical Association.

Max Davidson. http://www.laurel-and-hardy.com/archive/articles/2011-01-davidson/davidson-1.html.

Mittenthal Brothers. (content sponsored by Kalamazoo Public Library). www.kpl.gov/local-history/biographies/mittenthal-brothers.aspx.

Nineteen Twenty Five Catalogue of Pathépictures Selected for Educational, Religious and Social Groups. Retrieved from Media History Digital Library, 2011. http://www.archive.org/stream/catalogueofpatheoopath#page/n3/mode/2up.

Thanhouser Company Film Preservation, Inc. Edwin Thanhouser, biographical notes. www.thanhouser.org/people/thanhousere.htm.

BOOKS AND ARTICLES

Abel, Richard. *The Cine Goes to Town: French Cinema 1896–1914*. Berkeley: University of California Press, 1994.

Balio, Tino. *Grand Design: Hollywood as a Modern Business Enterprise, 1930–1939*. New York: Charles Scribner's Sons, 1993.

Barrier, Michael. *The Animated Man: A Life of Walt Disney*. Berkeley: University of California Press, 2007.

Beauchamp, Cari. *Joseph P. Kennedy Presents His Hollywood Years*. New York: Vintage Books, 2009.

Birchard, Robert S. *Cecil B. DeMille's Hollywood*. Lexington: University Press of Kentucky, 2004.

Chase, William Sheafe. *Catechism on Motion Pictures in Inter-state Commerce*. 3rd ed. New York: New York Civic League, 1922.

Christianson, Stephen G. "Triangle Shirtwaist Factory Fire." In *Great American Trials*, edited by Edward W. Knappman, 255–59. Detroit: Visible Ink, 1994.

Coe, Brian. *The History of Movie Photography*. London: Ash & Grant, 1981.

Crafton, Donald. *The Talkies: American Cinema's Transition to Sound, 1926–1931*. Berkeley: University of California Press, 1999.

Dardis, Tom. *Harold Lloyd: The Man on the Clock*. New York: Viking Press, 1983.

Fossati, Giovanna. "When Cinema Was Colored." In *All the Colors of the World: Colors in Early Mass Media, 1900–1930*, edited by Luciano Berriatúa, 121–32. Reggio Emilia: Diabasis, 1998.

Gomery, Douglas. *The Hollywood Studio System*. New York: St. Martin's Press, 1986.

Hirschhorn, Clive. *The Universal Story*. New York: Crown Publishers, 1983.

Hulse, Ed. *Distressed Damsels and Masked Marauders*. Morris Plains, NJ: Murania Press, 2014.

Jewell, Richard B. *The Golden Age of Cinema: Hollywood, 1929–1945*. Malden, MA: Blackwell Publishing, 2007.

Jewell, Richard B., and Vernon Harbin. *The RKO Story*. London: Octopus Books, 1982.

Katz, Ephraim. *Film Encyclopedia*. 3rd ed. New York: Harper Perennial, 1998.

King, Rob. "The Spice of the Program: Educational Pictures, Early Sound Slapstick, and the Small-Town Audience." *Film History* 23, no. 3 (2011): 313–30.

Koszarski, Richard. *An Evening's Entertainment: The Age of the Silent Feature: 1915–1928*. New York: Charles Scribner's Sons, 1990.

———. *Hollywood on the Hudson: Film and Television in New York from Griffith to Sarnoff*. New Brunswick, NJ: Rutgers University Press, 2008.

———. "Laughter, Music and Tragedy at the New York Pathé Studio." *Film History* 14, no. 1 (2002): 32–39.

Lasky, Betty. *RKO: The Biggest Little Major of Them All.* Englewood Cliffs, NJ: Prentice-Hall, 1984.

Lewis, Robert. "Edmund Lynch Biography." (unpublished manuscript, 1949). Merrill Lynch Corporate Archives, World Financial Center, New York.

MacGillivray, Scott. *Castle Films, A Hobbyist's Guide.* New York: iUverse, 2004.

Maltin, Leonard. *Of Mice and Magic.* New York: Plume, 1987.

Mebold, Anke, and Charles Tepperman. "Resurrecting the Lost History of 28mm Film in North America." *Film History* 15 no. 2 (2003): 137–51.

Movielab, Inc., v. Berkey Photo, Inc., 321 F.Supp. 806, No. 70 Civ. 3800 (S.D. New York 1970).

Official Films 1947 Catalog. (collection of the author).

Okuda, Ted. *Grand National, Producers Releasing Corporation, and Screen Guild/Lippert.* Jefferson, NC: McFarland, 1989.

Perkins, Edward J. *Wall Street to Main Street: Charles Merrill and Middle-Class Investors.* Cambridge: Cambridge University Press, 1999.

Read, Paul. "Unnatural Colours: An Introduction to Colouring Techniques in Silent Era Movies." *Film History* 21, no. 1 (2009): 9–46.

Robach, M. "Color in Motion Pictures." *International Projectionist* (November 1931): 11–13.

Salmon, Stephanie. *Pathé: À la conquête du cinéma 1896–1929.* Paris: Tallandier, 2014.

Schatz, Thomas. *The Genius of the System.* New York: Pantheon Books, 1988.

STV Inc., preparer. "Phase I Environmental Site Assessment of M895, 105 East 106th Street, New York, New York, 10029," prepared January 19, 2012. http://www.nycsca.org/Community/Programs/EnvironmentalDueDiligence/DueDiligenceRpts/M895/01M895Phase1ESA.pdf.

Thomas, Tony, and Aubrey Solomon. *The Films of 20th Century Fox: A Pictorial History.* Secaucus, NJ: Citadel Press, 1979.

United States v. America Corporation and (Republic Corporation), Civ. No. 1542–61-EC (D.C. California S.D. Central Division 1963).

United States v. Movielab, Inc., 70 Civ. No. 3100 M.I.C. (D.C. New York S.D. 1974).

U.S. Congress. House Committee on Ways and Means. *Photographic Film and Motion Pictures: Hearings on General Tariff Revision before the House of Representatives*, Part 5, Schedule N—Sundries. 66th Cong., 3rd sess., 1921. Washington, DC: Government Printing Office, 1921.

Walker, Brent E. *Mack Sennett's Fun Factory.* Jefferson, NC: McFarland, 2010.

Ward, Richard. *A History of the Hal Roach Studios.* Carbondale: Southern Illinois University Press, 2005.

Weinberg, Herman G. *The Complete Wedding March*. Boston: Little, Brown and Company, 1974.

Willems, Gilles. "The Origins of Pathé-Natan." In *Une histoire économique du cinéma français (1895–1995), Regards croisés franco-américains*, edited by Pierre-Jean Benghozi and Christian Delage, translated by Annabelle de Cröy. Paris: Harmattan, Collection Champs Visuels, 1997. http://tlweb.latrobe.edu.au/humanities/screeningthepast/classics/rr1199/gwrr8b.htm.

Yumibe, Joshua. *Moving Color: Early Film, Mass Culture, Modernism*. New Brunswick, NJ: Rutgers University Press, 2012.

INDEX

Italicized page numbers followed by the letter *g* indicate photographs contained in the gallery.

RICHARD LEWIS WARD is an associate professor in the communication department at the University of South Alabama and the author of *A History of the Hal Roach Studios*. He has published essays in *Film & History*, *Media History*, and *Studies in Popular Culture*.